TRY
AGAIN

TRY

AGAIN

An Ex-Con's Path from Prison to Prosperity

Nick Marshall

VIVA
EDITIONS

Published in the United States by Viva Editions, an imprint of Start Midnight, LLC, 221 River Street, Ninth Floor, Hoboken, New Jersey 07030.

Printed in the United States
Cover photo: Noella Diaz
Back cover photo: Noella Diaz
Design: Ashley Calvano
Layout and Design: Westchester Publishing Services

First Edition.
10 9 8 7 6 5 4 3 2 1

Trade paper ISBN: 978-1-63228-098-5
E-book ISBN: 978-1-63228-118-0

CONTENTS

CONTENTS

DISCLAIMER

This publication contains the author's opinions, ideas, and stories, some containing graphic imagery and mature language. It is sold with the understanding that the author is not rendering medical or legal advice in this book. If you or someone you know is suffering from addiction, depression/other mental health issues, or the like, please seek medical attention.

AUTHOR'S STATEMENT

I never set out to write *this* book. I thought I had sold a manuscript about my youth and how I made mistakes that sent me to prison. Instead, this version was the offer on the table. I couldn't be happier that I took it and, despite the uphill battle of writing it in four months, set out to the challenge. I finished the first, highly overwritten, draft in thirty-one days; thirty-one bottles of wine later. Over 190 hours spent alone at my desk, in my head, reliving the past twenty years of my life, pacing my apartment, smoking the occasional cigarette, and walking around the city during the "off hours" clearing my head (really just thinking and thinking about what the fuck I was writing, how it would come off, and if it was worth a shit).

With that said, this is what I remembered, clearly, that I felt worked within the context of this story. I changed names and likenesses of many people, I left others in (with their permission) and left so many others out as I didn't think they pertained to the story, not that they didn't hold a special place in my life at any given time; because they did. Many of the people who were left out held places, but I chose not to for my own reasons, as an author, as a story-teller, and as a human. There are some contradictions throughout, mostly due to my up and down financial situations against the timeline necessary to make the book better for the reader. But overall, I provided you with a glimpse of the past twenty years of my life since leaving the gates of prison.

Simply said, I left out far more than I have written. I worked off a timeline as it happened, but left a lot of what I did along the way out. Some of which not to bore you, other parts that weren't my place to tell, as it affected notable people/public figures. And while on that note, although I think he is one of the greatest living actors of our generation and I admire his work tremendously, I never actually met Mr. DiCaprio. For all of the salacious "night-life" stories I left out that you may have wanted to hear more of, I'm sorry this wasn't a "tell-all," but it simply isn't my right to write about. Yes, I've partied and been around some crazy shit and could have used that to try and sell books by naming names and presenting proof, but that is not who I am, nor is it my intention.

I set out to write a book about struggle. About life. About pain, suffering, mental health issues, addiction, and the choices people like me make as we are trying to survive, and succeed, in this thing called Life. I can only speak of my faults, fuckups, mistakes, small successes, and the myriad of failures along the way, which despite how low they affected me mentally, I continued to plow through. The "don't take 'no' for an answer" philosophy. The "work hard and continue to try and fail" mentality that eventually finds suc-cess. That is what I found when I started to write this book. The ability to find a way up the mountains that lay before us. To carve our own path within the rough terrain.

I hope that anyone who reads this is both inspired and warned. Life is hard. It is even harder when the deck is stacked against you. But that is not a reason to give up and complain and blame the system or others or any other factor you have no control over. Gut check yourself. Pull your pants on, tighten your belt, and set out to work hard to achieve whatever it is that you desire. Trust me, the impossible is possible. Godspeed to you all, may you find happiness from within the darkness and success where you felt you would never find any.

Thank you for reading.

INTRODUCTION

Prison changes a man. Changes a man more than you could ever imagine. The sheer dehumanization of it all. The violence. The sounds. It is not a place of rehabilitation. Instead, it is a place of survival, mentally *and* physically; for your will shall be tested throughout your sentence. Can you keep your sanity? Can you survive attempts on your person, or your life? Can you manage to do time, as they say, lest it do you? There is nothing about the experience that churns out productive members of society upon release. No tools that increase one's chances at success upon your release. Nothing *useful* that is. Just a bunch of false bureaucratic crap at the lowest of base levels that they use to get funding for these "programs" on the backs of the hard-earning taxpayers.

In fact, in most cases, chances are that the people who go through this experience return to society more of a criminal, as the entire system sets you up for failure so they can remain in power; power on a new level of invasiveness, from parole to counseling, to the various other nonsense that surrounds the business.

Because make no mistake, the prison system is a business. Big Business, or so it has become. A churning machine utilizing human beings and their indiscretions, mistakes, crimes, or socioeconomic classes against them.

If I had to compare it to something that would allow you, the reader, to truly understand the depths of hell that is a state prison, it would be being drafted into war.[1] However, when in war, you are fighting for something: your country, your life, your loved ones; an ideal. Yet in prison you are also fighting: for freedom, respect, dignity, and self-worth, in addition to your life and person. Though the main difference between the two is that those who end up in prison most often do so by their own poor decision making, as I did, which leaves no excuse.

I have seen people get jumped in the hallway, beaten and robbed of their commissary packs of food, cigarettes, and new underwear. I have watched people fight like gladiators, naked save their boxers and prison-issued boots. I have slept with one eye open, peering and listening as a group of young men beat another with a sock full of locks while he slept, praying I would not be next. I have gaped at someone getting shanked, and heard the sound that it makes when it pierces the skin (most likely the cracking of bone). And saddest of all, I have been witness to a man who was beaten so savagely that his skull was cracked open on the concrete of a dining hall floor; pieces of his brain scattered around him as the corrections officers (COs), who couldn't be bothered, finally got involved and called the infirmary.

And this is why many times throughout my bid I had to eat standing with one leg on the steel bench meant for my rear end, shoveling food into my mouth, head on a swivel for fear of being

---

1   I would like to make it clear that I do not believe serving a prison term and serving in the military bear the same weight, but there are elements that are comparable.

attacked while in a vulnerable position. I had to find times to shower when it seemed less likely to be jumped. How could I tell? That varied from day to week to month, unit to unit, and I slept so lightly that any sound drew me awake. I was on guard for my life, ready to fight if someone were to try and take me in the night. Yet I have never been to war. Never had anyone shoot at me. Never had to run from a bombing, or see people blown to bits in front of me; not as my father had. A young, poor high school dropout from a poor town outside Newark, New Jersey drafted into Vietnam, surviving his time with the award of a Gold Star for bravery, something I did not find out until ten years ago; he had never spoken of it, nor his time in Vietnam. Anything he ever did tell me, you will read about in these pages. And I only bring this up to say that these two things: war and prison, change a man. In vastly different ways, yet strangely similar.

What you are about to read is so many things: sad, frightening, hopeful, chaotic, unbelievable . . . and yet all true. This book is about struggle, addiction, hope (both loss of and holding onto), and most of all, perseverance. Not a moment in my life was truly "easy." Yes, there were many occasions where I made it *seem* easy, but that was mostly because I had certain tools that society allows for it to be made so. I was born in Westwood, New Jersey. A now tiny enclave forty minutes outside of Manhattan. By all intents and purposes, I should have never ended up where I did as I had opportunity. "Privilege," as they say now. And that is why my being able to write this story is so important to me. Because I may not have started as the underdog like so many others throughout this country, but I spent the past twenty-five years as one. And both before and during that time frame, I have met so many young men from inner cities. Lived with them; ate with them; laughed with them; taught many how to read and write, and even wrote their letters home to loved ones for them; met their families; and saw their struggles firsthand. And the biggest takeaways I have? They didn't all belong there. The system is rigged against them, always has been. And once they are in it, they have little chance to get out and live healthy, happy, clean, and crime-free lives, as according to Background Checks.org, recidivism in this country hovers at a staggering 70 percent within the first five years of release![2]

They are set up to fail once they have crossed the line of arrest, as nothing from that point on is "fair" or "just" as so many politicians like to say. From the corrupt parole system (as Meek Mill and Robert Kraft have brought light to) to the criminal justice system overall (cops, attorneys, and judges). So, why do I feel *I* have the *right* to tell this story? First off, it is mine and no one can take that from me. Second, the issues I dealt with, as a White, educated, privileged man, (add with that all my mental ailments—we'll get to that in a minute) pale in comparison to those who are of color, have little to no education, fucked up family bases, no shot, or such a small shot it's laughable, and that just pisses me off! And I want to be able to shine a light on these injustices. And maybe, just maybe, God willing, help someone, or many, in the process.

This story is about never giving up. No matter how hard it gets, no matter how close to ending it you are. No matter how you may be toiling slowly with the bottle or drugs to make it easier to end it, or to give up altogether and let things be what they may; what I like to call the "fuck it" attitude. Which is what landed me in prison in the first place, aside from the way I allowed all my anger, pain, and sadness to explode into the armed robbery I committed. I broke into a home dressed in black with masks, gloves, and a gun, and held seven people at gunpoint and robbed *only* their drugs— because I was "moral," or at least that's what I told myself.

---

2   "U.S. Prison Population vs the World." 2019. Background Checks.org. May 5, 2019. https://backgroundchecks.org/us-prison-population-vs-the-world.html

This is meant to be a sad, but inspirational tale, one that I hope many people can relate to because it is also about mental health (Post Traumatic Stress Disorder/Anxiety/Obsessive Compulsive Disorder/addiction—my issues) and struggle. The struggle to survive. To make it out from under the hand of The System. To "make it" in life, whatever that means for you. To make and keep friends. To love and lose. To be dead broke and then to have a little scratch, lose it all and have to start over. It is about this beautiful, and often horrific, thing called Life. It is a story about humanity and all its flaws.

I have made more mistakes than I can count (or remember). I have done stupid things, said even stupider ones. I have been violent (in my youth). I have been a great friend, and a worse enemy. I have allowed anger and resentment to get the best of me at times. I have been down on myself throughout most of it, suffered from severe depression, and even attempted suicide twice while I awaited my sentencing. Thank God I didn't succeed. And despite all of it, I am still kicking. Still living to fight the good fight, day after day, despite a massive debt load I have carried for five years, since I made the choice to leave nightlife, despite the money, as it was going to kill me. I entered a field that was just as vicious in many ways, only performed during the sober light of day, which is far better for my production level.

When I left prison, I had a few thousand dollars to my name, no debt, and *one* friend who wasn't a criminal or a gang member. Now, nearly twenty-five years later, I am more broke than even those few thousand dollars I had back then, but I am a wealthy man in terms of *friendship*. True friendships. Far more than I can count on my two hands. And to me, that says a lot. Because you can always make money, but you can't always make real friends. I was fortunate enough to be myself in front of them. To show them the true me; not the asshole doorman, not the prick bartender or manager, not the cocky jerk who was uninterested in useless banal conversations in various social settings; but the *real* me. The introvert. The Writer. The Thinker. The Artist. And lastly, the goodhearted man that I, and now they know, I am.

For them I am forever grateful. They have propped me up, supported me emotionally and financially (you know who you are and yeah, I owe lots of dinners, vacations, golf outings, and more, and one day, I'll repay you!), been my therapists as I could rarely afford one, have employed me, even when it was to their detriment due to my state of mind, and lastly, have shown me the love of making me Uncle Nick to their children, a gift I thank God every single day for.

And to everyone who knows only the "stage versions" of myself I displayed throughout my time trying to climb my way towards upward mobility, I apologize you never met the real me. And for all those who have come across me impaired by drugs and far more than copious amounts of alcohol, I am sorry as well, for I can be a whirlwind of craziness in addition to fun. For as any addict will only ever admit once they are finally ready to (and I finally am) this is a process, a journey; not a destination. And as I have decided to make this book not just about how I was able to go from prison to a highly notable person in a very insular world in a relatively short amount of time when I knew not a single soul who could "put me on," I also wanted to tell the truth of all the internal struggles I faced while doing so and still face today, though not nearly as much as a few years ago.

I want this book to be relatable to many. And I want everyone who is struggling mentally to know, you will get through it, with help, change, and most importantly, WILLPOWER. And equally as important to me, that every person who has ever left the gates of a jail or prison and stepped back into society as a "free" person, you have the power to metaphorically leave that experience behind those gates, not mentally, for that will always be with you, but through hard work and change. My grandfather, an Italian immigrant who made his way in this country, always told me to work hard and save my money. He said that no matter what the job was, if you did it well, people would notice. And from there, promotions and opportunities would come. Whether you are scrubbing toilets, flipping burgers, or shoveling shit, do it with everything you have and I promise you, if you continue in that vein, no matter how long it takes, you will find a way out.

I hope this book can serve as both inspirational and as a warning of what *not* to do at times. Because despite all this, I'm just a well put together FUCKUP who keeps failing and trying; who hopes that one day he will find the peace and success he has spent his whole life working for. This book is a good start.

CHAPTER 1

SAINT-TROPEZ

Saint-Tropez, France—2015

He who has a why to live can bear almost any how.
—FRIEDRICH NIETZSCHE

I woke up to a flight attendant shaking my shoulder. As I opened my Xanax-clouded eyes, I noticed she did not look pleased as she continued to shake me.

"Sir, your seat back, please!"

I mechanically performed the duty.

"Sorry," I smiled through my chapped, Xanax-infused, sleep-crusted lips.

She did not return the gesture. Instead, she walked away, and continued to perform her job as the captain spoke over the intercom in French, none of which I understood, but thought to myself how beautiful it sounded; a romance language, one I had the choice to learn in school. Instead, I chose Spanish as I thought it more useful to me in the States, not that I ever worked at it. The captain repeated himself in English.

"We are beginning our descent into Côte d'Azur airport. Flight attendants, crosscheck for our arrival."

I pulled the window shade up to reveal the aqua, azure, and navy blues of the Mediterranean beneath us fading into one another. All I could think about was what awaited me: the feeling of the lukewarm water, and the sun's rays shining down, transforming my skin into the sun-kissed bronze of a wealthy person who spends their days lounging on a yacht. Ah. The south of France.

As we made our way onto the tarmac, my thoughts were lost in the romanticism of the country, one I had never visited before. I wanted to take in those small pockets of European bliss, on what they call the French Riviera, knowing fully well I might never be able to afford to travel there on my own terms. It was a work trip, and one I was honored to be asked to attend, as the event I was "working" had one of the most exclusive guest list invites in the world: the Leonardo DiCaprio Foundation, supporting donations and awareness to climate change and our oceans.

We taxied for a few minutes before arriving at the terminal. Having heard the plane's engines cease and the ping of the cabin unfasten seat belt sign, I unbuckled and awaited the moment when I could stand and stretch my cramped legs after the longest flight I had ever taken in my life. I watched impatiently as the passengers in the various rows before me got up and attempted to retrieve their carry-on luggage from the storage above while the ones behind attempted to push past one another trying to get off the plane and to the luggage carousel first. I laughed to myself at the selfishness of people on planes. How is it that no matter where you are in the world, airplane passengers all act the same? It was no different there, despite the plane only having what seemed to be a few Americans, the rest French citizens, making comments about one another which I could not understand, but could feel, from the energy they exhibited toward one another. When it was my turn to stand, my legs almost buckled. I grabbed the seat back and steadied myself, shaking my legs out upon maneuvering into the aisle as I reached up and swiftly grabbed my carry-on, pulled it out over my head, and walked down the empty aisle before me. As I reached the gangplank, a feeling of excitement rushed over me. I was in Europe for the first time in my life and had one full day to myself to explore before having to work the next evening. I couldn't wait to get to the hotel, have some lunch and a glass of wine, then go to the beach and feel the sand between my toes and the warm embrace of the water as I dove in. I was lost in thought when I realized I was in the middle of the smallest airport terminal I had ever been and was, essentially, lost.

I hadn't planned for that trip very well. I was told I was going only two days prior and since I had never been, and it was on their dime, I requested to arrive a day earlier and settle in at a hotel, get a lay of the land, and try and make a bit of a vacation out of it. Surprisingly they acquiesced with my request and handled the bookings for me. The only issue was that everything I needed was trapped in my phone. I shook the device as if that would change something, until I noticed an icon in the top corner that advised me that I did not have service. *Of course, why would I?* I was in another country for Christ's sake. I quickly remembered that people had warned me, and told me that if I used WhatsApp, it would be free, and I wouldn't receive exorbitant international charges. I thought I made the right decision, only I didn't take into account the fact that it ran only on Wi-Fi. How would I get service in cabs, on the street, and the like? I would have to figure it out and adjust accordingly, on the spot. *Maybe I should have planned better.*

I approached an elderly woman running a kiosk of all that is French to sell to tourists on their way home.

"Excuse me, do you know the Wi-Fi here?"

She looked at me with a scowl, then a shake of her head. I

3

quickly remembered all that I had heard of France in the past: that they did not like Americans, further, that they *hated* Americans who made no attempt to speak French. Deflated, I smiled at her and walked away in search of a person who looked like they spoke English. I searched for Wi-Fi on my phone and found the airport's, however it was password protected. *Dammit.* I approached the airline ticket counter and was quickly introduced to a man who told me clearly, in English, the password and that the service was very spotty and only worked in two areas of the airport. I thanked him profusely as I headed to the exit area where cab drivers gathered to find new fares. I sat on a bench beside them and logged on. The bars came alive and suddenly a slew of emails flooded in. I scanned through them, all from the past night's correspondence of my coworkers at the club, of no issue to me at that point, and quickly found my hotel information.

I opened the Uber app and read that they did not operate in the country. *Shit.*

I thought for a moment before screenshotting the hotel address, knowing that I could forget it, or some other calamity that would leave me without a device to communicate in a country whose language I did not speak, and walked up to the nearest cabbie to ask for a ride.

"Sir, can you take me to Le Suffren Hôtel in Port Grimaud?"

He nodded his head and spoke to me in broken English.

"*Oui*, sir. Eighty euros."

"Do you accept cards?" I asked, showing him my credit card without being able to do the conversion rate to see how much he was robbing me for the trip.

"*Oui*," he nodded, took my bag, and began to lead me to his car, a white compact with a blue "taxi" sign on the roof.

He tossed my bag in the back as I entered the car. We drove off of the airport's grounds and onto a road on a cliff, overlooking the sea. I rolled down the window, let the wind whip against my face, as I took in the scent of salt, dirt, the ocean, and trees; all of which were in perfect bloom. I saw olive and lemon trees on some of the properties we passed, a mix between exquisite hillside mansions, small, run-down clay-style homes, and perfect little farm-style abodes. The ride took roughly an hour, but the views were so impeccable it made the time fly by as I was lost in thought, dreaming of a life that included that backdrop. As we pulled off the main highway and into a harbor, my stomach began to drop. No longer were there large homes with stately manicured gardens, but instead, a small port town with beaten-down boats, many stained yellowed from years of neglect and salt water. Nothing about the town screamed wealth. It was as if I had gone from Dune Road in Quogue to Seaside Heights on the Jersey Shore. I became even more disheartened when he pulled up to a shabby little three-story stucco building with cracked clay tiles in the middle of the harbor. Nothing about it rang "French Riviera," and I started to grow concerned that it was, in fact, the hotel that had been booked for me.

"Are you sure this is it sir?"

"Yes, Missur."

He exited the vehicle and locked the doors, prompting me to join him after I used the payment screen on the back of his headrest.

"Sir, this is Saint-Tropez, right?"

He laughed.

"Oh no, Missur, this is Port Grimaud. A small fishing village. Saint-Tropez, is weal—" he cut himself off as he gestured the money symbol with his fingers.

"Welcome to the *real* France."

He extended his hand, and I mine. He entered the car and I watched him drive away. I took in the town, one I was not expecting, but was determined to find the beauty in since I was there on my company's dime, and surely beat my dark, ground-floor railroad apartment with bars on the windows. I walked towards the hotel and into the lobby. A small desk cut into the door frame with a room leading to who knows where occupied the check in area. I tapped a silver bell on the desk and within a moment, a woman who had to be in her eighties wearing a house dress like my grandma used to do came before me smiling softly.

"*Bonjour,* missur."

"*Bonjour,* madam. I am checking in for the night."

She stared back at me blankly. *This language barrier is gonna be an issue.*

I pulled the phone from my side and showed her the picture of the reservation. She pulled a pair of reading glasses dangling on her necklace up to her nose, squinted, and studied the phone as I held it to her. Satisfied with what she saw, she nodded and returned to the room behind her. I heard the sound of things moving around before she reappeared holding a key with a large plastic charm and a few sheets of paper. She slid both across the desk and without speaking, simply pointed to the information, then looked up at me, silently asking if I understood her before she handed me a pen. I produced my credit card and she ran it through the processor. Satisfied, she pointed to the staircase that led to my room on the second floor.

I thanked her and made my way up the stairs and down the short hallway to my room. As soon as I opened the door, I felt a sense of happiness and calm, for the room was well kept, with a terrace view overlooking the harbor. There was a sense of history in the place. A world where people woke each day, prepared fresh food, went to work with their hands, said hello to their neighbors and lived long, fulfilled lives. I placed my suitcase on the chair, logged into the Wi-Fi, and began to WhatsApp my coworker. She welcomed me and told me to enjoy my night alone, then informed me not to be late for pickup the following night as we were there for work and had a very tight schedule to be kept. I Googled the address and discovered that it was located directly in the heart of Saint-Tropez, off the boulevard that ran through the town. It was a private residence and I wondered why I hadn't simply been booked there for the two-day trip, where she and my other coworkers were seemingly staying, instead of here, twenty minutes away, in a seaside working town. Yet with one look out into the sun-stroked harbor, I decided to enjoy my day. I Googled the nearest beach, and luckily, it was within walking distance.

I changed into a bathing suit and walked out of the hotel and through the small town. I passed a small crêpe station tucked into a building looking out at the water and ordered a traditional ham and cheese crepe and a beer. I scarfed it down as I sat on a bench facing the harbor, not having eaten anything since before my flight the night prior, and downed the beer in a few swigs. After I passed the end of the harbor, I walked up a hill into the other side of the town where small, picturesque houses dotted the landscape. When I reached the top, the vista opened up into a vast beach area neatly tucked into the rock formations on both sides. The beach was filled with families lying under umbrellas on the rock-style sand. I made my way to an empty area before the water and laid down a towel I took from the hotel bathroom. I quickly realized I had forgotten to pack sunscreen, but nothing was going to ruin that moment of pure bliss. I sat on the towel and watched as small rolling waves rippled against the shoreline. I gazed on as I noticed families playing together on the sand and people frolicking in the calm, green-blue water.

It wasn't long before I made my way out into the sea, floated around on my back, and lapped in the drift as the sun beat down and rejuvenated me. When I sat back down, something hit me: I was the only single person in their thirties as far as I could see.

I thought about that for a moment. The simplicity of life. The beauty and value of that, so far removed from the fast-paced world of wealth and vapidity back in New York. The world that brought me to the continent to perform my duties at a famous nightclub where we were doing a pop-up event. I laughed at myself and those thoughts as I laid down to rest in the sun. . . . When I woke I could feel my skin beginning to char. I looked at my phone. I had been asleep for over two hours, the sun began to wane in the sky as it was after five. I decided it was time to take a final dip, gather my things, and head back to the hotel to prepare for dinner. I showered, learned what a bidet was (and enjoyed the experience), then changed and ventured out into the town in search of a restaurant.

I came upon a small shack with outdoor seating on a hill, adjacent to the harbor. I managed to order some wine and food without being able to read the menu and proceeded to watch the sun fall behind the hills as I listened to the sound of the boats crashing against one another. It was peaceful; the antithesis of what surrounded me on a nightly basis: raucous crowds, people yelling and whining like little children, attitudes of expectancy, people impaired by alcohol or drugs, slurring, yelling, fighting; and that was just outside the club. After dinner and a few more glasses of wine, I ventured back to the hotel to get some rest. I laid on the bed with the French doors open, and listened to the breeze and the boats. I began to think what a simple life would be like. To live in that kind of paradise surrounded by nature, living off the land. Where people seemed happy and food was affordable suddenly seemed ideal. Only I chose to live a life of constant hustle. Of vast ups and downs, smiles and tears, and prayers. It's what brought me there. I couldn't be too mad. I just knew I wanted more, and that I was more than my job and the role I played. I hoped one day I would return under different circumstances. It's the simple things that matter; I tried to convince myself. Instead,

I lived in New York City and chased dreams. And when I woke the next morning, I would be living within one.

The taxi was waiting for me when I stepped out of the hotel. The nice woman at the front desk had called it for me. I slept like a child with the French doors open all night; a feeling of calm I have never had before. It recharged me. I was ready for whatever awaited me that day, as I had no idea what I was expected to do other than to secure a tuxedo and be ready to work, whatever that meant. Who was I to argue? We traveled further into the cliffs, through the rolling roads, the sea at our side. As we made our way, the landscape changed dramatically. The homes were suddenly larger, if you could even see them, tucked behind large shrubs and age-old trees, hanging gardens and various types of vegetation. As the driver pulled off the main stretch, the road seemed tighter, feeling even more cramped than Grimaud, as we were suddenly within the town of Saint-Tropez. Old, small European homes lined the tight streets. Carpets and clothes hung outside on lines. Cobblestone streets and small paved sidewalks. *This* was the Europe I had been excited about. I wanted to get lost on those roads, turned around and spun in every direction. I wanted to shop in little storefronts and grab a pastry and coffee. While lost in my reverie we came to a stop in front of one of the nondescript buildings. The driver pointed to the small, slanted numbers displayed on the stucco, next to a large wooden door. He helped me get my luggage from the trunk and drove off. I stood, without cell service, before the door and knocked. No answer. Only silence. It was then I noticed a bell. I pressed it and its sound reverberated against the walls. A middle-aged woman with a slightly worn face and a large nose peeked her head out from the door, sizing me up and down with judgment.

"Is this Traves de Conquetts?"

"*Oui*," she nodded her head.

"Unit three?" I inquired.

She opened the door fully and welcomed me in. I entered the courtyard. Cobblestones ran the length of the floor; a dank smell of cellar permeated the air around us. She pointed to one of the four, smaller, wooden doors facing one another throughout the courtyard. I smiled and thanked her as she closed and locked the main door behind me. I walked to Unit Three, which was painted in black script on the door, and knocked heavily. I waited as she entered what was most likely her unit. I knocked again and waited. After a few moments I heard some shuffling from within and the door opened, revealing an enigmatic woman in her late twenties, with long chestnut hair, emerald green eyes, round cheeks, and a chiseled face with perfectly pouted lips. It was as if time froze. I was taken, and it wasn't until she spoke that I came to.

"Can I help you?" she spoke clearly with the hint of an accent. *Was it German?*

"Oh, yea. I'm sorry, shit. You speak English!" I said clumsily.

"Fluently," and looked at me as if it were my turn to tell her why I was standing at her door with my luggage.

"Oh, sorry. I am here to meet Jacques. Is he around?"

"Oh! Are you Nick?"

"I am," I stated confidently, elated that she had already heard about me. What did she know? Or was it simply my ego and narcissism getting the best of me?

"Well, come on in, I'll show you your room."

She stood aside from the doorway and let me in. I stood in the foyer looking up at a cramped, tight apartment with a kitchen I could see at the back and a living area without a TV, only a couch.

"I'm Andrea," she said as she extended her small, fine hand. I took it in mine, soft as it was and felt a spark. I pulled back. *Was that real?*

"We're right upstairs," she shifted the conversation and walked onto the staircase.

I couldn't help but notice her slim, sinewy limbs and her formed figure which was on display from the cutoff jean shorts and tight T-shirt she was wearing. She led me down a tight hallway with four doors on one side. When we reached the last door, she opened it.

"This is you."

The room was small. It had a twin bed with a small throw blanket and sheets that reminded me of my grandma's house. A small bathroom was adjoined.

"Jacques said he would be back in a few hours to get ready. Here's the Wi-Fi."

She took my phone and tapped away before handing it back to me.

"We're going to head to town for lunch if you wanna join?"

"Love to. . . ."

"Cool, so why don't you settle and I'll see you downstairs in fifteen?"

"Cool."

I laid my luggage on the bed and took my tux out and put it on a hanger in the bathroom and searched for an iron. No dice. I stared at my wrinkled tux for a moment, hoping someone in the house had an iron. I took out my travel case and rested it on the sink, brushed my teeth, and looked in the mirror. All seemed in place as I threw some water over my face and patted it dry with a towel. I went through my phone and sent a message to my coworker that I had made it. She sent back the numbers of our driver in case of emergencies and reminded me that I must be ready to go by 3 p.m. I kept the same clothes on and made my way downstairs where Andrea and another stunning woman were standing in the foyer, ready to go.

"Hey Nick, this is Frederick, my best friend."

All six feet of her tall frame stood over me as we shook hands.

"Nice to meet you, Frederick. We waiting on anyone else?

"Nah, they'll all be back later," Andrea stated.

"Cool, you two lead the way."

I followed them down the cobblestones, through the wooden door (which I found out we had a key for), and onto the narrow street corridor. As we walked, they spoke in the language I thought must be German to one another. I didn't feel it rude as I did not know them and figured it was kind they allowed me to join them for lunch. Then Andrea turned back to me and said, "Sorry about the Dutch, but her English isn't so hot."

"No worries," I replied as they continued to chat, realizing how naïve I was about other languages.

A few blocks later we made a turn and we were out onto a walkway on the water. Before us sat the largest yachts I have ever seen. Hundreds of feet long, their tails resting against the base of the water wall. Multiple outdoor cafes faced the water. It was the antithesis of where I had been the day previous. No families, no simple people living a simple life, but instead, supreme wealth. The brands were everywhere you looked: Chanel, Gucci, Prada, and the like. The fashion and sunglasses transported me. It was what I had dreamed of. A tiny fish within a great pond. I was in awe and began to start feeling myself. As if I belonged there. But I didn't. I just happened to be there. *Act as if.*

"Let's sit over here and eat, cool?" Andrea asked.

We agreed and sat at an empty table in one of the café's facing the slips. The waiter came over and dropped menus before us and began rattling off questions I couldn't understand. Andrea responded to him in what seemed perfect French and turned to me.

"Do you know what you want to order? I'll tell him for you."

"You speak French too?" I asked, surprised.

"And German. The difference between us and you Americans. We learn multiple languages."

"I can speak a little Spanish."

She laughed and spoke to Frederick in Dutch. They laughed together. *At me?* I looked over the menu and decided on a simple burger and a Coke, then told Andrea.

"Anything to drink?"

"Not now, it's going to be a long night."

"But a fun one!"

The waiter returned and Andrea ordered for us, some wine and mussels for her and Frederick, a burger and Coke for me. We began to chat and I learned more about her and what brought her there. She worked in Amsterdam doing some sort of charity stuff, but spent a lot of time previously modeling in Paris, where she knew Jacques from his time there working in clubs. Although she was proverbially "out of the game," she was invited and asked to bring a friend to the event to help round out the guestlist so all the rich men had women around; a typical nightlife recipe. Beautiful women (models) bring wealthy men (money) and nightclub owners win (success/notoriety/celebrity).

That's the equation.

And I was there to get to know the wealthy men, befriend them, and get them to come to our events around the world and our clubs in NYC. I was the outlier as I was not a true "invitee" like the rest. I had a purpose, to network. But no, I was not on anyone's "you must know" list. More of a function of the system. A cog in the wheel. But I would use the opportunity to the best of my advantage. For my Rolodex. My future endeavors. For fundraising for making a movie—or so I thought. When the check arrived, I paid, attempting to be a gentleman, only to be taught a very important lesson: know where you are. I never expected a lunch with two glasses of wine to be $400 USD. I would have to work an extra shift when I returned to make that money back.

Lesson number one: this is not *your* world.

After smiling off the small heart attack from the price realization, we walked back to the house. Andrea and I couldn't stop speaking to one another. So much so, Frederick was a little aggravated, feeling like she was suddenly the third wheel on the journey. I could feel her sense of relief when we got back to the house to get ready for the event. She was happy to see me run off to my room, leaving her to her friend. When I entered, I immediately noticed my hanging tux and shirt, still rumpled. I went down the hall and knocked on Andrea's door and asked if she had an iron. Not only did she; she offered to iron it for me because I treated them to lunch, which I happily accepted, as I hate ironing. An hour later I was dressed in my formal wear and standing outside alone, waiting for a car to pick me up. And when the clock struck the noted time a large black Mercedes-Benz Sprinter arrived. A man stepped out and introduced himself to me as Jim, a six-foot-four monster who was a part of Mr. DiCaprio's private security detail, and informed me he would be my driver during my stay. *Now we're talking!* I asked him if I could sit in the front seat as I preferred that to the stale, dark back of a windowless Sprinter. He had no issue with it and off we drove, through the small streets of the town.

"Where are we going, by the way?" I asked

"Domaine Bertaud Belieu."

"Nice!"

"Been here before?"

"No. I just know wine. Never been to a vineyard."

"You should be in for a treat . . . overall," he winked at me.

Before long we came upon a vast piece of property in the

middle of the cliffs. The sign outside stated the name of the vineyard, but that was not all. The level of security at these gates as
we made our way up was unlike anything I've ever seen. You
would think the president was coming to town. We were stopped,
and I had to present my ID as the car was swept for bombs. We
were soon cleared and allowed to drive up the long winding road
where vines stretched out for as far as the eye could see. A large
building rose into plain sight. We pulled into a large driveway and
the car stopped.

"I'll be here when the event is over. Once you are ready, I'll
bring you to the club."

"Appreciate it, thanks."

"Enjoy," he smiled knowingly.

I began to walk up the stone stairs, onto the veranda overlooking the property. When I reached the top, I saw my coworker
dressed in a gown, taking photos in front of a lemon tree.

"Welcome!" she said and walked over to give me a hug,
"Damn you look good!"

"Thank you, so do you. Love the dress."

"Dope, right?" she stated as she spun around, the frills trailing
as she turned.

"This place is insane," I replied.

"It's a dream. Can you take a few shots of me for IG?" she
asked.

"Sure," I answered.

"Get some facing this way, then we can do some that way.
I want to get all these backdrops in."

I proceeded to photograph her for a few minutes as the event
staff finished setting up the various bars and tables for the cocktail hour. When I was done, I handed her phone back and we
stood overlooking the vineyard, its vast rolling hills out onto the
horizon.

"How do you like your rental, sorry it had to be with a promoter, but the hotels here were way too expensive."

"That's why I was out in a fishing town last night?"

"Better than New York, no?"

"True. Where are you staying?"

"With a client at his house. Sick!"

"I can't get the look?"

"He's not going to let a dude he doesn't know stay. Sorry."

"All good. So, what do we do now?"

"Have fun."

"Wait, I thought—"

"Honey, we are *guests* for this!"

"Really?"

"Yes boo!" she said and walked over to one of the standing tables where her purse was. She reached inside and pulled out a seat number and handed it to me.

It read: Table 12 Seat 4 and showed a small seat map for the table so I would be sure to get it right.

She looked at her watch.

"People should start to arrive soon, go get yourself acquainted."

I left her outside and made my way to the main room. It was a large hall, transformed with large flower arrangements, banquet tables, chairs, a stage with two large screens, and a podium. It was about the size of a wedding venue. It was grand, yet intimate. On the stage there was a shimmering, jet-black grand piano. I walked around a bit, admiring the flowers and the flatware. *It was an event fit for a king, modern-day kings*, I thought to myself. I had never worn a tuxedo before and had surely never been to an event of that magnitude. And although I was technically "the help," I was told to take part. To enjoy, have fun. Sounded easy enough, but I started to get a pang of nervousness in my stomach. *Who the hell was I to be here, in this room, with these people?*

I worked rooms every night; rich and powerful people, celebrities, it never fazed me, I felt at home. The difference was that it was my world, hospitality, within the club I worked for, that modicum of power I held which gave me the confidence to interact with anyone who entered. Why should this be any different? Though it was. I was not in my element. I was Cinderella at the ball without Prince Charming. And as I wandered around in thought, the lights suddenly changed and a band, which I didn't even notice had set up, began playing on the stage.

I shook my fears aside and told myself to act the part. That it may have been my first time in a room like that, but as an aspiring actor, writer, director, it would not be my last. And really, weren't most of the people in the room self-made? Probably not, but at least I could tell myself that and that they were only *people*. Like you, me, mom, and dad. And as I began to give myself the confidence I needed to get through the night without feeling less than, I found myself outside on the veranda again, watching intently as glamorous people began to arrive.

I found my coworker and sidled up next to her.

"You don't mind if I stay by you for a bit? Maybe introduce me to some people?"

"Sure. Relax, you seem nervous. You ain't never nervous."

"I am, actually."

"Just be yourself," she smiled and squeezed my arm. I don't think she had ever been that nice to me before.

I stood silently and watched as people began to flood the room. It was surreal as I watched people I had mostly only seen in movies, on red carpets, or nightly talk shows casually enter, grab a drink at the bar waving, smiling, and hugging one another like a high school reunion. I soon felt more at ease as I settled in, watching those people in their element. There was no pomp or circumstance, save the elaborate dresses and jewelry of the women, or the buttoned-up tuxedos of the men. They were no different than "normal" people at a wedding, birthday, or any other event. The thought calmed me, and before long I found myself strolling around, nodding to people whom I had only dreamed of working with throughout my years as a struggling artist. I stumbled upon the raffle section where the auction items were located by accident. I had taken a turn off the veranda that led me to a tent, aside from the main gala room where pieces of art and sculptures sat displayed on the wall or in glass cases; pieces by Rothko, Damian Hurst, and Warhol. I knew from the clientele, as well as the two security officers standing watch close by, that they were *real*. They were the reason we were there. Rich people bidding against one another to support the foundation. I had never been to an auction. I stood before one of the paintings in awe when I heard my name.

"Nick!"

I turned around and saw my friend from acting school. I asked myself why a person I had been through the trenches of training with happened to be at the exact same party? But then I immediately remembered who she was dating at the time.

Me: the help.

Her: a guest.

"How are you?!"

We hugged and she introduced me to a girl with her, a stunning model who graced the covers of various magazines. We exchanged pleasantries and talked about the elaborate event we found ourselves at. I informed her I was there for work and she then understood why she was running into me there, four thousand miles from home in a place I had no business being. I asked if she didn't mind if I tagged along for a bit as I didn't know anyone. She told me it was fine and we set out to get a drink at the bar. With the comfort of an old friend and hers, both of whom happened to be wildly attractive, I suddenly had no issue sparking up conversations with those around me; go figure. The small dose of confidence was what I needed, as no one likes the lonesome guy trolling around the bar. With my new friends in tow, I was soon chatting with some of the biggest movers and shakers in the world, speaking no differently than you would to Joe from the local pizzeria. The only difference was that most were famous. Though as I came to know, they were no different than you and me; they were just wealthier, more successful and in the public eye. For the most part they had the same insecurities as everyone does. One actress asked me if her dress didn't look a little off in the shoulders, to which I replied it did not, that it was perfection, as was she. She smiled, rolled her eyes and asked me who *I* was and how I made it to *that party* as she motioned her pointer finger at me playfully. When I told her, she laughed and said it made sense. She went on to say she was friends with one of my bosses and loved to come out to his parties. When I slyly asked her why we had never met, she said she didn't go out much anymore since becoming a mother, her party lifestyle being a thing of the past. As we spoke (and dare I say, flirted?) I really began to feel a sense of ease, so much so that when I looked over and saw Andrea make her entrance with whom I expected was Jacques and a gaggle of models, I smiled at her with a level of confidence I hoped would make her swoon, as if I belonged there speaking to that A-list actress. I excused myself for fear of overstaying my welcome and made my way from conversation to conversation. I was feeling more and more empowered as I went, so much so that I began to introduce myself to familiar faces from society pages. I was living a dream.

A little while later, I found my table and my seat next to a billionaire family of kids who often came to the club with whom I was very familiar and struck up a conversation. They introduced me to the others at the table: an art heir, a famous model, and some other businessmen whose names I had never heard. The servers swarmed the tables offering red or white wine, then food runners dropped off the first course. I ate, drank, and chatted about nothing of importance, mostly very superficial and without much substance, all while minding my table manners at each step; bread plate to my left, butter knife, salad fork. Soon the entrées arrived and I found myself carefully attacking a filet mignon, fork in the left hand, carefully cutting with the right, one piece of meat sliced at a time and gingerly placing them into my mouth, avoiding any spills. About halfway through the entrées, the lights dimmed and the stage lights went up. The master of ceremonies of the night introduced none other than Sir Elton John, who walked on and sat at the jet-black piano and spoke into the microphone saying his hellos to the audience and the host before belting out a few of his greatest hits.

At that point the guests, most of whom hadn't finished their entrées, nor did I, stood and began filming him, swaying along and bobbing to his tune. I sat in awe as one of my favorite artists of all time, whom I had never seen live, was performing so close to me. After his performance, he stood, bowed, and walked off as John Legend took his place. Playing two of his biggest hits, his voice reverberating around the room, couples engaged into one another, the girls swooning as many of the men remained deep in conversation with people I assume they were doing some sort of business with, or hoped to, walked around carelessly, working the room. The concert portion didn't last too long and dessert and coffee were soon served as Mr. DiCaprio took the podium. He thanked everyone for their support and donations to the foundation and then announced that there was still more work to do in helping the cause and began the auction. I sat in awe as forty-five million dollars was raised by roughly twenty-five individuals in the room! The most interesting item of the night was not the art, but when he took off the Rolex he was wearing and pushed the bidding up significantly as he added the final, off book item for the night. I couldn't help but sit there and think of how much debt I carried, how what I made in a year (and at the time I was doing pretty well) couldn't even buy the couch in one of those people's houses. It all seemed so attainable in theory, but up close, it was light years away. A few moments after the bidding ceased and the applause stopped, my coworker tapped me on the shoulder.

"Time to go," she said.

I rose, said my polite goodbyes to those who were left at the table, and set off in the Sprinter with her to the club for work. The dream receded in the background as I shifted my focus to the night ahead as we went over the reservation list, minimum spends, and the way operations would need to go. We arrived within ten minutes and were escorted by security to the world-famous VIP Room which was not yet open, but ready for us to take the helm and prepare for the afterparty. She led the fray, introducing me to the manager of the club. We walked the room as we learned the table numbers, where the service stations were located, and how the process would work from her running the door, to me getting credit cards (no IDs were necessary with that group as it would be an insult) and seating tables to the servers sections (which in France are men I found, not women) who would take over from there. After the walk through we held a preshift in which I went through our expected clientele, what their minimums would be, who needed champagne parades, what type of bottles they preordered, and all the other information needed to run a successful operation for the night.

Shortly after the clock struck eleven, there was a line outside the door awaiting our opening. When we got outside, the paparazzi had already gathered to await the celebrities and socialites who would be in attendance. As we went to take our stations, the general manager informed us that they had assigned their regular doorman to assist us so we didn't *ruin* any of their existing relationships. It didn't sit well with us, but it wasn't our first rodeo and we had to respect them to avoid ruining relationships on either side. And then, the night began as they usually do. Slowly but surely. The first hour was business as usual as our guests trickled in. The following hour picked up at a pace that I was used to, but as usually happens, our egos won on both sides of the rope (staff and guests), and nothing went seamlessly. The place got packed and everyone outside felt they were more important than anyone else and after a whirlwind hour or so of arguing, running, and sweating; it was all over. The club was full, the tables were sat, and I was done with work. I shook hands with the staff and went inside to drink and schmooze with our guests.

Around 2:30 a.m. the club began to thin out and I approached the GM (general manager) to make sure we had all the spends of our clients listed correctly before I left for the afterparty at a client's mansion. He gave me a bunch of numbers that didn't even match the minimums and it was then I knew he was trying to rob us. I thanked him for his time and effort, then snuck over to the service station and took photos of all the receipts so we would be able to win the argument in a few days when he would inevitably attempt to avoid paying our dues. I said my goodbyes to his staff and set out to find my driver to take me to the afterparty with Andrea, Jacques, and the girls. Upon getting into the back of the Sprinter with everyone, Andrea offered me some MDMA (ecstasy), which I hadn't done since my youth. I quickly partook, figuring I wanted to go on an adventure with her for the night. I downed the pill and swilled it back with a bottle of water. The ride wasn't long, and when the door opened, again I was in complete awe.

We were in the circular driveway of a massive modern mansion. Sleek. Glass. Built upon crisp green imported grass off a cliff overlooking the sea. A DJ played house music as people danced and frolicked in the moonlight. Some people were swimming, clothing *optional*. Others laid on chaise lounges, smoking, drinking, and talking. Andrea pulled me near the edge of the lawn where there was a large tree with a vast trunk and thick arms that held an immense display of greenery that filled it out. From a significant branch, two ropes were tied that led to a double seated swing. She sat and I stood beside her as she swayed softly back and forth, the breeze ruffling the trees enough that we could hear them through the music being played back by the house.

"This is beautiful. I've never been anywhere like this before," I said as the drug began to run through my body, filling me with a heightened sense of feeling.

"I love the south of France, it reminds me of Mykonos, only different," she replied.

"I've never been."

"I'm surprised, I mean, you work in this world. Don't you have to go and be around this scene?"

She was right. There was what we all referred to in nightlife as the "one percent of the one percent" cycle. Cannes during the film festival in the spring. Ibiza, Mykonos, the south of France, and the Amalfi Coast throughout July and August until Labor Day. Always making it back to New York in time for Fall Fashion Week.

"Truth is, I'm an artist. This is like a bartending job for me. I take it seriously, but it's not my life. I'd like to think my life is real. For the most part, all this is fake. Smoke and mirrors," I confessed.

"I can see that," she said as she drifted off in thought for a moment, gazing at the giant full moon, sea, and mountains in the distance. I followed her lead and took in the surroundings, the music a soft, underlying soundtrack in the distance. She grabbed my hand and the spark returned, running through every fiber of my being.

Then she spoke.

"I'm a yoga instructor too, you know," she looked at me and smiled. I smiled back and we locked eyes for a moment, frozen in our perfect world.

"I am a real person. Not like a lot of these other people," she added.

"Do you ever come to New York?" I asked.

"Sometimes. It's so much easier, and cheaper, for me to get around Europe though."

"Well, if there's a way . . ."

She nodded, then leaned into me and we kissed. The soft, supple feeling of her lips on mine. A slow, passionate kiss that shook me to my core. We pulled back and laughed.

"That was nice," she said.

"It was beautiful," I stated confidently.

"Oh no, the drugs seem to be talking!"

We laughed.

"You wanna go back to the party? I think my friend is going to get upset."

"Sure," I answered.

I helped her off the swing and followed her back as the music rose, the raucousness of the party was in full swing. We grabbed a drink and then I excused myself to go work the room for a bit, conversing with clients and strangers. As I moved from group to group, I kept looking for her. And sometimes I would catch her looking at me and we would smile.

When the sun began to rise and the party began to disperse, I found her.

"Wanna go back to the flat?"

"Yeah, I think so."

She looked over to her friend and walked a few steps towards her, calling out.

"Ready?"

Her friend nodded.

"But wait, do we have to grab Jacques" Frederick asked.

"I have a driver, if you don't care to wait." I stated, sure Jacques would find his way back.

They shrugged and we walked into the house and through the living area, out into the front drive where the Mercedes, and Jim, waited.

"Ready?" he asked.

"Let's do it."

"Where's the other guy and the others?" he followed up.

"Inside. You may have to come back for them."

He nodded and we entered the back of the Sprinter. . . .

We were ripped from our blissful slumber as her friend banged loudly on the door, yelling in Dutch. I sat up startled, in a daze from the drugs and trying to understand what was happening. It was then she looked at me and calmly told me they were running late to their flight and that the car was outside waiting. In the midst of my doughy-eyed evening I had forgotten that, I too, had a flight to catch. Though at that moment I was unsure of what time it was or if I was going to miss it, but didn't want to stay in that place alone, so I started throwing clothes on and tossing everything I had into my suitcase. I checked my phone, and discovered the numerous missed messages from my coworker and driver.

"You mind if I catch a ride with you guys?"

"Sure, but you have to hurry."

I rinsed my mouth with water and toothpaste and tossed my toiletry bag into my luggage. I rushed down the stairs and out the door and over the cobblestones behind them and into the smallest taxi I have ever seen. I stuffed into the back draped over one another as they told the driver in no uncertain French terms that he had to step on it. We couldn't help but laugh out loud as he took the notes to heart and performed his best Street Racer, peeling out from the small alleyway, whipping around a blind corner and out onto the highway north towards the Nice Côte d'Azur Airport. Her friend played music and we sang as we held one another. After about an hour, we hit traffic and the girls accepted the fact that they had missed their flight and booked the next one out. I knew my flight departed in the late evening and noticed the sun just starting to wane over the sky, so I assumed I was fine. The driver made a few twists and turns off the main road, onto those less traveled, and got us there unscathed shortly after. As we went up to security, the reality of life began to pour down on me. She was wonderful and I was smitten, but what could I do?

"Come to London with us. The flights aren't bad and there is another seat," Andrea stated.

In that moment it was as if my entire life stopped and I levitated out of my body and watched myself from above. There I was, at a crossroads. Do I follow her and risk getting fired, or do I roll the dice and let fate work out whatever was to come with us? And in that moment, one which seemed to last forever, but was only seconds, I gave her a hug, looked into her eyes, and said goodbye. I promised I would find a way to see her again. She kissed me and held me and didn't want to let go, as her friend, who was gripping her arm and pulling her away, detached us. I watched them go. And at that moment, I looked up at the flight tracker and saw that mine was about to board. But I did not move. I stayed and watched her, and she me, until she proceeded down the tunnel to her terminal and disappeared. I couldn't help but think of so many things. How beautiful she was. How magical I felt with her. And how I was too broke (an excuse?) or scared (real?) and how all the choices I made in life were no longer spontaneous. That I somehow did things the right way, or tried to, that the trip, the whirlwind of two simple days was not my life, yet it was. That I would see her again, or not. But no matter the outcome, no matter what the universe would bring, it would be far better from where I had come. As I took my seat at the window and put on my headphones, I played one of those songs that makes me cry, that one that lets me know everything's going to be alright, even if it isn't.

And I allowed Elton to sing "Daniel" to me as I thought to myself, *How the fuck did I get here?* and *If people only knew where I was fifteen years ago!* I fell fast asleep thinking I had an even brighter future to live and love if I kept on keeping on. . . .

CHAPTER 2

THE BEGINNING OF THE END

Kearny, New Jersey—September 12, 2000

I jumped from my bed as I was jolted awake, and attempted to make sense of my surroundings as my father yelled.

"What the fuck are you still doing asleep? You're going to be late!" he screamed.

Shit.

"I slept through the alarm," I said, holding my head in my hands.

"You look like shit," he retorted, stepping close.

"And you reek of booze! What's wrong with you?" he questioned, not amused with my behavior, but at a loss of how to address it.

"Who cares. What can they possibly do to me now?" I answered matter-of-factly.

"You need to get showered and changed and clean yourself up. We are going to be late," he fumed, accepting the fact that there wasn't possibly any more trouble I could find than being late to my sentencing day.

I brushed past him and into the bathroom. As I stepped into

the shower, a rush of emotion ran through me as the water poured over my body. It would be the last time I would shower in my apartment. The last time I would shower *alone*, for years. The last time I would have soap, shampoo, *and* face wash. The last time I would have a warm, plush towel wrapped around my body. The last time I would look at my reflection in a glass vanity mirror and brush my teeth with a real toothbrush. The last, the last. . . .

"You have fun?" he asked, careful to keep our last time together light.

"Not enough, that's for sure," I said as I entered my room and reached for the clothes I had laid out on a hanger the night before. In doing so, I noticed my breath; I did reek of booze. The smell made my stomach turn. I gagged lightly, tossed the towel aside, and got dressed.

"Nick, let's go!" he yelled from the other room.

The gravity of the situation sunk in and I put the pedal to the metal. I finished buttoning my shirt and began tying my tie as I entered the living room where my cousin Mark stood, next to my father, who was cleaning the crust from his eyes wearing nothing but his underwear.

"I guess this is it," I said uncomfortably as I completed my knot and pulled the collar down over it.

"Stay strong in there. Remember, anyone fucks with you, fight. And keep fighting, never stop," he said and moved in to give me a bear hug.

As we embraced, I felt the tears begin to well up in my eyes, but pushed them away as we separated. I looked at him.

"I love you brother," I said.

"Love you too. Call me anytime. Let me know if you need anything."

I nodded my head and followed my father down the steps that I have known so well over the entirety of my life. Each one felt like an eternity. I counted them as I went. There were more steps than years I have been alive and I remembered all of them. All the memories of my youth in that house. My *grandmother's* house. Every single Christmas in her living room. Opening the newest G.I. Joe and other gifts, some I begged for and others I never wanted. Fresh-baked apple and cherry pies along with her famous chocolate chip cookies. My prepubescent years of waking up on weekend mornings and raiding the cupboard for the newest Franken Berry cereal. Playing by myself with toys in the backyard because my cousins were far older and out chasing girls and parties. Innocence. Youth. Family. Life. Freedom. All the things I took for granted. When I finally reached the last step and opened the screen door to the porch, reality hit me. Only three more to go. One for each year I would be gone. I paused for a moment before stepping onto the red brick, fearing that once I did, everything I ever knew would be gone.

"Let's go!" my father shouted as he entered his car parked in front.

Torn from my memories I proceeded, watching each foot under me as it firmly planted onto the next step. When I reached the broken sidewalk, I turned and gave the house one last look. It was the second home I had left in my short twenty-one years on this earth. Yet it was the only place where family memories persisted, because I still had access to it. I would hold on to that house, those memories, during my time. And when I felt I had accepted that truth and my fate, I turned and entered the car. Silence, except the sounds of a burning cigarette and my father's inhales and exhales surrounded us for the first few minutes before my father attempted to talk around the issue at hand. He mentioned my mother meeting us, my brother sending his regards, and something about my aunt. I knew he wanted to say something, and waited until it came.

Soon he began to talk about his tour in the army; how he remembered when he was drafted into Vietnam. The fear and uncertainty he had felt. He had known men who did not return home and feared the same fate awaited him. He was living in my grandmother's house. When his day arrived, he had packed his bag, said goodbye to his mother and sister, and left for the base down at Fort Dix. He explained how ironic it felt to still be on US soil, yet so far from his old life. He opened up to me for the first time about his number being called, then placed on a large aircraft with the other men and shipped out to the jungles of Vietnam. Then it came. . . .

"My point is, the next few years will be difficult, but at least no one is shooting at you. You will survive. You may come home scarred, but you will come home *alive*."

As I listened, I stared out the window, taking everything in, knowing that I wouldn't have it again for a long, long time. Each house we passed, each tree, each leaf, each store, each car, each person; everything. It made me sad that I never noticed all of it before, at least not like I did at that moment. And I pondered about how beautiful life is. How much I would miss it. I had spent most of the years I could remember selling drugs, chasing money and respect, partying, and looking for something that I never found. Yet at that moment, taking in God's gifts of nature, I suddenly felt like I could do it. I would do it. I could get through it in order to get back to all the beauty that I took for granted. I would do whatever I had to and keep on the path I had begun. It would be hard, but I could do it. I vowed to make it in this life. I needed to make it. Somehow, someway. I refused to let all this life pass me by without a fight. I was going to fight. It was then I felt Hope return. She rested her hands on my shoulders and I felt strangely secure as we got closer to the courthouse in Hackensack, NJ. And before I knew it, like an amusement park ride you wish wouldn't end, we had arrived. And everything in my being wanted to get back on and ride again, only I didn't have any more tickets, or money, and I simply had to live with the memory.

The sun was shining brightly onto the stone facade of the courthouse. Blades of fresh grass looked as if they had been dipped in morning dew. Yellow, pink, purple, and orange tulips peeked out of the flowerbeds surrounding the imposing stone staircase that led to the large wooden front doors. I rushed to the bushes and dry heaved as lawyers and citizens stared at me; my father shook his head. I returned to his side and we made our way up the dreaded staircase. By the time I reached the top, I was nearly out of breath because of my hangover. After walking through the doors, we were held in line by the officers standing before a metal detector. I could feel the sweat dripping from my forehead and armpits, soiling my shirt. I wiped away at it with my tie. We proceeded through them, removed the contents of our pockets, placed them onto the conveyor belt as we passed, and gathered them on the other side before making our way to the elevators. When the doors opened on the second floor, I saw my mother. She was waiting on a bench outside the courtroom with a wad of tissues in her hands. She had never looked so beautiful, minus the tears running down her cheeks, as I approached. I reached out to her and took her in my arms, patting the back of her head softly as she cried. I promised her it would all be okay and asked her to be strong for me. I knew in that moment while comforting her, that the epiphany I had earlier was linked directly to her. It took my father's story for me to understand it fully. I may have been the one losing my freedom, but my parents were the ones temporarily losing a son. And as I already painfully knew from his absence that day, in my brother's eyes, he had already lost his only sibling years ago. If there was a time for me to grow up, it was then. I had to face my punishment and become a man.

I entered the courtroom with my head held high, holding my mother's hand firmly as my father followed behind us. I hugged and kissed her for what would be the last time, at least for a long time. She straightened my tie and looked me over, then sat down on an empty bench in the back of the room. I turned to my father and hugged him. He looked me in the eye and nodded, reminding me of all that we spoke about in the car with one look. I continued toward the defendant's table at the front of the courtroom where my codefendants were already waiting with our respective lawyers, and accepted that I was nearly late. I noticed the other young men's family members scattered throughout the courtroom as I looked at my mother and smiled, showing my strength, and not the true pain and anguish I was feeling inside. I found my father and did the same as the rumble of a loud baritone voice reverberated throughout the courtroom.

". . . the Honorable Judge Timothy Sullivan presiding," bellowed the bailiff.

The judge entered wearing the traditional black robe and proceeded to sit, enabling us to follow suit. I watched intently as he studied the paperwork before him.

"Prosecutor Ralph, the State agrees to the terms set forth in this plea agreement?"

"Yes, we do Your Honor," he replied.

The judge asked each of us whether or not we understood the plea agreement set forth. When the judge spoke to me, the prosecutor interjected.

"Your Honor, the State does *not* agree with Mr. Marshall's intended plea agreement."

"Your office arranged these pleas, Mr. Ralph, and you just stated to the court that you are in agreement with them. Did you *not?*" the judge asked, visibly annoyed.

"Yes, Your Honor, but our original offer was one more year

for Mr. Marshall. We agreed 'in term' pending your judgment on the matter so as to avoid the cost of further litigation to the State. We ask that you review his plea specifically, within the context of the severity of the charges presented in this case and suggest another year be added to his sentence."

This prick, I thought to myself as my attorney, Mr. Neary, interjected.

"Your Honor, the State offered the plea, whether begrudgingly or not, my client signed it, therefore this should be a moot point."

"Mr. Ralph, as I understand you have had over a year to plead this matter out. For the record, please state why are you asking the court to reevaluate the plea agreements?"

"Mr. Marshall both planned and partook in these events Your Honor, therefore subjecting him to a stricter penalty than his cohorts. My intention was to expedite the process and avoid the cost of trial to the State by offering him the same plea as the other defendants. My hope, being that you would understand the State's side and rule with us."

The judge scanned the paperwork again.

"They all did it, right? *Together*?" the judge asked.

"Yes, Your Honor."

"Then that's it, they all get the same sentence. If you had wanted so direly to force Mr. Marshall into a higher plea, then you shouldn't have offered him the plea that you did. Motion denied. At this time, I would ask that each defendant recount their level of guilt for the court so we may accept the pleas they have been given."

We each recounted our versions of the events of that fateful evening as the court reporter furiously typed away, implanting the truth of that night into the record. Tears were rampant throughout the room. You could hear the audible sniffles and gasps from the onlookers. I was the last to speak and was forced to stop on multiple occasions throughout due to my own crying. Mr. Neary placed a fatherly hand on my shoulder in consolation, helping me get through. When I finished my story, each lawyer was given a chance to speak, none as brilliantly as Mr. Neary. He lambasted the prosecution for going after us the way they did. He reminded the court that besides that one mistake in our young lives, nothing had indicated that we were threats to society. All of us were college students from good families. What kind of example would it set by throwing away a young man's life for one mistake? He argued that rehabilitation is the answer, not incarceration. The judge seemed to be listening intently to everyone before he spoke. I couldn't read his demeanor, and hung on his every word as he opened his mouth to hand down his decision, my last hope for a miracle.

"The aggravating factors in this case outweigh the mitigating ones by four to three. Any other option than incarceration sends the wrong message to our society and other youths who may act the way these young men did. Hopefully this will remind people that you may not run around brandishing weapons and committing robberies in our towns and cities, no matter who the victim may be. Gentlemen, I hope that you will use this time to reflect on the mistakes you have made. You are all young enough that upon your release you may have an opportunity to live a full, clean, and straight life. I accept the pleas as set forth. You are hereby sentenced under the No Early Release Act, and remanded to the State of New Jersey for a period of three years, with a one-year stipulation without parole eligibility. Bailiff, please cuff them and lead them away."

I shuddered as he hammered down the gavel. Neary grasped my shoulder tighter in his hand and gave me an encouraging pinch before he released it. I turned to him and shook his hand while thanking him for his effort. He informed me that he would check up on me soon and told me to call if I needed anything. I could hear gasps from the benches behind us as the bailiffs approached us with handcuffs drawn. We held our hands in front of us, waiting to be cuffed. I turned enough so it would be hidden from my mother's view, then looked up over my shoulder towards her. She was crying hysterically, wiping her tears over and over with the same used tissues. I stared until I caught her eyes. When I did, I smiled, then mouthed the words, "everything's going to be okay."

I looked to my father and nodded my head like a man before the bailiffs led us through the exit. As the door closed behind us, I never looked back. We left the people who care for us in the courtroom trying to pick up the pieces we had discarded.

CHAPTER 3

BERGEN COUNTY JAIL/CRAF

Hackensack/Trenton, New Jersey—January 2001

I was awakened by the sound of keys jangling as they turned in the lock of my cell door. I opened my eyes and saw the corrections officer standing over me in the doorway, the faint morning light reflecting against the stark fluorescents that line the tier outside.

"Marshall. Get your shit. You're going down," the officer stated emphatically.

I went to the sink and splashed water over my face. My distorted reflection stared back at me through the plastic mirror. It was real. I was going down to state prison.

I rolled my bedding into a ball and dragged it down the stairs along with two large plastic bags containing my book collection. I dropped the bedding beside the officer's bubble and said goodbye to the Corrections Officer (CO) on duty as I walked up the gangplank for the last time.

I was placed in a holding cell and given a bologna sandwich and milk, although I couldn't bear to consume it. I heard a commotion and peered out of the window but couldn't see anything.

Then I heard keys rattle. The sound grew closer; louder. Then I saw them: state corrections officers. They were large, fit, and well-built men, nothing like the mostly rotund county COs. Their uniforms were dark blue and they wore large utility belts with gun holsters around their waists with heavy black Hi-Tec boots on their feet. These men commanded your immediate respect. It is their business and you are their commodity.

"Who's Marshall?" one asked.

"That's me, sir." I said out of respect.

"Nicholas Marshall, SBI #340523C?" he asked.

"Uh, yes sir. I think," I stammered

"Why are you hesitating? Is that you and is that your number?" he asked, aggressively.

"Yes, it is," I stated.

"When you are addressed from here on out, that is your name. You will remember that number, because that is your name. If you forget that number, you don't exist. Are you getting me?"

This is very different already.

"I understand, officer."

"What's your name?" he demanded.

"053423C, sir."

"That's not your number. Your number is 340523C. Now step in here and strip down to your essentials," he said as he pointed to a small room. It was empty with only a metal chair in the middle of the room. I entered and began to undress myself under his watchful eye as he pulled on blue rubber medical gloves. With all my clothing in a pile before me, he began the search. He grabbed my jawbone in his hand, then placed his fingers inside my mouth and ran them along my cheeks and gum line, carefully searching for any contraband.

"Hands and arms out. Spread your fingers. Run them through

your hair. Show me the bottoms of your feet. Wiggle your toes. Turn around. Bend over and spread 'em."

With his search complete, he handed me a green jumpsuit that read "NJDOC" in large black lettering emboldened across the back and a pair of gray canvas shoes.

"Put these on and sit here when you're done," he said as he reached for the chair.

I did as I was told as he walked away. I heard his boots clacking on the linoleum and then, the faint rumbling of what sounded like chains in the distance. He returned carrying large shackles in his hands. He knelt down before me and proceeded to shackle both of my legs, securing them around my ankles. He cuffed both of my hands in front of me, and tied everything together by securing a chain that ran from my ankles to my wrists. I had never felt so caged in my life.

He left the room and returned with my laundry bag filled with books.

"Do you really want these?" he asked.

"Yes. I want to take them with me, sir."

"You will have to mail them home at your own expense when you get to CRAF."

"Okay."

He tossed my laundry bag inside the large clear plastic bag.

"Stand up."

I rose.

"Arms out."

I followed his direction. He yanked at his handiwork to make sure I was secure before handing me my bag of books to hold and led me out of the room. With each step I took, the cuffs tightened over my limbs, cutting off my circulation. I was forced to arch my back as I walked to avoid the piercing of the cuffs. I assumed the getup prevented prisoners from running, but it surely left little room for walking.

I followed him out of the doors to the holding area and down the small hallway toward the garage that I entered through months earlier. It seemed like an eternity. The cuffs continued to pinch my skin. The weight of the bag caused my biceps to bulge. I began to sweat. I looked at the CO in the bubble and nodded. I could see it in his eyes. That look; *pity*. I had seen it before.

I was led through large iron doors to a waiting bus. It was large and looked exactly like a school bus, only different. It was painted white and all of the windows were blacked out with the darkest grade tint, black cages bolted over them. On the side of the bus was a large decal colored yellow with blue shading, it read: NJDOC. The letters loomed over the bus, making the vehicle look smaller in comparison. Over the entrance door there was a decal of a small blue dove.

Another CO awaited me brandishing a 12-gauge shotgun. He held it out before him, the barrel lying in his left hand, the pump ready to be pulled, the brown wood of the handle resting in his elbow joint. The sight of an armed man holding a shotgun so close to my face frightened me, though I showed no reaction as I passed. Instead, I held my head high as if everything I was witnessing was as commonplace to me as it was to the other inmates who were about to surround me.

I'm definitely not in Kansas anymore, Toto. I really wish I could simply click my heels.

The CO helped me up the stairs and onto the bus. Every single eye was on me. Sixty or eighty eyes, all white as a cloud with brown or black colored pupils, stared at me. I was the only White person aboard, save the COs. I shuffled down the middle aisle scanning each row for an available seat. Staring back at me were men with scars running the lengths of their faces, tattoos covering their necks and arms, and teardrops running from their eyes. Nothing I have ever seen or experienced had prepared me for that moment. No ghetto or block I had ever been on was quite like that. It was as if every hardened criminal who had spent their lives running in the shadows of society sat staring at me. It was the real deal. The Big Time. I had graduated.

I continued toward the back, looking some of the men I passed in the eye; an attempt to muster pride and toughness onto my outer being so they couldn't see the fear inside my soul. I arrived at an available seat toward the back of the bus and turned around, faced the front, and shuffled my feet into place between the two benches as I plopped down on the seat made of hard, molded plastic. Using my hands was not an option as the cuffs did not allow for leeway.

As I looked around, I noticed all three officers were armed with what looked like Glock 9 mms on their belts. They stood at attention on the other side of the cage, watching us. As we drove, the volume rose to an ear-piercing level as inmates spoke and called out to one another.

"Shut the fuck up back there! Keep this shit up and there's gonna be problems. Try me motherfuckers!" the CO bellowed.

I looked out the window and saw marshland. We were passing the Meadowlands. I remembered my youth; going to the fair at Giants Stadium (now MetLife Stadium), eating cotton candy, and riding the Zipper while flirting with girls from other towns. The memory was brief, for it was difficult to escape the severity of my situation.

I began to pray silently that I would one day be back in society, living a clean life. *Please God let me survive. Allow me to change. I promised myself I would. I cannot break while I am in here. These chains cannot hold me forever. Please God help guide me through this.*

As we passed Newark Airport and approached the oil

refineries, I could see snow beginning to fall; they were large, full snowflakes. The kind that falls when the air is so crisp you can almost taste it. Snow began to stick to the pavement as the cars whizzed by, stirring it up into the air. It was beautiful.

It brought me back to the days when I was very young, before I was getting in any type of trouble. I thought about sleigh riding down a large hill by one of the local schools that had been shuttered for the snow day. I bundled myself into snow pants, grabbed my sled from the garage, and walked nearly two miles to the school in a snowstorm where I traveled off the beaten path, up into the woods and created my own, more dangerous sled run through the trees before coming out onto the main hill where the other children played.

I would return home, soaked and cold as the night crept in and the streetlamps illuminated the snow, making it turn almost orange in hue as it continued to fall. I would walk into the house, kicking the remnants of snow off my boots before heading down to the laundry room and discarding all my wet clothing into the washer. With a warm change of clothes, I headed to the kitchen where my mother had prepared hot chocolate with marshmallows. My toes, nearly frostbitten, would be brought back to life by warm ski socks with heat packets that she gave me.

Then I thought of my mother and our ski trip together. I was barely twelve when she took me to Park City, Utah, just the two of us. We were skiing Deer Valley and got caught in a heavy snowstorm. Because I always had to push limits, I attempted to go down a black diamond with moguls, even though I was far from an expert skier and had never attempted them before. It took us nearly an hour to get down the run as she stayed behind me worrying incessantly while I tumbled into deep powder nearly every five feet. When we finally made it down to the safety of the resort, she cursed me for putting myself in danger.

I smelled that air again; the fire burning and woodchips roasting. It caused me to snap back to reality and look up, noticing that the smell was real; smoke from a fire rose in the distance. We traveled through the backwoods of leafless trees. Everything around looked dismal, as if the life had been sucked from it.

It was then that I saw it. A large brick building that looked like the prison from *The Shawshank Redemption*. Outside of the building, there was a large fence, nearly thirty feet tall with three tiers of razor wire on top of it. A large sign outside it read: Central Reception Administration Facility, CRAF, Governor Christine Todd Whitman.

I had arrived.

We stopped outside the gate as an officer carrying a large mirror attached to the end of a pole walked around the bus and tilted it under the carriage, while another officer approached the window. We were cleared to move once the pole officer motioned to the other. The large, fence-style gate opened before us.

The bus pulled to a stop in an empty courtyard. The large, old building loomed over us. The driver opened his door and pulled the shotgun off the back gate. He placed it in his hand, holding it by the barrel, and walked around to the passenger side door. He stood a few steps back and brandished it before him. The guard in the back of the bus took the shotgun displayed in front of him and positioned himself at the rear of the bus, aiming at our exit door. The third CO unlocked our cage then stepped off the bus.

"Single file, one at a time," he said.

He grabbed each one of us by the arm and helped us down. His grip was firm and fleeting.

With all of us standing in a single line outside of our bus, the passenger CO swept the inside of the vehicle. Satisfied that no one remained aboard, he signaled another officer who radioed something to another. At that point, a large cast iron door on the ground level of the building swung open. Two guards appeared, flanking the doorway.

"Take 'em in," one said.

Our formation was led to the doorway by the passenger guard. He handed a stack of folders to one of the COs standing at the doorway and disappeared inside. We remained standing in the cold with the snow falling over us as we shivered in our thin jumpsuits. The cold steel of the shackles began to freeze around my skin.

Soon we were cleared and escorted through the doors. The room was small and dark. Inside, a CO sat within a cut out room, surrounded by file folders. He told us to hug our right shoulders against the brick to keep one side of the staircase clear.

I saw the dust from the brick's erosion fall off as my body touched against it. The hallway smelled of a dank odor, like the basement of a condemned house. A single yellow colored bulb hung from the ceiling by a long string wire. Against the color of the faded brick, it created an orange light, illuminating our surroundings as we slowly ascended the stairs.

"Shut the fuck up and don't make a sound. Single file to me," another CO said.

Then a different voice was heard from the landing of the stairs.

"Next five! Step all the way down, goddammit! You must not'a been a smart boy. I said all the way down. There ya go, that's right. Drop your shit in front of you."

I heard an inmate below me talk to someone close to him.

"Dat's dat little mothafucka I told you 'bout. I wish to God I saw him on the street. I'd cap his ass; he only like five foot and shit."

I waited. The group before me entered, then I heard the voice again, repeating nearly verbatim his past instructions. Soon after, the doors swung open and it was my turn. I entered to the voice speaking directly to us, saying the same thing, into an abandoned industrial shower stall. There was a lip in the floor about four inches thick and showerheads jutting out from the concrete in the wall behind us. Facing us, lined up along the lip, were five COs wearing blue rubber gloves and five cardboard boxes resting on the floor below them.

I looked at the man in charge: the voice. The other inmate was right. He was a miniature Black man, standing all of five feet tall, sporting a shiny, freshly shaven bald head.

"Unlock 'em," he said.

With each of us paired with an officer, they stepped forward and began to unshackle us.

"All right, welcome home. Strip down and throw your jumpsuits over yonder. You can toss your shit in the boxes in front of you, then get your asses down nice and naked and seal 'em up. Fold the edges and make 'em look right."

I dropped my bag full of books in front of me, took off my jumpsuit, threw it aside, then placed my books in the box and began to seal it as instructed.

"Won't you look at this shit. We got a smart motherfucker in here. White boy reading books and shit. Maybe you shoulda' read more books when you was out on the street and your pale ass wouldn't have ended up livin' here."

I ignored him as I finished my task then stood up to begin the standard search procedure. As we were being searched, Shorty walked up and down the aisle with another officer taking pictures of any tattoos that look like they could be gang related

"This that smart mothafucka. Ain't ya? Readin' and shit. Well, you ain't reading no shit in here. Those books is goin' home. Whereva' the fuck home used to be. Let me see this shit," he demanded as he grabbed my arm tightly in his hand and studied one of my tattoos.

"Take a picture of that shit. You in a gang motherfucka? Some kind White boy-Asian gang or some shit I ain't familiar with?"

I stared ahead in silence.

"Take a pic of that one too," he added as he pointed to another tattoo.

"Let me find out you're in a gang, and I swear I'm gonna have some fun with yo' pale ass."

"Pick your shit up and clean yo' dirty asses."

We stepped over the lip and lifted the cardboard boxes that contained our belongings and followed the guards. We were escorted through a small hallway, still naked, to another area where a guard was seated on a stool outside a large shower stall.

The area was as old and decrepit as the building itself and reeked of mildew. The walls were adorned with lime green tiles, the caulk between them completely gone, remaining in place only from the glue behind them. Soap scum was caked onto their surface. The floor was the same, nearly brown with dirt stains. I smelled a faint whiff of urine throughout.

Two shower heads jutted out from the wall, and neither had faucets. A silver push button released a leaky stream of water from the showerhead for a few seconds. The soap came from a hand dispenser plastered on the wall.

One of the five men with me stepped in front and pushed the button standing under the head as if he had done it before. He pressed the soap dispenser, lathering soap onto his hands and all over his body. The water stopped as he began to lather. He had to push the button again to restart it. He repeated it a few times until all the soap was gone from his body. He turned, looked at me, and said, "You better hurry up you ain't got all day."

I jumped in and pressed the button as he stepped aside.

"HOLY SHIT!" I screeched.

The water was freezing cold; I mean ice cold! I danced in and out of it, wetting my body enough to lather as I shivered while yet another inmate stepped under, then out to lather, as I stepped back in.

I was sharing a fucking showerhead!

The guard signaled that time was up. We were forced out as soap still covered my body. I took a hand-size towel and patted myself dry upon exiting while goosebumps covered my freezing body as I stood barefoot on the cold concrete.

We were then ushered to the area where we left our cardboard boxes and were given XX-jumpsuits. I found my box and carried it down the hall to another room with two large cages. We were told to stack our boxes in a corner as we grabbed bologna sandwiches and small milks from a bin before being locked inside one of the cages.

There were at least fifty inmates piled inside. I knew no one. I was glared at by each set of eyes as I entered. Nearly one hundred individual eyeballs, differing in color from jet black to light brown to hazel, stared at me for the few seconds it took me to enter the cage and find an area to sit, which there wasn't. I could feel those eyes, each one of them measuring me, making judgments about me, sizing me up as I walked by holding my bologna sandwich. Again, I was the only White person besides the corrections officers.

I stood and stared out the window at a dismal courtyard. There was a basketball court with two red rims hanging from dirty, once white backboards, the net having long since been torn down. Some rusted free weights laid in the snow. Two guard towers, one at each corner of the yard, held two guards; one inside, another outside monitoring the perimeter with his shotgun. I took a bite of my heavily processed sandwich and tried to ignore its taste.

After what seemed like an eternity (there were no clocks on the walls), people began to be called out of the cage in groups. I waited as the cage became less and less crowded. Then I waited some more. The cage was nearly empty when my name was finally called.

I met the officer at the entrance. He unlocked the cage and motioned me to grab my property box before escorting me over to a large desk where two inmates served as his workers.

"SBI number?" he asked.

"340523C." I remembered. *Good start*

"Do you have anyone you wish to send your belongings to?"

"I can't keep anything? It's only books."

"No."

"My mother."

"Address?"

I gave him the address.

"You understand you are responsible for the shipping fees? They'll be deducted from your commissary account. If you do not have enough money in the account, the money will be deducted from your daily pay once you start to work."

"That's fine."

"What size shirt are you?"

"Medium."

"Pants?"

"Thirty-two."

"Shoe?"

"Ten."

"Just a minute."

One of his inmates gathered the things from the list he had made and presented it onto the desk in front of him.

"One undershirt, medium. One pair of boxer shorts, also medium. One pair of state-issued shoes. Please sign here on the bottom. Follow that officer over there."

They escorted us down a low-ceilinged corridor that looked like something from the medieval times. The room they sat us in had a line of bulletproof windows opposite benches where nurses performed intake procedures on the inmates. When it was my turn, I sat before a nurse and placed my arm under the glass for her to give me a shot and a scratch test. She asked me questions and had me sign a form before I was told to go see the dentist in a small room across the hall.

I sat in the *Little Shop of Horrors* dental chair as a masked man prattled around in my mouth with his tools, shouting notes to an assistant who sat at a computer across from him. With no glaring issues, I was let go.

"All right boys, it's quarantine time. Follow me."

What the fuck does that mean?

We were led through different corridors and up a set of stairs. All of the movement in that facility was strangely orchestrated. When other inmates were being escorted in line formations, we were held up to let them pass. We were told to have our right shoulder on the wall while they walked by, hugging their shoulders against the wall opposite. We were not allowed to talk or associate with anyone in the hallways. You could almost hear a pin drop.

We arrived in the quarantine unit, a cellblock rectangular in shape with all cells running along the right side of the room. They were very old and had bars, not solid steel doors like the county jail. Two bunks were bolted to the concrete wall over one another. The toilet-sink combination was standard steel. They called my name and assigned me a cell with another inmate.

Soon after settling, the food arrived. An inmate placed slices of white bread onto a small shelf between the bars of our cell then slid our food trays through a small opening between the bottom of the gate and the floor. Another came around to pour us iced tea from a large, garden style, watering pot. I stood and ate my meat loaf using my top bunk as a table.

When I was finished, I slid my tray back under the bars of our cell. The inmates collected our garbage and cleaned the tier. I sat on the floor where I could see the screen and watch *The Simpsons* until I was interrupted by a CO who had come onto the tier.

"Listen up! Ya'll r' bein' given body and hair cream. Strip down naked, take the body cream and apply it to every part of your body immediately. *Every* part of your body. Once you do, get dressed and go to sleep. I'll be waking you up at 5:30 a.m. to put the hair cream in for fifteen minutes. It's gonna smell like shit and burn, but you have to do it. Everything you have on now will be discarded tomorrow. Now make sure you put that cream on. I've seen what happens if you don't and it ain't pretty."

The inmates who dispensed the food began handing out the creams to us. When they were finished, they left the runway and the place went dark for a moment until an orange night light was placed on. My cellmate and I stripped down and applied the lotion. The smell alone almost made me vomit up my dinner. It was horrid. Within minutes the tier was consumed by it. Once I had covered my entire body and used up the whole bottle, I put my jumpsuit back on and placed one of the provided sheets on the mattress of the top bunk and climbed up. I wrapped myself in the other sheet like a mummy, trying to ignore the rancid smell that filled the room.

As I laid there, staring at the ceiling, I thought of Hope. I spoke to her and asked that she carry me through that portion of the journey. She promised me that she would, but as quickly as she came, she went. It was a torrid love affair between us. I fell asleep searching my mind for her image and prayed that she'd come back soon to continue holding me up. I simply couldn't live without her.

I was woken by the sound of the cell door as it slid open. The officer entered, shouting with two inmates in tow.

"Get up! Time to get up!" he said as he obnoxiously wrapped

his nightstick along the cell bars while he walked down the runway.

I hopped down from my bunk, grabbed hold of the shampoo-type cream, and applied it to my hair. It was sticky and gross, and smelled like gas.

"Strip naked and throw every single piece of material in these here piles."

He pointed to the mounds he had created in front of him.

"Jumpsuits here, underwear there, sheets over there. After you've done that, go back into your cell. You'll be handed sponges and buckets with bleach. You're to wash your cells down; mats, toilets, everything. Those cells better reek of bleach. Otherwise, I'll have you cleaning it on your bare-ass knees while I stand over you making damn sure you get each and every crevice. When that's complete, and only after that's complete, I'll call you out two at a time for showers."

We did as we were told. I was covered in the sticky lotion that I was forced to sleep in. My hair was dripping with goo and burning. I was completely naked on my hands and knees inside a four by six cell with a sponge in my hand while another grown man, a complete stranger, was naked next to me doing the same.

When we finished, the CO cleared us, and allowed us to shower. After a timed two minutes, he called us out and I was handed a towel and fresh jumpsuit from one of the inmates as I returned to my cell. I put it on and sat up on my bunk while the inmates began to serve a breakfast of grits and a boiled egg. I ate it feverishly. Eating was my action of the day. I was a dog waiting for my master to feed me.

Shortly after breakfast was over, names began to be called. I was summoned from my cell with two other inmates. We met another CO at the outer cage where he escorted us through the corridors, past a bevy of offices, arriving at another cell block.

The setup was different from the quarantine unit. It was larger and had cells on both sides. In the middle of the room were six small iron picnic tables and chairs bolted to the floor. There were four TVs, one in each corner of the room. I was given a cell number, then handed two sheets, a toothbrush, toothpaste, and a roll of toilet paper.

I entered the cell to a large Black man sitting on the edge of the bottom bunk, fluffing his hair with a plastic pick while looking into a mirror propped up on the bars of the cell pointed awkwardly away from him. Our eyes met for a brief second. It was enough. He was large and intimidating. I went about my business, placing my sheets on the top bunk while standing on the toilet, careful not to intrude on his space.

"What's your name?" he asked as he continued to pick his hair and look into the mirror.

"Nick. You?"

"They call me Doc." *Silence.* He still had not looked up at me.

"You look like you belong in Hollywood or something. What you down for?"

"Armed robbery," I answered without hesitation, hoping the gravity of my crime might in some way gain me the clout I so desperately sought.

"Shit. Little Nicky's down for some shit!" he said with extreme condescension as he laughed heartily.

I paused momentarily as if awaiting more conversation. When it didn't come, I continued to go about making my bed as he picked his hair. After a few minutes I had had enough of the tension and decided to ask him a question.

"What about you?" I asked meekly.

"Aah, many a things Nick, many a things," he said as he continued picking and looking in the awkwardly placed mirror.

I was not sure what to make of Doc. He was older, close to forty maybe. He was even more well-built from what I had originally noticed. And there he was fucking with me. Yet it didn't seem to be in a menacing or malicious way, it was almost playful.

"Your first time, huh?" he said with a smirk and finally looked me in the eye, his dark brown eyes penetrating the depths of my soul.

"How'd you know?"

Suddenly I felt I could tell him anything, such is the power he wielded when looking at you.

"The way you came in. The way you looked at me. I could see the fear in your eyes. You're nervous, not sure what to expect. Maybe somebody's gonna make you his bitch, maybe you're gonna have to fight, you don't know just yet but you're tryin' like hell to mind your own. Hoping you can just slide on by. At least you've learned that."

The truth in his assessment stung me.

"Not your first time I take it."

"Nah, not my first time Nick," He was no longer looking at me, instead he continued to pick his hair and simultaneously look at something through his mirror, but it wasn't his hair. It bugged me.

"Can I ask you a question?"

"You just did." Silence. "Go ahead, but don't make it no stupid question, like something personal you hear?"

"Why do you have the mirror like that?"

He laughed. His bright white teeth shined through his otherwise dark features.

"Oh, that. That's so I can see the TV."

"But you can't hear it."

"I know Nick, I know, but it keeps me sorta busy. Ya dig?"

I smiled, nodded my head, and jumped off the toilet and onto the floor before him.

"So, Nick, tell me how you ended up here, in this situation I mean. Like I said you don't seem the type. Where you from?"

"Westwood."

"Ha, ha, ha! Now where the fuck is that? Sounds like that shit outta *Boyz in the Hood*, when the White dude comes to my man's house in Compton and says he's from Westwood. I thought that shit was all made up."

"It's a place in Bergen County, I think there's one in Cali too."

"Bergen County. Wow, Nick. You outdid yourself, didn't ya? Bet you Westwood is a nice place, big houses and shit. Bet you come from a good family too. So, how'd you get all mixed up in an armed robbery?" He smiled.

There was something soft in his demeanor, something safe and friendly, and I opened up to him because of it. I told him a lot of things. Things I hadn't ever told anyone. I told him the truth about what I felt brought me to doing my crime. I let my guard down and admitted to him that I was a fake gangster. A wannabe. I told him about being bullied and left out of social life by my peers and that once I started running with the wrong crowd, people began to respect me out of fear. And instead of realizing it meant nothing, I let my ego take control and create a monster. All the while he listened intently, not saying anything, until . . .

"That some deep shit Nick. But listen, we all got problems, it's how we handle them. You fucked up and ended up in here. Now it's up to you to get through it and change, if that's what you want. And that's what it sounds like to me."

Soon dinner arrived and Doc knew the food runner. The runner paid his respects and gave him an extra tray. Doc offered me half, to which I gladly accepted. We sat, ate and talked some more.

"Still though, all that shit you told me and you end up here for sticking a drug dealer, ain't that something." he said, shoving a chicken nugget in his mouth.

"Irony."

"You're actually lucky. You done that shit around my way, you'd be dead. We don't fuck around with no police. The game got its own rules."

The cells opened and we were allowed out on the floor for one hour. We went outside and hung out on the tables where Doc introduced me to some people. I could feel him give them looks to leave me alone. I tried to watch TV, but most of them were set to *Cops*, which till this day, I still can't bear to sit through. I walked to the other side of the tier and noticed a TV set to the local news. It was a Philly station. They reported on a local kid who just graduated from Penn summa cum laude on a scholarship. I listened to him speak about opportunity and hard work. And that's when I felt it; how far away from life I really was. Depression washed over me like a migraine. I stopped watching and went back into my cell and laid on my bunk thinking before our daily hour of freedom was even up.

When the hour ended, Doc returned to our cell.

"Why you didn't stay out? You gonna be in here till tomorrow sometime. You should take advantage of the time outside this cell. Good for your mind."

"I wasn't feeling it."

"It's your bid," he said, flippantly.

"They don't have any books in this fucking place either."

"I'll get you some books tomorrow," he said with the bravado of a man who gets things done.

"You can do that?"

"I can do a lot of things. They might not be what you want to read, but they'll keep you busy."

"You read Doc?"

"Yeah, I read. What? N***as don't know how to read and shit? I spend a lotta' time in the law library."

"You know I ain't mean it like that."

"I know, was just fucking with you."

"Why don't you tell me a bit about you? I mean I told you every-thing about me."

"What do you wanna know Nick?"

"Well, where you from?" I asked.

"Newark, you know where Newark is?"

"Of course! My family's from Kearny and I was living there for a while when I was on bail. I used to hang on Mt. Prospect."

"Mt. Prospect, huh Nick? Now why the fuck you up on Mt. Prospect? You shouldn't be hangin' in Mt. Prospect Nick."

"That's what I've been hearing. I did a lot of drugs."

"Oh, Nick, drugs are bad man, drugs are bad. Fucks your mind up. You gotta stay off that shit."

"Yeah, I know. At least now I do. So, what did you do, this time, to get here?"

"Attempted murder," he said without hesitation, hint of regret, remorse, or concern.

The way a person might answer a question, like, "What nation-ality are you?"

"Oh . . ."

The comfort I had suddenly vanished. I listened on with com-plete amazement as he continued to speak.

"You see Nick, I dealt drugs on the street. That's why I know they'z bad news. And some motherfucka fucked me. I run a busi-ness and I can't have no one fucking with my business. So, I shot him in the leg. I ain't try an kill 'em, just shot 'em. A little warning that if he fucked me again. Then I'd kill 'em."

"Uh, Doc, have you ever, uh, killed anyone?"

Silence.

"Yes."

Silence

I am sharing a cell with a murderer!

"I'm not proud of it Nick, but I had to, it was him or me. And it wasn't gonna be me."

"Have you ever been shot?"

"A few times. In the back once, got grazed on the shoulder another time running from a drive by, not fun, Nick. Life round my way ain't no fun. It's a constant struggle."

I was sad for Doc. I couldn't empathize with him, but I strangely understood his viewpoint. I suddenly felt comfortable again.

"How long were you down for before?"

"I was down for a murder charge years ago, did about nineteen years for that. Then I got out, started doin' things again and I caught this one about a year ago."

"How long were you free?"

"A few years."

"You have family?"

"Yeah, I gotta wife and a few kids, it was nice bein' out there with them. That was real nice."

"How long you got this time?"

"Ah, this ain't nothing, like seven, it should go pretty quick. I'm used to it," he just rattled off, as if *seven years* was *not* a long time to be incarcerated.

"You ever think about giving it up? Just be married and enjoy your kids. Get a regular job?"

"Nick, Nick, Nick, Nick, Nick. I'm sorry man, but don't no jobs go to a guy like me. I might be book smart and well-read and all that, but that don't translate into dollars. I'd be working for nothing, if I could even get a job. They just look at me as a murderer and that's all I'll ever be. Most anyone won't hire me. This is all I know. All I'll ever know. I just hope my kids get a shot at something better."

I wanted to tell him to lead by example for them; make sure

they get an education that isn't only from the streets. But what could *I* say?

"You're fortunate Nick. You got people who love you, who would probably do anything for you. You should take this as a lesson. You got a real chance when you get outta here, more so than almost anyone else in here. And not only cause you White, believe that."

"I'm starting to."

"That's enough for tonight, I'm bout' to take it down. See you in the morning."

The next day, the COs had informed us that we had a choice for our daily hour out of the cell: remain on the tier and take a proper shower for the first time in days, or go outside to The Big Yard. I couldn't resist getting some fresh air, no matter how cold it was; I needed it even more than the shower I would have been taking for the first time in three days.

I watched eagerly as the clock ticked away. I grasped the bars of my cell and pressed my face between them, sniffing the air like an animal. At 12:57 p.m. I was hopping from foot to foot in anticipation. Doc had been watching me with slight amusement for an hour as he laid on his bunk picking his hair.

"Take this, it'll be cold out there, don't want to get sick," he said, holding a brown state-issued canvas bomber jacket. I didn't hesitate to grab it, and examined it as if it were some strange life form. I thanked him.

How the hell did he have a jacket? Nobody had a jacket. Then again, no one had a chess set in their cell or got two food trays like he did. I guess that is what "times in" can afford you: all the shit no one else can get their hands on.

The cell door opened and I rushed off towards the back entrance where a line was forming. I shuffled into formation and kept my head down, trying to blend in with the other inmates, although that was not so easy as I was the only one with a coat.

We were escorted down a back staircase that descended directly into the yard. At the landing, a guard unlocked the door and let us out. The movement was like being caught in a caribou stampede; hundreds of gray body masses rushed at the open doors that represented freedom. Soon I was standing inside a giant square gazing up at the large wall with its razor wire as inmates poured out of various doorways from the building, heading to their respective groups scattered throughout the courtyard. Some began to play basketball and handball with the nearly frozen balls stuck to the damp grass, others went to the weight area and began to work out.

I noticed a small group of White men, maybe seven of them in a yard with over two hundred inmates. They were all older. Most had visible swastika tattoos or otherwise racially inspired pieces. I went to approach them, but stopped myself; their group was *not* for me. Instead, I made my way towards a group of Black and Latino men working out on a pull-up bar. Careful not to cause myself any trouble, I nodded to the bar as a sign of asking permission to work out with them. The Black man nodded and I began to go "around the world."[3] Soon, more people joined our workout. Not a word was spoken between us.

My hands were quickly red from the frozen bars and my nose was running from the cold. Even with the coat, I was freezing. My adrenaline could not take my mind off the weather as it consumed my being. I ceased working out as my hands were nearly numb,

---

3   Name for a prison style workout that consists of various sets of pull-ups, push-ups, and dips.

only I could not go inside to warm them. I was stuck there until the next movement was allowed by the guards.

I was relieved when I heard the calls shortly after I stopped working out.

"Line up, time to go back inside."

Inmates slowly shuffled toward the doors. Hundreds piled upon one another, forming lines and clusters to get back through the small double doors. I was stuck in the middle of the merging crowd. My breathing increased. I was getting nervous. I looked around and thought about what I would do if a fight broke out. The thought was interrupted when I was squished through the doors and onto the staircase where I could breathe again. I returned to the tier, *safe*.

After days of worry over what prison I would end up in, I received word that I was up for classification. I was escorted through the corridors and into a part of the prison I had not yet been to. It housed a small cage similar to the holding cell when we were first brought in. It was full of inmates waiting to be classified.

I sat in the cage silently watching as men entered and exited the classification room. The reactions were like an *American Idol* audition. Inmates left excited or cursing: "Bayside baby!" or "Man fuck ya'll. I hope ya'll mothafuckas die in hell!"

The next two years of my life rested in the hands of a few administrators behind those doors. The balance of my *entire life* rested behind them. I didn't want to become an animal in order to survive. I wanted to coast through my bid and go home. If I was forced to adapt to an array of daily violence and live like a savage, I would have to. But in doing so, I would lose Hope forever. She would not like who I might have become. I would not be worthy of her love.

They eventually called my name. I sat in a single chair in the middle of a somewhat large room where a CO was stationed at each doorway flanking me, while a large desk with seven people, congressional hearing-style, rested before me. They stared at me for a moment, uncomfortably, before speaking.

One man, sitting in the middle, ran the show. He was in his mid-forties, had bushy jet-black hair, and a black mustache. He wore cheap-looking oval brown glasses and seemed to need them only for reading as they rested over his nostrils. My attention hung on each word that left his mouth.

"Nicholas Marshall, crime of armed burglary in the first degree, no priors. . . ." Etcetera. Etcetera.

Then they spoke only to one another. I could not hear them. They fuddled through my paperwork. They had decided.

"Mr. Marshall, this is a very serious crime you are convicted of."

"Yes, I know sir, I—"

"You are going to Mountainview Youth Correctional Facility. I hope to never see you in that chair again."

"Sir, that isn't Bordentown is it?" Bordentown was known by its moniker, Gladiator School. It was gangland. Each and every day you would have to fight for your life, *literally*.

"No, it isn't, would you rather—"

I was so relieved and elated that I interrupted him.

"No, sir! Thank you so much!" I said, as I sprung up from my chair and headed to the door, careful not to say another word.

Hope had returned and kissed me passionately.

When I got back to my cell I told Doc the news.

"Congratulations Nick, that should be a nice little bid. Now it's up to you."

I continued my days at CRAF the way I had been. It was awfully boring, but I had Hope with me again. We cuddled at night. I held her tight and she told me that she'd always have my back. I was falling in love with Her. She was becoming irresistible.

One morning the CO shook me awake. It was time for me to

go. I said goodbye to Doc before being escorted to a holding pen where I sat awaiting the transport van to take me to Mountainview. I thought about the past two weeks. Three hundred and twenty-two hours locked in a four by eight space with another man. I couldn't wait to get to the green pastures of Mountainview Youth Correctional Facility and begin to do my time.

CHAPTER 4

HALFWAY THERE

I honestly don't know how it happened. I was nearly two years into my sentence when I heard that I could apply to be in a halfway house. Upon doing the research, it seemed highly unlikely that I would be accepted, based on my crime, length of sentence, and a myriad of other reasons. But that didn't stop me from taking the chance. I'd hoped that a bit of luck would come my way, considering I kept my head down and stayed out of the common trouble one in prison could easily get into, with drugs, gangs, and . . .

So, it was quite a surprise when I received the news that I had been accepted into one and would be leaving sooner than expected. I was keen to keep the news to myself, for fear of someone hearing and attacking me or setting me up in some way that would negate the gift and send me back down to the compound in maximum security. And since they don't provide you a specific date for security risks during transportation, you simply have to wait each day out and see when your name will be called, like so many of the other men who have been granted the same gift. Unfortunately, the days between receiving the news and waiting to be called were arduous. Previously, each day was simply another off the calendar. The anxiety of potentially leading to a far more human experience, was grating. After a few weeks I got so depressed I couldn't get out of bed. I started to curse myself for applying. My reality was I had a year or so left in my sentence. I had mentally accepted that for years, and I was teasing myself with the hope that another step toward freedom was coming, constantly thinking of *when*?

And like anything else, once the mind has accepted the situation you are in, you are able to live through it. And as I did, each day got slightly easier, as I no longer thought about the *when*, but the present and getting through each day, same as the one before and the one after; the prison mentality. Until my name was called . . . I jumped out of my bunk like a rocket leaving a silo and rushed to the officer's bubble. Upon arriving he told me to grab my things as a van would be there to get me, and two other inmates, shortly. I returned to my bunk, with my secret out, and gave away all my commissary: my Walkman and anything else that I had worth giving. I would no longer be needing it where I was going. As we walked to the small van, I asked to sit in the front seat. The officer had no issue with it and I happily indulged. It may seem trivial, but to someone who had to be shackled for twenty months, the simplicity of someone trusting you enough not to cause trouble and allow you the humanity to sit in a seat and control a window was absolute heaven to me. The entire ride to the house was filled with excitement, fear of the unknown, and dreams of what my future could be like as I never looked back on the prison we left behind. It wasn't until about an hour into the ride that I noticed we were headed deep into the bowels of Trenton. We parked outside a nondescript standalone building, the perimeter of which was covered in concertina wire; I began to question whether I had made the right decision. I was met by a "counselor" (the new corrections officer) who stood outside the entrance to the building holding a clipboard. We were cross-checked by both parties, to confirm that we were in fact the inmates requested. Once we were proven to be, the CO said his goodbyes and left us standing outside with the counselor who began to provide us the rules of the house and temper our expectations. As we were not in a halfway house, but an "assessment center" called Bo Robinson Assessment & Treatment Center. For the next sixty to ninety days, depending on our participation in the "program" would determine if we were to make it to a halfway house, and far more importantly, which one.

It was a bit demoralizing, but I was there already and not one to step backward. I was soon sitting on a large, twin plastic mattress (with springs!) in a small room with four bunk beds. No one spoke or greeted me upon entry. Most were watching small portable TVs, others listening to their Discmans, wearing street clothes, not the usual brown prison uniform that I had arrived in. I decided to embrace the situation as a step up and in the right direction. Over the next few days, I was able to settle in and learn what was actually taking place. We were widgets in a system; a for-profit system. That was how they got money from the State for our "housing and treatment." I use the latter term loosely, as the programming was complete nonsense and provided absolutely no useful life skills for any of us when we were to be set free and return to the streets to seek work in the real world. Though the perks outweighed the nonsense, overall.

On her first visit, my mother brought me sushi and clothes that I had left in storage with her as well as my old Discman and some of my CDs. Those small reminders of being human far outweighed the issues I had with the house and the way they treated us. I kept my head down and played the part and after seventy-five days, I was finally given a classification appointment. I sat before a board that informed me I would be going to Tully House in Newark, a sister house owned by the same group, where I would need to "complete the ninety-day program" before being allowed to seek employment; not a true halfway house at all. That angered me, as it reeked of corruption in the highest form. Add that to the fact that it was a private operation and collecting taxpayer money for their own coffers while using us as widgets in their machinery; it was tough to swallow. And so, a few weeks later I found myself being transferred to Tully House in the back of a caged van, a reminder that I was still very much an inmate, not a human, once again. Upon stepping off the bus and into the reception area, we were greeted by another counselor. Only they had a whole new script. He went on to tell us of the rules of the house, followed by the requirements to complete the program (twice daily Narcotics Anonymous/Alcoholics Anonymous meetings, various "classes," one on one counselor sessions, and other "activities"). At the end he asked who wanted to stay and who wanted to go back to prison. I was surprised at the amount of men who stood up and said "fuck this place, send me back," and I just watched as they were handcuffed and shackled and led to a waiting room for the Department of Corrections (DOC) to pick them up.

I assumed that although I didn't care for their programming, nor their business model or anything else about the place, it was still a small step up from prison and that if I kept my head down, I could get through the nonsense and through to the end goal of going out to get a job for my final months of my sentence. And that is just what I did, no matter how much it killed me to participate and keep my views to myself. Add to that the rate in which they locked people up every day, it was not easy. Each day, at least two men would be handcuffed and sent to the waiting room where DOC would come and get them. And as each week passed, nearly half of those same men returned, having to start the program over. It was the greatest scam against the taxpayer I have ever seen. As each time we passed through the revolving door of the facility, they got paid. Eventually I managed to navigate the system and survive, and as I was nearing the end of the programming portion, I had my eyes set on a final way out. And that way out came when one of the other inmates told me that he was going home and that there would be a space for me at the place he worked when my time came to leave the halfway house and look for work. He told me he worked at a moving company with some other inmates where they loaded vans in the warehouse all day long and ate breakfast and lunch off a food truck that visited daily. It seemed like a great, mindless escape where I could simultaneously get exercise. A few weeks later, having completed the obligatory programming, I was finally allowed to search for work. And because of that inmate's help, I didn't have to go to the glass factory, or the supermarket, or any of the myriad of awful jobs the house had contracts with for far below minimum wage, but could do something that could potentially be useful upon my release for a fair wage.

My parents dropped off some of my old dress clothes the week before during a visit and the day had finally arrived. I got ready in front of the small mirror in my communal room, and pulled a tie around my neck for the first time since my sentencing and combed my hair to look presentable. Not being able to sleep, I awoke at 4 a.m. and was ready well before the 6 a.m. breakfast call. Armed with my travel pass, I awaited my release when the clock struck seven. I walked out the front door, through the gated turnstile, and out onto the streets of Newark. I walked up the block and out onto Frelinghuysen Avenue, and waited for the bus with the other inmates who had work permits. The area was a run-down industrial zone. A place I had feared prior, but having become part of the problem gave me a sense of security. The bus arrived, I paid the fare, and took a seat. I watched as the city of Newark passed by me; project houses where dealers were still out in the early morning; the large, tree-filled park that sat in the middle of the city; and a series of row houses. Eventually the city changed and we were in a land of strip malls and small, beaten-down homes, in Elizabeth. I snapped out of it when another inmate tapped me on the shoulder and told me we had to get off at the next stop.

We stepped out onto the sidewalk and made our way through another industrial area filled with junk yards, barking dogs, and trucking depots. After fifteen minutes, we reached the doors of Reliable Van and Storage. There was a food truck outside, just like the ones I used to frequent when I pumped gas in my early teen years. I had cash in my pocket and ordered my old go-to, inhaling the fumes of burnt butter, bacon, egg, and cheese as they fried it on the small griddle. I sipped a black coffee, real coffee, not the powder I had been drinking for years that I bought from the commissary. I sat on the edge of a dock bay and ate, feeling as if I were the king of the world. *The little things.* After I finished my coffee, I was approached by Jake, the head of the garage workers.

"Nick?" he asked, a barrel of a man, six foot three, with large Cossack hands.

"Yessir."

"I'm not a sir, I'm Jake. Come inside and chat."

"Got a resume? Not that you need one. I mean, you'll be loading trucks, fuck do I care?"

"Actually, I do," I presented my resume to him. He began reading it over. His face contorted as if he was reading something foreign.

"So, wait. You can type? Know how to use a computer, email, man phones, all that?"

"Uh, yeah . . ." I replied, surprised by his reaction.

"Sit here for a second," he said and disappeared through a back door, leaving me alone in his office. I looked around and saw various hunting trophies, taxidermy, and pictures of him with various kills. He returned with a short, stocky man in his fifties, with a thick red beard and rosy alcoholic cheeks.

"Nick, this is Junior, he runs the logistics department."

I stood and we shook hands, I sat back down, he stood over Jake as he sat.

"We were thinking, how about we give you a job inside? Get a desk, computer, phone, all that jazz. You can be Junior's guy. He'll teach you the ropes of the business. That work?" he asked. I looked at them, dumbfounded.

"Are you serious?"

"The pay's better too, but you gotta wear office clothes, something like what you got on."

"Of course!" I blurted out.

"Okay, you're hired. You start tomorrow," Jake said.

"Good to meet you, seven thirty sharp. See you then," Junior said and left.

Jake walked me back through the garage, shook my hand, and said goodbye. I returned to the inmate who got me the interview.

"Thanks again."

"You get it?"

"No. I got a job inside," I said, pointing to the office.

As another inmate walked past me he said, "Figures . . ." and shook his head in disgust.

Upon returning to the house, I went to my counselor to tell her the good news.

"Ms. Brown, I got a job! A good one with a desk and computer and good pay!"

"Woah, woah. Mr. Marshall. I'm not sure that's allowed," she said, deflating my ego.

"What do you mean? It's a *job*!" I pleaded.

"You're not allowed to have internet access, or a phone. You can't take it."

"What? Why?"

"It's not good for your recovery . . ." she stated seriously.

And that was the exact moment when the nonsense began and didn't end. I took the battle to the head of the house, and eventually, raising every flag I could, I won, but it took me a week and a lot of legal threats. One of the many pieces of bureaucracy that is the system. I wasn't going to let them win, and they didn't.

CHAPTER 5

RELEASE DAY

The final two weeks of my prison term dragged on longer than any other after I received notice that I was to report to the Union County Parole office in Elizabeth, NJ. I received a term of three years supervised release, and I was nothing short of devastated. My attorney and I had signed the plea deal under the impression that it would result in no parole since I was required to complete 85 percent of my sentence of three years. Thus, I would be "maxing out," as the system calls it. That is when an inmate is not given parole at any time during their sentence and at no point is someone ever to fulfill the full sentence, the 15 percent differential is always the bureaucratic "gift" of sorts. Not in my case. As I was one of the first cases to be sentenced under the law and it was unclear whether there was a traditional parole attached or a type of probation after or as it should have been, nothing at all but true freedom. Each permutation was a vast difference in what my life looked like for double the amount of time I had just served. There I was, completing my time without incident, ready to tackle life as an upstanding citizen, never to perform a crime that could land me back in prison, only to be told I had three years of *parole* hanging over my head. And God forbid I violated in any way, I would be sent back to prison for the remainder of three more years. After years of mental preparation and fighting my way through my hell on Earth, two weeks before my release to society, I found out that I essentially had received a *six-year* sentence and there was *nothing* I could do about it.

Not only was it unexpected, it was downright crushing to have to report to a parole officer for another three years of my life. I was thrust into the depths of depression I had felt prior to entering prison. For years I had watched people be released, then show up back on the same tier or a different prison or camp only months, sometimes years, later. As that is the system. Once you are in it, good luck getting out. I had to face that fate head-on as a participant, not an observer. That was my mindset day in and out for those weeks. A shell of myself at first, though as the days waned and the sun rose, I found myself slowly accepting my fate as there was no other choice. Then one day I awoke and that final day had arrived on the calendar. And although it was suddenly filled with the joy of impending release, only hours away, it was layered with anxiety and fear of what parole will be like and the effects it would have on my plans for my future. Because everything I had planned for, every goal I had written down, everything I dreamed of doing, or places I planned on going to, in that moment stood subject to bureaucracy; the worst part of the world we live in. And just like that, after two years, six months, and twenty days of incarceration, I was going to be a (somewhat) free man in less than twelve hours.

After breakfast, my name was called by the security of the house and I was taken by van in the early morning to East Jersey State Prison (more commonly known as Rahway State Prison). As the van pulled up, the grass was still wet with dew from the previous night and the sun sparkled off the Golden Dome. I remembered the nights just a few months earlier in which I cried in that Ad Seg (Administrative Segregation) cell, having been wrongfully re-incarcerated after the counselors at Tully House thought I had deviated. In reality, I was in the back warehouse loading a moving truck for a cross-country haul on the holiday, where they didn't ask around to see, and sent me back to CRAF (Central Reception Administration Facility) in Trenton where I spent two weeks, again. It wasn't until the board read a letter from my boss Vinny explaining where I was and what I was doing that they sent me right back to Tully. That Golden Dome represented my freedom and acted as a deterrent (reminder) for my future. *Never again will I see the inside of a prison cell.* I followed the security guard inside the jail, through the front door, almost as if I was a visitor, and not an inmate. I liked that feeling. Inside the lobby we sat in a waiting room filled with various photos of NJ state troopers, past and present governors, and historical photos of the prison. I thought about all the history and pride that surrounded the place, from a law enforcement and gubernatorial level, though not seemingly from a societal one. After a few minutes of contemplation in the waiting room I was escorted inside an office.

I was presented documents with no instructions except to sign it then hand it back to them. Apparently, they stated that I had been a prisoner for such-and-such amount of time and I was being freed on such-and-such a date, that I had served the time myself, that I had paid or (in some cases) still owed X amount of dollars to the State or local authorities for my crime. Then I was presented with a form to sign regarding my parole. I was thrown by the document's verbiage. I asked the officer on duty exactly what it meant.

"You have three years parole. If you violate, you go back to prison," he barked.

"But I'm maxing out tomorrow," I said.

"What? Let me see that again," his brows furrowed as he surveyed the sheet.

"I can't quite explain it, but it looks as though you still have to serve out three years of parole. You're going to have to talk to the parole office about this; above my pay grade."

He handed the sheet back to me to sign and once I did, he gathered all the paperwork and I was escorted out to the lobby where security awaited. We walked out of the front door to the van. As I climbed in, I looked back at the prison. It looked the same as it was when I entered, except that the Big Yard was open. I watched as inmates performed their outdoor routines that provided one hour of sunlight for the day. I couldn't take my eyes off those men. They were downtrodden. Their movements were slow, lethargic; almost rehearsed. I felt for them, yet I never wanted to walk another day in their shoes. Parole scared me. The thought made me shudder as I closed the door and the van pulled away. I said a silent prayer as the Golden Dome glistened over us and we made our way back to Newark:

When I walk out of that God-forsaken house tonight at 12:01 a.m., please let me be moving on. Moving on to a new life, one with new challenges and new hardships and earned success. Don't ever let me take the easy way out again for fear of winding up back here.

When I returned to the halfway house, I saw Ms. Brown, my counselor whom I had a hate/hate relationship with as she represented the absolute worst of the system to me, in the hallway.

"Mr. Marshall. I'm told you can leave tomorrow morning at 9 a.m." she said with a plastic smile.

"No, no. I'm aware of my rights and I'm leaving at 12:01 this morning. I'm not spending another minute in this shithole."

"Mr. Marshall! *Language.* You are still under my custody, I'll remind you. And per the rules, you are only allowed to leave at midnight if you have someone picking you up, which you haven't applied for. We can't just release you onto the streets of Newark at midnight, I'm sure you understand."

"But you can leave us there at six o'clock in the morning? If a ride is all I need, I'll have one waiting."

"The night security will have strict instructions not to let you go until your ride has arrived. And they will have to present ID before you are released into their custody."

"They'll be here," I said as I began to walk away.

"It's been a pleasure Mr. Marshall, I'm sure I'll see you again," she poked.

I stopped and turned to face her.

"You'll never see my face so long as you live, Ms. Brown."

I headed to my room and changed, seething from my conversation but thankful it was the last one. I headed to the ombudsman to get my money before catching the bus to work. When I arrived, I called my mother.

"Mom, I'll come pick you up at work for lunch tomorrow after I see the parole officer."

"I can't wait to see you, I'm so happy Nicholas," she said.

We had a short, banal conversation and I returned to work. But I couldn't focus and spent the rest of the day jerking around the office, chatting with coworkers, and walking around the grounds, basically playing hooky at work, too excited to focus on anything but going home for the first time in so many years. Though time managed to drag on. I checked the clock every ten minutes and only five had gone by. It was the most anxiety-provoking day I had in a long, long time, but eventually the clock's hands ticked into the evening hours and I was off for my final walk to the bus and trip to the godforsaken halfway house. Upon my exit, I was met with a lovely, New Jersey spring day. The air was filled with the scents of blossoms and the breeze was warm. I had never enjoyed my trek through the dingy streets of Elizabeth as much as I did that day. I stopped at my local pizza place for the last time and said goodbye to the owner. I told him I had found a new job and would no longer be around. He offered me my usual chicken parmesan, on the house. I deferred and tried to pay him, but he wouldn't accept it. Instead, we shook hands. I left thinking about the nature of most people, which is innately good. That is what I strove to become: a good person. A person who lends a hand, an ear, or a dollar. There is something uplifting in doing good for others, and I would try to live that life upon my release, as best as I could.

When the bus arrived, I got on for the last time. I vowed to myself to never take a bus again, if I could help it, so long as I live. I took a seat and watched the neighborhood pass me by. Memories of all the feelings I had during the trip I took the first day I was allowed to apply for work came flooding back and before I knew it, the bus arrived at my stop and I headed down the dead-end street to the gates of the house. I sat on my bed and ate my dinner, then started to pack my things, giving my roommates anything I would no longer need or want, which was pretty much everything except some notebooks and books, and then, I waited. I was so excited I could barely contain myself. I couldn't sit still. I bounced from room to room talking with anyone who would listen, watched TV, paced back and forth; anything to keep me busy. But it was only 8 p.m. Others watched TV or played games in the rec room, then would head off to sleep only to wake up there again the next morning, nothing changed. Except for me, everything was changing, and no one wanted to be around me as my energy reeked of freedom, something no one else was going to experience the next day, let alone weeks or months to come. Before I knew it, it was 11 p.m. Lights out. Count up. The last count I would ever be a part of. I sat on the edge of my bed watching the clock as my roommates drifted to sleep. In less than one hour,

I would be free. It would all be behind me. I would start fresh. 11:45 p.m. I couldn't take it anymore! I double-checked that I had everything and headed to the front office. I said hello to the night guard I liked, not acknowledging the other whom I couldn't stand. I looked up at the camera and saw that it was raining; *pouring.* The raindrops hit the ground intensely forming massive puddles in the unevenly paved street. My focus turned to the clock. It was 11:59 p.m. One minute to go. *Holy shit! It is finally here.* The clock struck twelve. I looked at the camera again: rain. No car lights. 12:02 a.m. *Nothing.* 12:05 a.m. . . .

"You know if no one comes to pick you up by 12:30 I have to keep you all night."

"I know. Trust me. They'll be here," I responded.

I couldn't believe dad fell asleep. *He's never let me down before, ever! Why tonight of all nights?*

Then I saw lights. Headlights coming closer down the street and stopping at the gate. *Holy shit. Holy shit. Holy shit I am about to do it, walk through that gate for the last time.* I watched him exit the car as he pulled his jacket over his head and ran through the turnstile into the vestibule to show his ID to the guard at the gate.

"It looks like you are free Mr. Marshall. Good luck to you."

"Thank you, the same to you Wali. You will never see me again. Mark my words."

"What about alumni?" he asked.

I gave him a look that asked: "Are you kidding me?"

He nodded his head in understanding with a slight smile. I grabbed my bag, headed to the door, and waited until he buzzed it. I listened to the sound of the lock click open. I would not miss that sound. I walked through the lobby, each step more hurried. I pushed the door open and the rain poured onto me. My hair was instantly soaked. I broke into a jog for the turnstile exit. I got to it and pushed. Still locked. I buzzed. I waited. One . . . two . . .

three . . . four . . . *come on, open the goddamn gate!* I pushed. Still nothing. I was getting anxious, so I pushed again. Finally, it released, and I was pulled through and spit out into *freedom!* Good-fucking-bye! Goodbye Tully House; and gray and red colors; and meetings; and plastic chairs and benches; and cuffs and cages; and steel bars and vans; and correctional officers; and prisoners; and shitty food; and violence; and hate; and jackhammers and pickaxes; and fights; and bathrooms with no doors. Goodbye *forever!* I walked towards the car and paused. Never before had rain falling on me felt so good. I almost started to cry. After two years, six months and twenty days, I was free.

I opened the car door elated. I no longer cared that he was late or that I had parole.

"I'm sorry champ, I fell asleep."

"I don't care. You're here. I'm free. That's all that matters."

"You want to stop anywhere?"

"Home please. I just want to go home."

CHAPTER 6

THE FIRST DAY OF FREEDOM

Westfield, New Jersey—April 2004

I woke up in a queen-size bed, buried inside its soft white cotton sheets, wrapped within a large duvet cover as the sun poked through the small window of the basement room. I sat up and listened to the sound of silence; my new reality. No more horns, sirens, loud cranking of gears, slamming of cells, or yelling of guards and inmates. Simply the silence of an early morning in suburban New Jersey. I took it all in for some time before shedding the comforter and stepping onto the carpeted floor, my toes curling as they felt the threads between them. I threw on a T-shirt and headed upstairs to make coffee and start the day. I paused as I made my way up the stairs as I passed a wall of photos. I look at my father, his wife, her girls, and my brother. Noticeably missing were any photos of me. I thought about that for a moment before proceeding. That I had been missing from their lives for three years; essentially dead to the world, the family, and society. I was a person not spoken about. Rarely thought about by most. A distant memory of a person; as if I were dead. And I guess I was, to nearly everyone else. That lost soul in the ether of heaven, one you think about in church, or in passing, not a part of everyday life. Yet there I was, again. Reborn. It occupied my mind as I climbed the stairs and made my way to the kitchen. I grabbed a pod from a case on the counter and placed it into the coffee maker. I watched and listened as it made a hissing sound, pushing the transformed dark brown water into a mug. It was a new invention called a Keurig.

"Morning son," my father greeted as he entered the room, freshly showered and wearing a golf shirt and slacks, his feet covered by thin red dress socks.

"Morning, Pop."

"First day of the rest of your life," he said as he walked up to me, grabbed my shoulder and gripped it with his hand, moving past me to make himself a cup of coffee.

"I guess so."

"What time do you have to go to meet your parole officer?"

"Nine, then off to work," I replied.

"You're gonna be fine, son. Just keep your head down, work, and do the right thing. This will be behind you before you know it."

"That's the plan, Dad."

"The car keys are hanging on the rack near the front door. I gotta get to work. Need anything, call me."

"Thanks dad, I should be fine."

He left to finish getting ready and I returned downstairs to my room. After showering and putting on my work clothes, I grabbed the keys and stepped out onto the front porch, into the brisk early spring air that cooled dramatically after the previous night's rain. The grass was frozen, and cracked as I stepped onto it. I sat in the car, the cold leather seat sending a chill through my body as I turned the key, blasted the heat, and allowed the engine to warm up before putting it into gear. As my hot breath fogged the windows as the cool air pushed through the vents, I thought about prison. Those mornings in the camp when I had to go to work in the forest.

The freezing cold air. The texture of the mandated jackets they gave us. The smoke of the exhaust pipe of the vans that transported us. It sent a chill right through me. I shuddered at the thought of it, as I returned to reality and placed the car in reverse, backing out of the driveway and onto the street. As I made my way down the streets and onto the main thoroughfare, I watched people. The mothers with their children rushing them to the corner to wait for the bus, or the fathers pulling out of their driveways as their wives stood in the doorway waving to them. People in their cars drinking coffee, talking on their phones, or vibing out to music as they wait for a traffic light to turn. It all seemed so simple, so normal. *This is life*, I thought to myself. More importantly, this is *free* life.

I drove through the suburban town's streets to the highway and off the exit ramp into the urban town of Elizabeth. The settings could not be more juxtaposed. The small plots of land with nice houses that peppered the town my father lived in were different than the broken-down row houses that littered the Elizabeth landscape. I was all too familiar with it as I had been "living" there for nearly the last year of my sentence, in the halfway house, taking the bus through the project areas of Newark into that small city to go to work. I pulled up to the parking garage, got my ticket, and found a parking space. I nervously walked through the garage and out into the street as I made my way to a nondescript building where police officers and thuggish youth stood outside smoking cigarettes, careful not to cross paths with either side. I entered the lobby to linoleum and fluorescent lighting, the two pieces of décor I had become all too familiar with, and pushed the elevator call button. As I stood waiting, I read the sign displayed on the wall:

PAROLEES ONLY—NO FAMILY
NO WEAPONS. NO DRUGS.
SUBJECT TO ARREST.

I had reached my floor. Folding chairs lined the perimeter of the space, occupied by people of various ages. One Spanish male in his thirties wearing a puff down coat, playing on a gaming console. Another African American male in his sixties, nodding off as he waited, and yet another African American male in his twenties, texting on his cell phone. A heavy-set Latino woman in her late twenties sat holding what looked to be a six-month-old wrapped in a blanket. I walked up to an enclosed desk, with a plastic window that separated me from the receptionist disinterestedly playing with her nails. I stood before her for a few moments, waiting for her to acknowledge me.

"Excuse me, miss?" I asked.

She looked up at me with dagger eyes.

"What?" she asked, perturbed.

"I'm here to check in."

"Name?" she questioned as she pulled a ledger from her side and opened it.

"Nicholas Marshall."

She began flipping through some pages until she found my assignment.

"You got Mr. Carson. Take a seat. He'll call you soon."

She turned, shut the window, and picked up her cellphone. I knew the interaction was over. Why would I expect any sort of friendliness? I was a criminal, *right?* I sat in a chair and looked around. I had become all too used to these settings: government buildings in disrepair, bad lighting, and miserable people. I hated them all. I wanted to feel the light in life again. That light of the genuine kindness of most people. The citizenry that I had given up over my poor decisions. During my time working while at the halfway house, I learned what that was like again. The way my coworkers treated me, despite being a convict. I yearned for that life. One filled with hope, love, "and—

"Marshall!" I heard my name called, drawing me from my reverie.

I looked over at an open door next to the front desk. Standing within its frame was a large man, roughly fifty years of age, who looked a lot like the rapper Ice Cube. I stood.

"You Marshall?" he asked, and I nodded.

"Come inside," he said and stepped aside from the doorway. "Down that corridor, make a right at the last row of desks," he instructed.

I did as I was told, understanding that in the prison system you don't follow officers; they follow you, keeping an eye on your every move. I thought it was funny. Not because I had committed a crime and it was their protocol for safety, but because I didn't consider myself a criminal; just a kid who really messed up. Yet there was another example of what certain parts of society thought about me and I acted the part, walking through those offices filled with cubicles and parole officers and offenders, making my way to his desk which he pointed out to me. I sat in the chair before it as he made himself comfortable and opened a folder. He read through the charges and laughed.

"Shit. You don't look like much of an armed robber."

"I'm not, sir."

"Well, surely not that good at it considering you're sitting here," he continued. "Let me tell you how this is gonna go. You're going to get a job and piss clean. You do that, we good. I see you livin' on down at your pop's place, nice suburb and all, but I'm gonna say this anyway. You ain't allowed no contact with criminals. None. Not your old squad, no one you met inside, and nobody on the outside. You do, I'ma lock you back up. That cool?" he asked.

"Understood, sir. I actually have a job already, but was thinking about getting a different one."

"Oh yeah? Why would you do that?" he asked sincerely.

"Well, I was a bartender and server before I went in and I would like to go back to school during the day, so that would be the only way I could do both."

"Not sure how I feel about that yet. Let's see. Few things you need to know. You can't sleep anywhere other than your paroled address, and I make house calls at all hours, so best you be there if you're not working."

"What if I wanted to sleep at my mother's house?"

"Not happening. Also, you can't leave the state without permission."

"They live in New Jersey," I replied.

"Don't care. You can't stay. It's the rules. I ain't make 'em, I just enforce 'em. And for now your curfew is 9 p.m."

"Curfew!" I exclaimed.

"Yeah, nothing good happens after nine. And until you show me your level of responsibility, you're gonna have a curfew. Don't break it, otherwise—"

"You're locking me up?"

"Bingo."

I nodded my head, but couldn't help but think what difference it made? So long as I played by his rules, how could they tell me where I could, or couldn't, sleep and work? So long as it's legal and I pay taxes and I stay out of trouble, what gives?

"You gotta come see me every two weeks for now. See how you do. If you ain't a problem, I'll push it to a month. We can be friends or enemies, up to you. I don't like doing paperwork, so don't make me. Understand?"

"Understood," I replied as he reached his hand into a box on the floor and pulled out a cup and urine stick.

"Come on," he said as he pointed me in the direction of the bathroom.

"Fill it halfway and close it tight. And clean off any dribble," he said, handing me a paper towel as he stood over me as I unbuttoned my pants at a stall.

I couldn't pee right away, after a moment, he turned on the water hoping to encourage me, then returned to watch. I shook off, sealed the cup, and handed it to him. With gloved hands, he placed the cup on the sink basin and opened it, placing the urine stick inside.

"In the future, be ready to go when you get here. It'll speed the whole process up," he said as we waited for the colors to turn. Satisfied, he pulled the stick from the cup and showed it to me, tossing it into the trash bin along with the gloves.

"You're good to go. Toss the contents in the toilet and I'll see you in two weeks."

"What if I need to reach you?" I asked.

He pulled a card from his pocket and handed it to me.

"Thanks," I said as I placed it into my back pocket.

"Don't fuck up," he demanded as I reached the front entrance.

I nodded, and exited into the waiting room, which (now) resembled a prison visiting hall, far more people of all ages, *waiting*. When I left, I began to think about what I was going to do. The meeting sparked a mess of feelings about parameters that I didn't see coming. Everything laid out seemed far more restrictive than rational. I had already served my time, all of it; now more bullshit. I was stuck deep inside my head, thinking of ways I could make it work. To be able to live an honest life, while still having a semblance of true freedom under the guise of "rules" seemed so daunting as the stakes were literally freedom or prison. I thought of the guys around me in the pen who always said they would rather max out than be on parole, that the whole system was set up to bring us back. Well, they were right. Most of them lived in the system, which isn't fair. Which led me to think, *how can I beat it . . . ?*

Once I arrived at work, I booted up my computer. My phone

was blinking with voice messages. I began to listen to them and take notes so I didn't adversely affect one of our moves.

As I was typing out an email, Vinny's assistant stood over me.

"Vinny would like to see you," she stated.

"Okay, I'll finish this email and head over."

"Now," she spit and walked away.

What now? I told them I would be late as I had to go to the parole office upon my release and had no control over scheduling. I rose and racked my brain about what I did as I made my way to his office through the cubicles and eventually into the executive wing where I knocked softly on his open door.

"Come in!" he barked.

"Hey Vinny."

"Sit," he stated as he finished whatever he was reading and typing on his screen.

I remained seated in silence, twiddling my thumbs and looking around until he spoke.

"Nicky!" A glow came across his face.

"I wanted to congratulate you on your release. What surely is to be the beginning of the rest of your life. Your honest, good life, that is," he winked.

"Thank you, Vinny. That really means a lot."

"And, in honor of that, I've been thinking. I understand the difficulties that face you now. Society is not a friendly place to those who have been taken into the system and I feel we've gotten to know you well here at Reliable over the past year. The real you, that is. I spoke to the team and we would like to make you an offer."

"An offer?"

"Yes. Well, a promotion really. We would be taking you off hourly and moving you to a salaried position of fifty-two thousand dollars a year, with two weeks paid vacation and a full medical and dental package aside from that, effective immediately."

I sat frozen in the moment before I spoke. My mind was reeling. There I was, seated in the oversized leather chair with a high back, making anyone who sat there seem inferior to Vinny, his perch at his desk looking down over you like a feudal lord. My current position in life. My future. My dreams. It all ran through my head at a frightening speed.

"So . . . ?" he asked and I was suddenly back into the room, before him, having never physically left.

"Vinny, this is . . . wow. What can I say . . . ?" I stammered.

"I'm confused you haven't thanked me yet."

"Thank you, thank you, thank you. For believing in me, for this kind, and generous, offer. But . . ."

"But?" his brow furrowed as he sat back in his thick leather chair.

"But this isn't the direction my life is heading," I stated confidently while holding firm eye contact.

He was silent as he looked me over, the poker game about to begin.

"Entertain me then, as to where your life is going. With no disrespect of course, simply the reality of what you face."

"Well, here's the way I look at it. While I was out on bail awaiting sentencing, I got into Tisch, the New York University film program, as a director. And even though they wouldn't defer me three years, that accomplishment was probably the only one I had ever made in my life, and the hope of that was what carried me through the hell that was prison. It fueled me to teach myself to write. How to watch movies. How to gather the tools to become a storyteller. So, as much as I need a job and this offer would be amazing for the right person, I'm not the right person."

"But you need to have a job while you are on parole for the next few years, from what I understand."

"Yes. I do. And I've thought that through too. I am going to wait tables and bartend at night while I go to acting school. You see, the way I figure it is, I can't do three plus years of college at my age, nor can I afford that, so, if I go to work at night and acting school during the day, I'll be able to make a living, save some money, and prepare for my life once I am off parole and don't have any restrictions. Plus, it's not like I have many other options. I can't trade bonds, securities, hold a real estate or any license for that matter, shit, I can't even take some bullshit government job because essentially nearly every career is off limits to an ex-con. Save hospitality and entertainment."

"Or a moving company . . ."

"Yes Vinny. It's a great opportunity, as I said, for the right person. Which I am not."

He sat for a moment before he began tapping his pen on his mahogany desk, thinking.

"Okay. I see you are passionate and I know you to be driven, so, I'm going to help you."

"That's very kind but—"

He held his hand up as if to say "stop, I'm talking."

"Where are you going to work? Huh?" he asked, clearly frustrated with me.

"I have no clue, but I'll figure it out."

"Well, I have a clue. I'm a regular at a very busy, famous place in New York. If I asked them to give you a job, they would."

As he said the words New York, my mind began to rush. The thought of being back in the city I loved so much, the only place I ever wanted to live . . . and make it. But Carson's words were fresh in my mind as well. *"You cannot leave the state."*

"Vinny, that's incredibly kind, I mean, beyond. I would love that, if we can make it work."

"There's a catch." *Always is.*

"Shoot."

"If I do this for you, I would like you to give us a real chance in your new position. Three months. You stay here for three months, work a few nights, weekends, whatever you can handle. I want you to experience both sides of life. The service industry is tough. I have a lot of friends who do it for a living and they all fly by the seat of their pants. I'm offering you some stability. Do we have a deal?"

"You drive a tough bargain, Vinny."

"That's why I sit in this seat," he smiled. I stood and thrusted my hand out.

"If you can get me that job, we have a deal. Three months from when I start."

He shook my hand and I left the room. As I made my way back to my desk, I couldn't stop thinking: *how am I going to pull this off with Carson?*

CHAPTER 7

PONTE'S

F.illi Ponte, New York, New York—2004

The next day I called the number on Carson's card throughout the day, leaving multiple messages on his machine stating I needed to speak with him. Around six in the evening, as I drove home for the night, an unmarked number rang on my cell phone.

"Hello?"

"In all my years doing this work I've never had a parolee chasin' me down. What the fuck you want Marshall?" he asked.

"Oh, Carson, it's you, sorry no caller ID came up. I have a job opportunity that will allow me to go back to school."

"That bar shit, huh? Not sure how I feel about that."

"Yes, sir, and it also happens to be in Manhattan."

"Oh, hell no."

"Sir, I beg you. If there is any way you can let me try, at least let me go to the interview to see if I can get the job, then we decide? My boss got it for me. He's a regular there."

"He did? Well. . . ."

"He wants me to succeed in life, that's all."

"When is it?"

"I don't know yet, next week maybe."

I detected the heavy breathing of a smoker on the other line as he decided.

"Come to the office Friday morning. I'll set you up with a travel pass. For the day. In and out."

"In and out! Thank you and see you Friday!"

I hung up the phone feeling like I had my first win of the season. Over the next few days, I went to work, falling into my new routine. Vinny sent me an email with the manager's information and told me to reach out to set up an interview. When I got to the parole office to pick up my pass, Carson was waiting for me by the desk.

"Here you go Marshall. Don't make me regret this."

"No sir." I took it, thanked him again, turned to leave and stopped.

"What now?"

"What happens if I get it?" I asked.

"Let's cross that bridge *if* we get to it."

I left with dreams of my future. My interview was at 4 p.m. on Tuesday of the following week. I had to ask for a half day at work, which was frowned upon, but part of the bargain. My journey led me to Route 9, which would take me through my old haunts in Jersey City. Memories of the life I led that landed me in prison flooded my mind. The parking lot where I got robbed; a motel where my crew robbed a drug dealer from the city; New Jersey City University's campus, where I had met the professor who had changed my life and made me apply for NYU. I drove through the city, sat in traffic, and watched the "normal people," those who had no idea of the world from which I had just come, and it all felt as if I had never left. Nothing had actually changed, not the architecture, not the restaurants, the gas stations, or the strip malls. Things were simply as they were. I soon found myself outside the

Holland Tunnel, sitting in more traffic; one thing I was certain I did not miss. I looked up at the buildings, a vast gap where the World Trade Center used to be, and encountered an instant flashback. I remembered arriving at its terminal via PATH Train on my daily commute to work for a brief year in an attempt to go straight before my inevitable incarceration shortly after. I felt the chill of that fateful day when the towers went down; I watched the news from my prison camp, alone, while everyone else was at work. Tears formed in my eyes for the people forever lost, and the way it changed the entire world.

Snapped back into reality, I paid the toll and drove through the tunnel. I arrived at the parking lot where an African man stood at a podium outside the front doorway. He asked if I had a reservation. I told him I was there to meet Mario, the manager. He asked for my keys and led me inside where he used a phone and mumbled something indecipherable. A moment later, a large, rotund man with thinning hair and a toothy smile appeared with his hand extended.

"You must be Nick, Vinny's guy?

"I am. Thank you for seeing me."

"Let's sit and talk."

He led me through a beautiful ground level bar and dining area, the floor made up of imported Italian tiles. We made our way up the stairs into an elaborate bar area with dark mahogany wood, a copper bar, and a glass back bar with expensive bottles on display. It was a classy joint, nothing like the places throughout the city I worked at years ago. An old man sat at the corner of the bar, alone, drinking a martini. His hands were like meat hooks, swallowing the glass in his hand as I watched him raise it toward us and take a swig.

I sat in a deep-set leather chair as he took the seat across from me.

"So, you're a friend of Vinny's?" he asked.

"I work for him, yes."

"He said a 'friend,' and any friend of Vinny's is a friend of ours. Do you have your resume?"

I pulled it out and handed it over to him. He looked it over and chuckled.

"You like working in Chelsea I see," he laughed.

"I played to my strengths," I responded, as he grabbed his belly as he chuckled.

"A lot different here. Not that I have anything against that, just know that here, well, here's a . . . how do you say? It's a special place. A place in time, if you would. A certain . . . *type* of clientele."

"I get along with everyone, no judgment here."

"Good. We like that. You see these guys here? They've been here for years. People don't leave Ponte's. It's like a family. It *is* family. Family owned. Family staffed and a lot of the people who come are . . . *family.*"

And as soon as he said it, reality washed over me. The man in the corner. The name on the door. The way he was speaking. It all made sense. I was about to work for the mob. And I had no issue with it. Shit, I liked it even more. What better place for a person in my shoes?

"I haven't worked in a restaurant for a few years, but I'm a quick learner and a hard worker."

"Vinny says as much. He also told me about your . . . *situation.*"

And just like that the cat was out of the bag. I assumed he was good with it and remained silent, allowing him to add or see what my response would be.

"I believe everyone deserves a second chance."

"Thank you."

"Alright, since I brought you out from Jersey, want to trial for a bit?"

"In this?" I was wearing a white button-down shirt, a tie, and slacks.

"Pretty much what our staff wears around here. If you work out, we'll get you a jacket and put you on the schedule. How's that?"

"Let's do it," I said and rose from the leather chair.

He led me to the bar where a tall, fit Korean man stood with his arms on his hips, like a statue, smiling ear to ear.

"Edward, this is Nick, show him the ropes."

"You sure boss, he doesn't look much like a bartender," he asked.

I scanned the empty room thinking how I used to work at busy places, pumping out drinks, and how this guy just judged my skills solely based on my appearance. *How hard could this place be to run?*

"He's a friend of Vinny and says he knows what he's doing," Mario stated.

"A friend of Vinny! Well then, welcome. I'm Edward."

"Nice to meet you, Edward."

"I'll leave you two to it," Mario said as he walked off.

"All right. Welcome. I think we should talk about the rules before we start. First off, this is *my* bar. You do as I say. I like things where they belong. Where I like them. This isn't a democracy. It's a dictatorship and I'm Mussolini."

The man in the corner laughed.

"Give the kid a break Edward, Jesus," he scoffed.

"Nick, this is Big Lou. Big Lou's here almost every night. He drinks Stoli. Bone dry, up, stirred with three olives speared over the glass. That's all he drinks. Remember his order."

"Hey Big Lou." As his hand enveloped mine, I couldn't help but think what those hands did for a living, but had a few ideas.

"Don't take anything he says too seriously, kid. He's a cantankerous old fella," Big Lou said.

"He's not that old," I argued.

Edward and Big Lou laughed.

"The guy's fifty! You'd never know it with that glassy Asian skin he's got though."

"Just five years younger than Big Lou here. . . ."

"Go shit in your hat," he replied as they laughed and Big Lou tapped his empty glass with his long sausage fingers.

"You're up," Edward turned to me.

I hadn't been behind a bar in years. I took a moment as Edward stepped aside and gathered myself. I ran my hand over the well, pulled a few bottles by their neck to see what they were pouring and how he had it arranged, then looked over the glassware, the condiment tray; familiarized myself with the lay of the land. I grabbed a mixing glass and some ice, the Stoli and stirrer and, just like riding a bike, skillfully whipped up the first drink I had made in three years. I placed a bar nap down in front of Big Lou and then a glass and strained it all away before stabbing three olives and hanging them over the rim and waited. I could feel him and Edward looking over me, approvingly. When the drink came to calm, Edward nodded to Big Lou and he took a sip.

"You're hired," Big Lou stated.

"I'll let Mario know," Edward responded.

"Good work kid. Pay attention and you'll do great here."

"Thank you."

Edward went over standard operating procedures, Micros, the point-of-sale system, and other things I would need to know in order to work a full shift. After a few hours and four more customers later, Mario asked if I had it all down. Edward responded that I did. Mario looked at me, told me I was hired, and said he would be in touch with a schedule over the next few days. I thanked him, said my goodbyes, and rushed off into the night to my car for the drive home. I arrived back at my house a little over an hour later.

As soon as I exited the car and walked up to the house, I decided that the arbitrary agreement I made with Vinny would probably not last the full three months. I would live up to the agreement as best I could, but between the commute and all the hours working two full time jobs, I didn't see it lasting a full three months as this opportunity could be the key to the beginning of the life I wanted; the first steps toward that life that I knew I had to take.

The next day Mario emailed me a schedule. I received the best shifts! Three days in a row, Thursday, Friday, and Saturday nights. The email went on to state that shifts began at 4 p.m., and that I would need to account for travel time as lateness was not accepted. I would also need to get permission from work to truncate my hours on Thursdays and Fridays in order to make it in on time; and lastly, permission from the parole board to work out of state. Arguably the most important piece I still needed to handle.

I left a message on Carson's voicemail early in the morning when I arrived at work, exhausted, the next day. I performed my work diligently, as usual, even though the day felt like the beginning of the end, having gotten what I wanted . . . almost.

Vinny called me at my desk in the afternoon.

"Congratulations. I heard Mario liked you and gave you some shifts."

"Thank you, Vinny. This wouldn't have been so seamless without you."

"No need to thank me, just remember our agreement," he said, and I could hear in his voice that he fully expected me not only to live up to the agreement, but that if I didn't, things between us would no longer be kosher.

That evening, Carson returned my call. I informed him that the interview went well and that they wanted to hire me. He explained that he would have to get it formally approved, so he would get back to me. Before I let him off the phone I pleaded my case. I said that as I already had a pretty good job and was simply obtaining another one that would eventually allow me to go back to school in the attempt to have a more promising future, the request should be seen as a positive, not a detriment to my living out my term on the right side of the law. I went on to say that I'm sure he had seen and dealt with far worse situations to tackle every day. He wasn't very moved by my reasoning, simply restating what he had at the beginning of our call and hung up. I emailed Mario thanking him for the opportunity and informed him that I was working through the parole office to obtain the proper permissions to legally be able to take the job. He was very understanding and told me that there was no rush and I could start the following week or thereafter if need be. As I drove home from work that evening, stuck in traffic on the Garden State Parkway, I started thinking about my future. About what it really could, or would, look like. If I was denied the job, I would rail against the injustices of the bureaucracy and the system; one that doesn't work for the poor or disenfranchised and constantly subjugates people caught up in it (which now included me, despite my socioeconomic background).

It was then that I observed the people in their cars as they passed me, the various walks of life. Suddenly, I noticed that so many didn't seem happy. It was as if they were stuck in a routine. One they had accepted as "their" life based on security, their position, their families' "wants" for them or simply, all they thought they *could* be. I dreaded that life and felt that if I were denied any opportunity that presented itself based on arbitrary rules, I would become angry and resentful and perhaps, return to a life of crime. I pushed those thoughts from my mind almost as quickly as they came for fear of acting on them and losing my freedom again at some point.

Then I thought about the people I worked with and the way they treated Vinny and the other executives like some godlike figures. People who sat above them on the hierarchy of life and who's table they would never be invited to eat at. I thought about prison. About what it really means to be stripped of everything you know of yourself: your money, your status, your position; and be placed in a room, preverbally naked together, being told when you can eat and sleep and how suddenly the playing field is leveled down to nature. Only the strongest survive. People on the outside are seemingly no different than prisoners when you think about it; they are controlled too. They just do it with various comforts convicts don't have: freedom, couches, beds, grocery stores, bars, gyms, zoos, movies, and forms of entertainment that allow them to think that they are free, but in reality, they are just cogs in the ever-spinning wheels of society.

Having been removed from that for so long, I had a mission. To succeed. Being stripped of everything, including your humanity, is so eye-opening, it forces you to look onto society in a different way. We are all the same in the end, all human. That's the base truth, however it's the choices we make that separate us, and given my second chance at life, I refused to become a cog. I had to stand out. Had to make something of myself. To tell my story, others' stories. And if I didn't, what was the point of everything I went through? To experience all of that just to spit me back into the world of recidivism, poverty, crime, a job, love, hate, happiness, and family. All these things mattered and drove us as humans, but my need to move was predicated on having felt the true feeling of nothingness with the concrete and iron bars from which I came and wanted more from life, so much more. The ultimate freedom:

financial freedom. The type where you don't have a boss. Where you can go where you want, when you want, however you want. And in order to get there, I had to be a cog, for as long as it took, but never one that is stuck. Instead, one that is always moving forward; even through setbacks; perhaps we will call it a wheel.

Those thoughts consumed me throughout my ride home and into the night as I sat on the porch, staring at the moon. My new routine of needing to be outside as much as I could, daily, taking in the weather, the cool gusting wind of the early spring in North Jersey. I was trying to balance all that drove me with the ability to appreciate the simple things: walking outside your house, down the street, running errands to the local shopping centers; anything to make me feel human again. And I am aware these routines and thoughts directly coincided with the way I viewed other people and their routines. It was a cruel game in my mind, where one moment I would look upon someone in the grocery or at a traffic light and think of how I would never want to end up like them: a car full of crying kids, angry, cursing at a traffic light, or being rude to a grocery store checkout clerk. But at the same time, loving the ability to do any one of those things. To be grateful to freedom, for freedom. Over the next few days as I got deeper and deeper into the routine of my new life, I sat at night and contemplated how to get away from it; toward something better. I had yet to hear back from Carson, and my anger grew by the day. I complained about the injustice and nonsense of it all. I hated the system for keeping me down, when all I wanted to do was the right thing.

And then I got the call.

"I got your job approved. Here is how this is going to go. You have the ability to travel in and out of New York City, daily. But you can't ever stay the night. You dig?" Carson asked on the other side of the receiver.

I was so excited and relieved. I felt as if things were going to start moving in my favor, *for once*. And then I thought about the way my brain constantly went toward negativity and that I would need to address that, lest I be allowed it to take over and cause me to make choices that would be detrimental to my end goals.

"You won't be sorry," I replied.

"And if I am, you'll be locked up."

His words sent a shiver through me. The reality that I faced on a daily basis. The constant threat of being sent back. It seemed so unfair. It was so wrong the way they handled everything. The bar was low, very low, for returning. I mean, if I was late to my parole appointment, they could lock me back up. It wouldn't be for long (I had already gone through that in the halfway house, sent to CRAF again, and experienced firsthand how the checks and balances of the system worked—or pretended to) but they would still do it. No skin off their back to send a convict back to prison. Even if the parole board and all the bureaucrats would simply send you right back to freedom. A game of ping pong, but with humans instead of an inanimate object.

"That's not gonna happen with me, sir."

"We'll see. Next Friday at 6 p.m. Be ready to pee," he said and hung up the phone.

I wrote down the date and time and set various reminders, then emailed Mario that I would be there when he needed me. The next afternoon, while at Reliable, I heard back about my schedule and uniform. I was to start the following Thursday, smack in the middle of my next parole date. I called and left a message for Carson but did not hear back all day. I was frustrated with the lack of response, as well as the arbitrary rules that were affecting my making a living and getting back on track. I picked up the phone at the end of the day to call again, then thought better of badgering my PO and stopped myself, lest I began to piss him off. Another day passed and I was all nerves. I didn't know what to do. How was I going to call my new boss and tell him that I had an issue with my schedule, already? Angry, I went to work out at the company's gym after work, pushing all my feelings into weights against my body. I returned home, made myself a sandwich, and watched a mindless movie in the basement by myself which was becoming my routine, preferring the silence of being alone to that of entertaining my father and his wife in conversation. It had everything to do with the cacophony of where I had come; silence became a gift to me. I ate it up, as I did my alone time. Something I hadn't had for many years, privacy. I soon made my way to bed and dreamed of how things could be.

"Son, wake up," my father stood over me in his underwear.

"What?" I asked, my eyes filled with sand from a deep sleep.

"Your parole officer is upstairs in the living room."

"What!" I shot up out of bed, nervous, as why wouldn't I be, even though I had done nothing wrong.

"Relax son, get dressed and go upstairs," he left me and I did as I was told.

When I entered the living room, Carson was standing, looking over photos of the family in his puff down jacket.

"Mr. Marshall," he said, looking me over as I rubbed my sleep filled eyes.

"Morning Mr. Carson," he handed me a plastic cup and I took it.

"Leave the door cracked," he demanded as he followed me toward the guest bathroom.

I did my thing, easy to do first thing in the morning and handed it to him. He looked at it, looked around and said, "You're good. Toss it."

Surprised and confused, I did as I was told.

"Can you show me your room?"

"Sure."

I took him downstairs into the basement into what was my makeshift room.

He looked around, touched some photos then spoke.

"I got your message. You're good. Go to work. Moving forward we are going to have to find a day and time that works for our schedules to get together in the office."

"Ah, sure, sure thing," I said, my mind reduced to putty as I tried to understand his angle at that moment.

"Look, you seem to actually have your shit together, unlike a lot of others on my caseload. Come see me in two weeks. Are Tuesday evenings better?"

"I think I can make that work."

"Good," he nodded and set off up the stairs.

My father was pacing in the living area, now dressed, all nerves as I followed Carson from below.

"Mr. Marshall, I'm sorry for this inconvenience. I hope not to make it very regular. Thank you for understanding and your hospitality."

"Of course. Anytime," my father stated with no hint of irony.

"Tuesday. Two weeks."

"Yessir."

My father and I stood stunned, side by side, his hand on my shoulder, as we watched Carson walk down our driveway, and drive off.

"That was . . ."

"Weird . . . but I'll take it," I said, moving to make a cup of coffee.

"He seems nice, considering."

"I don't trust any of them, Pop, but yea, he seems nice enough. Until—"

"Let's not think about that. Just stay straight," he said and walked off as I prepared my coffee.

I arrived at the parking lot across from Ponte's and smiled as I handed the valet my keys.

"I'm Nick. You're going to be seeing a lot of me."

He nodded and smirked, English not being his forte.

I entered the building and joined the staff for a preshift meeting. Mario introduced me to the busboys, servers, and the other manager on duty. I said my hellos and took my seat as I was handed a notepad and pencil. They began the meeting by discussing the reservations on the books, who was coming and what VIPs we would need to be on the lookout for. I listened, eyes wide, as I learned a famous actor and popular athlete were to be in attendance. The chef was then introduced. He was a short Latino man in his mid-forties. I immediately thought to myself that he seemed out of place with all these Italian waiters and managers. I had worked in various kitchens before and seen every walk of life cooking and serving food, but it was rare that the executive chef of an Italian restaurant was Latino. It would be one of the many things that were unique to the restaurant. An uncanny sense of loyalty that I would soon learn and benefit from, but that day I was simply observing my surroundings and the various juxtapositions of that particular place, its staff, and customers. And once he began speaking, I was quickly scared and understood why I was given note taking materials. He began rattling off the daily specials, seven of them, not including the house specialty, the "angry lobster," which was a pan-fried lobster with spices, served whole with claw crackers and a bib, ranging in size from 1.5–6 pounds, on that particular day. I struggled to keep up, knowing little of the various ingredients he spoke of. I watched as the waiters seamlessly followed along and filled their pads with the night's offerings. After that, the wine director was introduced, opened a bottle, and began to pour glasses for everyone to taste as he explained its copious characteristics, which food it would pair well with and its price, a staggering one hundred and seventy dollars per bottle! It was unlike any restaurant I had ever been in, nevertheless worked at. It was a whole new league. One that left me feeling like I had a lot of studying to do as I made my way to the bar with Edward, who did not have a notepad.

"You make sure to write all that down?" he asked.

"I did. I think."

"Make sure you do, we need to keep our cheat sheet behind the bar in case anyone wants to eat with us, which rarely happens, which is why I make the newbies like you do it." he chuckled from ear to ear and held his belly.

He walked me through the side work of the bar, which is parlance for the preshift set up. Organizing and marrying liquor bottles, cleaning and lining up check presenters, filling napkins and straws, cutting fruit and stabbing olives, counting out the cash draw and filling out the preshift requisition sheet; making sure everything was ready for service. Once the bar was ready, we waited for people to arrive. Which I soon began to realize, was not what I expected it to be. Gone, it seemed, were the days of old New York regulars (alcoholics?) who frequented the bar each night, swigging martini after martini and regaling tales to us bartenders and fellow patrons. Instead, we served as a holdover for those waiting to dine and most times people told us they preferred to wait and order a drink at the table. It was as if the bar was the barrier of entry, a formality of sorts to the diners who came (mostly from Brooklyn, New Jersey, Staten Island, and Long Island), not a hangout spot; other than a few old school guys, like Big Lou. I spent my first night learning that overall, our income would be vastly dependent on our tip-out from the dining floor. Edward assured me that coupled with supreme generosity of the few regulars who did sit and drink with us, I shouldn't worry. As I stood under his watchful eye behind the bar, and made all the drinks that came in from the tickets on the floor so I could earn my keep, I thought about how time passes. While I sat at my desk at work each day, I would shift between manning the phones, sending emails, chatting with coworkers in the kitchen area, or surfing the Internet in moments of downtime. At Ponte's, when there were no customers or order tickets, we stood in silence, or spoke to one another, which wasn't something Edward loved to do; instead, he preferred to stand in silence, his arms folded, almost military in precision, and waited to perform his job duties.

It reminded me of prison; sitting alone in my cell, no book, no music, only the sound of silence. I shuddered at the thought of being back there, the cold hard steel, the cacophonous sounds of the cell block. The yelling, crying, and screaming; the rattling of the CO's keys or the click clack of their boots against the linoleum floors as they counted us, or made their way through the tier. I suddenly became unsure if the job would be good for me; mentally or financially. But I was there and it was only my first day. Surely things would change. Around eleven Mario told us it was time to wrap it up. Edward instructed me to remove all the bottles from the well and clean them and their stations with Windex, then remove all the candles from the tables and bar, stack them neatly on a serving tray, and store them on the bar for the next shift. When I completed that, he went over the closeout system on the computer and showed me how to run reports and reconcile the till. When we were done, we sat and waited for Mario to check our work and count us out, making sure our numbers were right. He didn't come for some time, closer to midnight, nearly an hour after he told us to begin closing. As we sat, I watched the clock grow closer to the new day and thought about work at seven in the morning. When Mario arrived, it took all of five minutes to go over our work, tell us we were good, and say goodnight. I said my good-byes and went to find the valet to get my keys, only I couldn't. He was gone. With growing concern, I rushed upstairs and found that it was normal and that he had placed all keys of cars still in the lot inside the drawer of the host station. Relieved, I grabbed them and rushed to my car to begin my commute home.

As soon as I turned the corner off the West Side Highway, traffic. I cursed it, and asked myself how in the world was their tunnel traffic on a Thursday night at midnight!? I settled, turning on music and trying to relax, knowing fully well sleep would be a luxury on those dual work days and nights. As I waited in the tunnel, I began to laugh to myself, thinking of how much I slept upon my first few weeks in prison, usually fifteen to eighteen hours, so depressed I was that I only rose for meals. After a few weeks, I began to adjust and realized there was no way I could do my entire bid in sleep, and embraced the nightmare that temporarily was my life. Parole would be no different; a means to an end. Nothing lasts forever. I would get through it. I arrived home a little after 1 a.m. and entered the house as quietly as I could. As I closed the door, my father stood in his underwear before me.

"Everything all right son?" he asked, concerned.

"Yeah Pop, work ran late, traffic," I answered.

"Okay, get some sleep," he said and returned to his bedroom.

It was then I realized how much stress I had caused him. His eldest son, having put them through all that hell. My ruination of a life. Stuck living in his basement with his new family, a scourge on them and their routines. I went to bed thinking that I would someday, somehow, make him proud. Proud where he wouldn't have to worry about me, that he could rest his head at night and not have to think about where I was, or what I was doing. Confident that I was doing well and right. I dozed off to the dream of that, of being better. . . . When the alarm went off, I sprang up as if I hadn't slept a breath. It was six thirty, and time to get my ass in gear. I hit the shower and grabbed a coffee in the kitchen as my father met me in the hall.

"You get some sleep?" he asked.

"A little."

"You sure you gonna be okay with all this?"

"It's my only way out, pal. It won't be like this forever," I told him.

He smiled and patted me on the shoulder.

"Have a good day son."

I arrived at my desk on time and began my work day. It was Friday, which was usually the best day of the week, as the weekend was hours away. And in the past, my twenty-four-hour furlough home once a month. But since I had two jobs, my weekends would be spent working. I had no social life, nor did I care to. I was on a mission to change my life. Friends and girls would have to wait. After I ate lunch, it hit me. I began to fade. I nearly fell asleep at my desk after having a cold cut sandwich. My eyes felt like sandbags, my mind like a cloud of nothingness. I simply wasn't used to it. My routine had been set for so many years. Up at six, lights out at ten. Repeat. Every day, the same. No holidays or variation to the schedule. I was out for nearly three weeks at that point and as things changed, my body struggled to keep up. I grabbed a coffee and took a walk around the yard where the various moving trucks were loading and unloading. When I sat back at my desk, I felt energized. I wrapped up all my work over the next hour, then headed to the city. I was met with Friday afternoon traffic, a recurring theme it seemed, and I would have to start to account for it. I listened to music as I inched along Route 9 toward the Holland Tunnel. I called Mario and let him know I would be a bit late, with apologies. He was not pleased.

When I arrived, Edward looked down on me and shook his

head. I apologized profusely and asked if there was anything I could do. He replied there wasn't as he had to make sure we were ready to open. I told him he would not have to make a single drink all night and he laughed and said he hadn't planned on it anyway. I soon found that Fridays were different. They were very busy and there was a lot to take in. First off, Fridays were goomah nights. Which meant that all the men would come in with their girlfriends/mistresses. It was our job to greet them politely, remember their names, pass no judgment, and not say anything about the men's families or wives. That was the code. One that would be reversed on Saturday nights, as those were reserved for the wives and families. That was explained to me in no uncertain terms by Edward, as our tips, and jobs, *depended* on it. The night flew by. It was invigorating to feel the energy of a lively bar again, one I hadn't felt for years. The thrill of meeting strangers and getting to know them. People from all walks of life. I missed it. And before I knew it, it was over. Edward and I were closing the bar out.

"Good work tonight."

"Thank you. It was a lot of fun."

"As a reward," he took a bottle of Macallan 25 off the shelf, poured two glasses, and handed one to me.

"Thank you."

I had never been much of a drinker. Prior to prison I was into hard drugs, "club drugs" as they were called. But all of that was illegal and I wanted no part of it anyway. Instead, I (would have to learn to) partake in alcohol, *socially (now)*. I took a swig and the dark liquid warmed my body and calmed my nerves. We sat and chatted about life, our upbringing, family, and goals as we waited for Mario to close us out. He offered me a second, but I reminded him I had to drive home. He poured himself another and I a sparkling water as we continued our talk. Soon I was safely home, sleeping like a baby with no alarm as Saturday morning was to be my first day to sleep in all week. The following night I returned to work and it was similar to the night before. The routine began to set in until I woke up on Sunday with nothing to do. I had a true day off, all to myself. It felt strange having nowhere to be and no one to spend it with. I went for a run in the neighborhood, through the empty streets and suburban houses and after I couldn't run anymore, I walked. I walked and walked and walked. The feeling of being free, of coming and going as I pleased was so new to me despite having experienced it for a majority of my life. The routines I had at work grounded me. They kept me moving towards something. But at that moment, although free, I felt utterly alone.

I hadn't felt the embrace of a woman in some time, since I had an affair with a woman at work while I was still in the halfway house. I began to question what my life was, and what it would become. I had one friend who wasn't a criminal, my buddy Tony. He was the older brother of my childhood best friend. We had randomly reconnected when I was working at a bar in Chelsea while out on bail, awaiting my fate. He walked in one afternoon for lunch with his business partner and recognized me. We began talking and I told him about what had happened in my life. He offered to manage what little money I could save while working before I went in and stay in contact with my mother, and that in three years whatever I could save would be worth more with his guidance, giving me a leg up when I got out. He stayed true to all of these things, except for the fact that he lost most of my money in the market. Such is life. But he offered friendship; a far more valuable commodity than money. And although we hadn't had time to hang out since I was released, we planned on it. And as I sat there walking the empty suburban streets with houses filled with families and children, I felt the pang of sadness and loneliness rush through me. It was a strange feeling, having finally been freed, only to feel the exact same things that I had for years alone in those places I tried to forget.

When I arrived home, I took a long, hot shower and decided that it was just the beginning for me. It was to be the course of events that would lead me out of that hell and into a new, fruitful life of friends and happiness; and dare I say, love. And when I dried off and put on comfortable clothes, I retreated to what allowed me to escape other than the way books had in prison; movies. I decided I would plough through with the help of cinema. And that one day, it would all be behind me and I would be *normal* . . . whatever that meant.

I received my first paycheck from Ponte's the following Friday and was surprised. I ended up taking home almost half as much as I did for my entire work week at Reliable. I was excited and wanted to celebrate. I called Tony and asked when he could hang out. He suggested we should go to a bar in Hoboken, NJ the following week. Initially I thought that wouldn't be such a good idea, but after running through the various rules I had from my parole officer, legal, responsible drinking was not on the list; at least it wasn't verbalized like all the other things I wasn't allowed to do. I asked Mario for the following Friday night off, to which he had no issue. I worked all week as if a sun-filled Caribbean vacation awaited me. My mood became festive. It was as if all my problems and concerns dissipated. What I never realized was how important socializing was to humans. I had been alone for so long and only interacted with inmates, persons that held power over me, my father, and coworkers; only at the bar I could feel alive again. I was a social being; I needed it to survive.

When Friday came, I rushed home from work to get ready. I was twenty-four, and I hadn't been out since I was nineteen. I looked through my closet attempting to find something to wear to a bar. I decided on some jeans and a button-down shirt. I put on far too much cologne that I found in my father's bathroom, and slicked my hair back. I was going to be a young man for the night, not an ex-convict. I was going to be normal and forget about my situation and try to enjoy my life, socially. I had my father drop me off at the train station to avoid drinking and driving.

"Nick, be careful. No trouble please?" he pleaded as I got out of the car.

"No sir, just good clean fun," I winked and left.

I'm sure he was scared to see me go and I took that into consideration, but at some point we were going to have to get past my past. A night out presented an opportunity to do so, legally.

I bought my ticket then sat on a bench and waited for the train to arrive. Various types of people made their way onto the track; some dressed to go out for the night, (as it was the train into the city) some coming home from a long day at work, and others simply taking the train to their next destination. When it arrived, I took a window seat, and placed my ticket in the holder for the conductor to punch as he made his way up the aisle. I had so many thoughts (fears) as the towns raced by me. *Was going to a bar really okay for me to do? What would happen if it wasn't? Was I risking my freedom?* I had no hard answers, so instead I told myself that so long as I didn't do anything stupid, all would be fine. I arrived at Hoboken Terminal and made my way to the bar where Tony told me to meet him. I was a few minutes early and there was a long line outside. I thought of the days when I used to run around the city when I was a drug dealer, from club to club, schmoozing doormen, and making a scene. What a far cry from that it was: frat bros, sloppy girls, khakis, midriff shirts, and tattered baseball caps. Not what I was used to on a night out.

I saw Tony walk up and wave, smiling from ear to ear.

"Nick! Great to see ya buddy! It's been a long time!" he said.

"Sure has man. Thanks for meeting me."

"Sorry it took so long. I've been so busy with work."

"All good. It's nice to be out and about. My first time in a long time . . ." I said, trailing off into my mind of thoughts about my past. He grabbed me by the shoulder.

"Don't worry buddy, things are different now. Come on, let's go in."

We stood in line and talked about life, our families, and how things were going for me since my release. Before long we were at the front of the line, showing our IDs to a bouncer and entering the bar. The place was packed with boys and girls drinking, yelling, and dancing to bad hip-hop music. We found our way to the bar and ordered some beer. I attempted to pay but Tony would have nothing of it.

"I owe you money!" he said.

"It's fine, it's only money. Friendship is way more important," I replied.

We clinked glasses and drank. We couldn't really talk much due to the noise, but it was more of the scene he brought me there for anyway. A cute girl passed us and I smiled. Tony watched me as she continued on.

"Go talk to her. I'll stay here and hold the fort down."

I went over to her and tried to say hello, but the smile was wiped from her face as she turned and looked at me with disgust, as if to say, "What are you doing next to me. Get away?"

Defeated, I returned to the bar. Tony laughed and put his arm around my shoulder.

"It's a numbers game buddy. Keep your head up and try again, the only way you'll ever succeed."

I shrugged. I was rusty. I didn't know how to be social in these situations anymore. I was great with the shielding of a bar between me, when I held the power of someone having to come to me to ask for something, then it was easy to strike up a conversation with anyone. But when the playing field was leveled, I was clumsy and awkward. I needed to work on it. As the night passed, I made a few more face-planting attempts until one girl came over to me and began gyrating to a song she seemed to like. And then I remembered what my strong suit was. I took her hand, dropped my beer at the bar, and danced. We grooved and moved and it was fun and free and I felt like I hadn't in years, glancing back at Tony, who was smiling as he rooted me on. As the songs transitioned, we moved closer together and soon we were kissing and I was loving the moment . . . until her friend grabbed her hand and pulled her away and she was gone through the crowd.

I turned back to Tony, who held a fresh beer out to me.

"Win some, lose some," he said and we clinked and drank.

"She was cute," I said, excitedly.

"Look at you, getting your sea legs again," he encouraged.

"Like riding a bike . . ." I said in jest and laughed.

The night continued on, though I was starting to feel a bit hazy, when I noticed the time. The last train was leaving soon and I needed to make it.

I said goodbye and he walked me out.

"You gonna be alright to get back?" he asked.

"Yeah, train's right there," I pointed in the direction of the station.

"Call me if you need anything, it was great seeing you! Look forward to doing it again."

I left towards the train and arrived at the platform with time to spare. I was not drunk, but *buzzed*. Giddy even. I looked around at people my age: a couple making out, a girl vomiting in a trash can as her friends surrounded her and held her hair back, and an older, well-dressed couple returning home from a date night.

Normal people, living a normal life. If they only knew where I was just a few months prior. When the train pulled in, I took a window seat again and as we departed, the strangest thing happened. I began to cry. Not a sob, but more of a soft, tear-filled wash of emotion. To think that I gave all social interaction and freedom up for one stupid day, one extremely poor decision, and there I was trying to put it all back together. It seemed so nonsensical. So stupid. I began to get mad at myself, but stopped as I had been down that road all too many times. It was done. I could not change it; the act or the result. I could only change the future outcome. Those thoughts occupied my mind as the train sped off towards my stop. Upon arriving I found a cab waiting in the lot and proceeded home. It was just after midnight. It was then I thought about my curfew. I had forgotten all about it as with my work I had exceptions. As far as Carson knew I was supposed to be at work and would be arriving home around the same time anyway, if he had decided to pass by. Though it still sent a chill through my spine to think of what could have happened and it drained the happiness and freedom of the night from my soul. Why were these arbitrary rules in place? At that moment, what had I done wrong? What had I done *criminally*? Nothing! Yet there I was, shaking with fear as I curled up in bed and started to cry. Three years of *this*? I was only months in. Where was the freedom in that?

I woke up the next morning with a slight headache. After some coffee and a workout, I began to feel like myself. I was prepared to tackle the work night that laid before me.

The evening went as Saturdays usually did, the one or two bar steadies mixed with a slew of the outer boroughs. Edward had excused himself to use the restroom and left me to man the bar. We were about halfway through the night when Mario made his way over and motioned his fingers, which meant to pour him a shot of Limoncello, his drink of choice through the night that kept him even, which was usually reserved for Edward to perform, but seeing as I was the only one there, I reached for the bottle.

"No. Jameson," he demanded, a fire in his eye I had never seen.

I did as I was told. He shot it, grabbed a lemon from the tray and sucked through it to mask the smell of alcohol before returning to the floor. He reached for a napkin, wiping his mouth and fingers then looked at me for a moment, before . . .

"You're gonna be a captain on the floor, starting next week," he stated.

"Nah, Mario, I'm a bartender. I don't have a clue how to do what those guys do. And there's no way I can remember all those specials."

"You want to be an actor, no?" he asked, it having been a topic we discussed at some point, although I had done nothing yet to pursue it, too bogged down by two jobs.

"Yeah . . ."

"Well, it's great training to become one. You start training Tuesday. And it will be full-time. I'll speak to Vinny, maybe he can lighten your hours or something."

With that he returned to the floor as Edward came back behind the bar.

"What was that about?"

"I don't know, exactly."

Edward noticed the Jameson on the service counter that I had yet to put away.

"He must have fired someone. He only drinks whiskey when he's hot."

"That'd explain it," I said.

"Explain what?" he asked

"Me starting floor training next week."

A large smile came over him and he began his belly laugh chuckle.

"You should be happy! You're gonna make the big bucks," he turned and grabbed the Jameson and poured us two shots.

"To you! Cap-i-tan!"

We tossed them back.

"But if it's such a good opportunity, why don't you do it?"

"Me, Asian man, that dining room? Oh no. I like the bar. My bar. Been for years. That room, Italians. You Italian, right?"

"Jersey-Italian."

"Same thing, all these guys, wise guys. And then the real Italians, like Luca and Marco." Everyone else, American-Italian," he winked and laughed again.

I arrived the next day for training on the floor. I hadn't been out from behind a bar and on the floor since I was a morning server at the Washington Square Hotel five years earlier. And it was no WSH. It was the big time. Captains and back-waiters. Seven daily specials. A large wine program. Tableside fileting of fish. Serving from the right, cleaning from the left. Women first, the person who ordered always served last. It was a crash course in high-level hospitality. Leave your personality at home. You are a servant, not an entertainer. I was introduced to Luca who would become my mentor of sorts. He was a sharply dressed Italian from Rome, with strong features, and the physique of David. He was a career waiter, having served in dining rooms all over the world. He was in America on a tourist Visa living the life that Europeans tend to live in America: one without care or consequence. They work to live, unlike Americans, who live to work. He was effusive, if not nasty. He was unsure if my skill set would translate to a dining floor, but Mario insisted he trained me. The first night was gruesome. I had to read the specials off the notepad, a HUGE no-no, even though it was my first night I was expected to memorize them. I spilled driblets of wine on a tablecloth as I moved from glass to glass. I cleared peoples' plates before others were finished. I was a complete mess.

After the shift, I was reminded of each and every mistake I made and it was noted on my closeout report. I was so disheartened, I went to Mario and asked to be put back at the bar.

"No. This is your new reality. Embrace it. And once you start seeing the difference in your checks, you'll laugh that you ever asked me this," he encouraged me.

I returned home that night determined to get better.

Over the next few shifts, things began to get easier. I made mistakes, was corrected, and made sure to never make the same mistake twice. By the end of the week, I had my first real test; a Saturday night. The floor was twice as busy as it had been during the week. I was given a small section of four tables to man by myself throughout the night. I had managed to get the memorization down to only using the notepad as a cheat sheet, masking it as a device to take the customer's orders. If anyone needed assistance with the wine list, I would seek help from a manager and listen, taking mental notes of what was said so as I continued to grow I would be able to answer customers' questions on my own. To be a better captain, I spent my off-time in the kitchen, learning the food, each dish's preparation and plating, and assisted in running the food to give me a grasp of every job in the restaurant. By Tuesday afternoon of the following week, I was shot. I fell asleep at my desk after eating lunch and was shaken awake by a coworker who informed me it was probably not a good idea. I thanked him and went to get some coffee where I ran into Vinny.

"Nicky, you don't look so good, are you sick?"

"No, just tired. Been a lot the past few weeks with my promotion and all the additional shifts."

"Mario told me. Congratulations. All seems to be good here as well, from what I hear," he said, fishing.

"Yup, here on time, stay as late as I can and get all my work done. So that's good."

"Things like this build character. Think of how many people in your situation would die to be in your shoes right now," he said, and left with his coffee as I sat stirring sugar into mine.

Thursday night the staff decided to go out to The Ear Inn for drinks after work. I had always declined, but that night, I needed a release. A drink or two couldn't hurt, *could it?*

I saddled up to the bar with Luca and a few of the other staff members and ordered a pint. We spoke about the night and some of the customers, their demands, and the way some of them treated us. It was fun and relaxing and I could see why so many servers needed to drink after their shifts; a reward for "service." To anyone who has never been in the service industry, you wouldn't understand the expectancy of people when they sit down to dine. It is as if the caste system were immediately put back into effect. People can be monsters. After an hour or so, having consumed two beers and a shot, I bid everyone adieu and walked over to my car. Upon starting it, I yawned, which should have been the first sign for me to stop in my tracks. However, knowing the rules, I couldn't risk staying the night in Manhattan, sleeping in a car, no matter how safe it technically was. I decided to press on instead. As I traveled through the tunnel, I began to yawn again. I opened the window and stuck my head in the breeze to help me stay awake. Only as I passed over the Pulaski Skyway and came off the ramp into the merge, I dozed off and hit the median. I immediately woke and gained control of the vehicle, looked around, and searched for other cars; there were none. I held both hands on the wheel tightly and sat up straight. I was scared shitless. My breath had become short spurts. My mind utter mush when I saw the exit for Reliable and drove straight for it.

I kept my head out the window as I drove, one hand on the wheel, in control, the cool air keeping me awake until I saw the entrance to the parking lot. I pulled in, parked the car, opened the door, and bent over myself to hurl. Only nothing came. It was fear-based. I was shaking. My hands rattled like the tail of a snake. I turned the car off and sat in silence. The cool air began to rush over me as I placed the seat back. As I laid down, an epiphany hit me: I could NOT remain in the driver seat. Not that I was drunk, my blood alcohol level was legal, based on the amount of drinks I had had and the hours in between, but I envisioned what it would, *could*, look like if a police cruiser had come by and noticed one car in an empty lot and a driver passed out in the driver seat. So, I moved over, pulled the seat back and closed my eyes. I woke to the rising sun. I wiped the crust from my eyes and sat up, looking around. Not a car in the lot yet. I noticed the time, 6:20 a.m. I was safe. I grabbed my backpack from the car and headed into the office. I placed the key card over the employee entrance and went to my desk, grabbed the emergency pair of work clothes I had stashed and headed to the gym to use the showers. I stood under the hot water and thought hard about the night. The risks I took, the worry my father must have had, and the fact that it was mainly due to exhaustion, though having even a few drinks with such a lack of sleep could have derailed my entire mission and sent me right back to the pen.

I decided a few things right there and then. NEVER again would I get behind the wheel of a car having had so much as one drink. The thought made it clear that I was not ready for a social life, especially in NYC where a majority of social gatherings were at bars, restaurants, or nightclubs. Second, that it was time to quit the day job. Vinny had been good to me, but over the past few months, it was becoming clear that not only wasn't it manageable for the long term, but that Vinny was my only protection against the cogs in the employment pool who seriously resented my leaving each day at three in the afternoon and still collecting a salary. It was time to cut the cord and take the next step toward whatever my future was to become. I returned to my desk clean and booted up my computer, aiming to get all of my work done and provide Vinny with my notice later that day. Around noon, I knocked on Vinny's door. He invited me in and told me to sit. I made my way to the high-backed leather chair opposite him and sat waiting for him to finish his typing.

"What's going on Nicky?" he asked.

"Vinny, I can't continue on like this in good faith. Between both jobs, the hours, and the commutes, I sleep less than five hours a night and it's catching up with me."

"I don't sleep more than four and I'm twice your age."

"You have better genes," I slyly stated. He was not amused, and I continued.

"Our timeline is nearly up and I have to be honest I'm not going to make it to, or past, month three."

He sat for a moment, disappointed. The smile had disappeared from his face and he felt that it was a direct affront against him and all he had done for me. It hurt to see him like that, as I knew I would not be in either of those positions without him, however, I was honest and upfront and wasn't that most important? He sat there long enough to begin to make it uncomfortable for me until he spoke.

"All right, what can I do? I can't force you to stay. Will you at least be an adult and provide me two weeks notice in writing so I can inform your superiors and delegate your work load?"

"I can and will," I said and stood. I reached my hand out and he took it. I looked him dead in the eye.

"Thank you, Vinny. I will always remember what you have done for me and will be forever grateful."

"Two weeks," he said and released my hand, turning to his computer. I took it as a sign to leave.

The next two weeks came and went and I have to admit, it

wasn't clean. I was so over being there, so exhausted from working five nights on my feet in the restaurant that I was a walking zombie. I was late a few days, having slept through my alarm and while there, I couldn't focus, or didn't want to focus, as I was mentally checked out. But alas, after the following Friday, I was finally released from my day job. It was freeing in more ways than one. Reliable was my job while I was in a halfway house and there was still the stain of that fresh on me, so leaving was bittersweet, but necessary. . . . I told them to mail my final check and drove home that night after leaving Reliable for the last time. I was ready to officially close that chapter of my life.

CHAPTER 8

THE PLAN

Westfield, New Jersey—2005

I had been out for nearly four months by the time I arrived to see Carson for the first time since he had to cancel our last visit. After peeing, clean as usual, we made our way to his desk.

"Pay stubs," I said as I presented both.

"You're making more than me," he huffed.

"Not for long," I replied.

He stopped writing and looked through me.

"What do you mean?"

"I've decided to leave Reliable to pursue my studies."

"Go on . . ."

"I've been given a promotion at work and I am a captain now, on the dining floor."

"A what?" he asked, perplexed.

"It's a glorified waiter, we just make a lot more money, as you see . . ." I pointed to my pay stub.

"Some racket," he sniffed and continued writing.

"Since I have my daily pass and all is going smoothly, I'm not a problem to you and don't intend to be, I'll be traveling into the city to find the right school, maybe attend some auditions I can find online. I want to start moving toward something that will get me out of the service industry."

"You're funny, you know that?"

"Why?"

"I spend most of my days chasing my caseload down to just go look for work, here you are quitting a job, which if you didn't have the other job would be an issue, so you know."

"I'm aware. As I said to you from the beginning. I have a plan. I can't remain stagnant. I have to grow."

"So long as you keep working and stay out of trouble, we good."

"Appreciate you Carson, even under the circumstances."

"See you in two months," he said, looking up at me as I stood to go.

"Really?"

"If you don't fuck it up, it'll only get better."

I left feeling like I had finally started to win. I woke up the following Monday to find that everyone was gone from the house, off to work and I was alone to enjoy the silence of the summer morning; the birds chirping, the wind softly rattling the trees. It felt good to have the day to myself, though I was unsure of what I would do each day to occupy my time productively. I decided that over the next few weeks I would look into some of the acting schools that were listed online. I would have to match schedules, deliverables, and pricing. I had a lot to decide on. I didn't have any debt at that time, except a small car note that I took on to have a nice enough car. I wasn't paying rent at the time either, but was still frugal enough to ensure that I was using my forced living situation to save nearly every dime I made so when I was able to move out and start a life on my own, I had a little scratch to do so. As I sat on the porch drinking coffee and thinking about the next steps I would need to take, it dawned on me that I would have the next few weeks or months of mornings like that. Simple, Peaceful, and Alone. It made me smile and warmed my heart. The only thing I was missing was a good book. And so, that was to be the first step: the bookstore.

I went to the local Barnes & Noble later that morning and began my search. I got a few books on acting, some on film, others of fiction. I always liked to have an array of reading materials, each to suit a different mood or need for my own research. Upon arriving home, I set about finding schools. After a few hours, deep into the Internet rabbit hole, it seemed I had a very big decision to make; take on massive debt and return to a local college to achieve some sort of degree, (though I had no idea what would be worth such debt, given the roads now closed to me because of my crimes), or attend an acting school. I spent the day taking notes, brainstorming, and planning my attack. When I finished, I had a pros and cons list, in addition to a real-world assessment of what I was facing. On one side I took my current weekly earnings (which varied as I was in service and worked on tips) against the cost of school, against the average cost of an apartment in various cities close to New York, *if* I were able to convince Carson to put forth the paperwork for a transfer to another district, which seemed unlikely. All told, it seemed pretty clear that I simply couldn't afford college. The numbers were staggeringly against me, and that was before I added in things like interest and potential penalties. The math made my decision pretty simple. I could afford to go to a trade school, for which I had no interest, or attend acting classes, and that was about it. I went to the movies that night; my first time in a theater in many years. Afterward, I walked around the town, looked into little shops, and got some ice cream, something I hadn't done since I was a kid. I was reprogramming myself to prepare for what was to come.

Prior to prison, all I did was take drugs, sell drugs, and chase girls. I was so lost I gave up what was left of my childhood for nonsense. And although I didn't have a social life during that early time of my release into society, I had myself; and a little bit of freedom. And for that I was so truly grateful that I learned to embrace the time alone, instead of being bitter at not having a social life and friends, or starting a career after college, as all the people my age were doing by that point. Instead, I learned to take things as they came and enjoy the little things. I returned to work the next afternoon and was back in the saddle. Each night after I was cut and I drove home, I knew I would have the entire morning and most of the day to myself to work on my future plans. And as happens in life when you set your mind and heart to things, opportunity meets drive and things come to you. One night at work, during a relatively slow shift, I was picking up drinks at the service bar when Edward asked me to come back, as he wanted to introduce me to someone. I gave him the lip service I usually did and told him I'd be back once all my tables were situated and I had a minute to chat. After sending in the food orders, I returned.

"What's up?" I asked.

He introduced me to a man in his mid-fifties, seated at the bar drinking a scotch, and said "I want you to meet one of our regulars, Max."

"Pleasure to meet you, Nick. Edward tells me good things," he stated, a kindness in his eyes.

"Uh, thanks," I replied, unsure of what it was.

"Edward tells me you want to be an actor. You have the face for it, that's for sure."

"I do? I gotta get in some classes, find an agent, all the things," I stated.

"Max is an entertainment attorney," Edward said.

"What's that?" I asked.

"I do the legal for people in the arts. Contracts, other things."

"That's cool," I replied, still unsure of where it all was going.

"Like I said, you got a good look. Ever think of modeling? Doing commercials? You could probably get started on that right away, without classes," he asked.

"I used to model, but I've always been told I'm not tall enough to really make it."

"That may be the case, but there are ways. How about this, there is an agent in my office, well he used to be an agent, now he's an attorney, but I can set up a meeting for you and let's see what he says, couldn't hurt."

"Really? That would be . . . amazing!" I could see Edward smile out of the corner of his eye, his master plan taking effect.

"I would love to help. And who knows, maybe one day you'll make it big and you'll be a client of mine. That's my only ask."

"Of course!" I exclaimed, knowing nothing about the industry, what would come and that it was surely a false promise, but one I needed to make.

"Edward, pen and paper please?"

He did as asked and handed both to Max who wrote out a name and a number.

"Give him a call in the office tomorrow, I'll give him a heads up so he takes the call."

"I really can't thank you enough, Max." I said, taking the paper and folding it into my pocket.

"Like I said, if you make it."

We shook hands and I returned to the floor, on cloud nine, thinking of how nice people were. It brought a tear to my eye, which I immediately shook off so no one would see me emotional. The rest of my shift I was dreaming of the next steps and the possibilities to come. That and the fact that most people were good and wanted good for each other. A part of humanity I missed within the bars and concertina wire that confined me and the other degenerates of society, and that isn't limited to the criminals, as I've seen more corrections officers, administrative persons, and counselors who need serious counseling and anger management themselves. The next day, around eleven, I called the office. A receptionist answered and I asked to speak to Goldstein. She told me to hold, then came back on the line and asked what the call was in reference to. I explained that Max had told me to call. The line went silent until . . .

"This is Goldstein."

I went on to explain how I met Max, when Goldstein stopped me and said that Max had already given him the heads up. He would take a meeting with me and see what he could help with, *if* anything. He went on to temper my expectations of the results of the meeting by warning me that usually the people he dealt with had degrees in theater from colleges, universities, or conservatories (whatever that was, I had to look it up). He then provided me with some days and time that would work for him and we settled on a date two weeks out. I thanked him and hung up the phone with hope in my heart. It was time to get to work and research the programs so I would be prepared to speak somewhat intelligently on the matter. Over the next few weeks, I spent all my free time researching the business and the education associated with it. I began with NYU, as I had gotten in, and it was the one dream I couldn't afford, nor stomach if they didn't grant me readmission, but figured starting there would lead me to the right place. I learned about Tisch's various programs: directing, acting, writing, etc. Then I correlated that to focus it down to acting schools. I found out about Yale, Julliard, University of Southern California, and a small group of others that really stood out for the famous talent they were responsible for. All of which required too much money and time to complete.

Then I discovered what a conservatory is, which is a school

focused on acting and all the elements within it: movement, voice, speech, and accent work, and different techniques such as The Method or Meisner. And then I realized that most of them required large amounts of time, similar to universities, and although cheaper, still out of my budget range. And although I probably could have stretched it, I would have to take on a sizable enough debt and that concerned me. As I still had my mother's comments in my ear about artists being broke most of their life and I didn't think it practical to take on debt of that magnitude for a career that was so unforgiving and temperamental. That all led to me looking for classes. I found a few that looked decent enough, nothing spectacular, but they were all affordable and had minimal commitments of eight to ten hours of class a week in their advertisements. That would allow me to continue working full time at night and keep saving for when I was able to have my own apartment. On the day of the meeting, I chose what I thought was the coolest outfit in my closet: a white V-neck T-shirt, blue jeans, and boots; a throwback to a Hollywood idol I dreamed to resemble, James Dean.

I made my way into the city and parked my car in the Ponte's lot as it was free to me as an employee, then set off to take the train to Midtown where Goldstein's office was. I realized I hadn't been truly "in" the city since my release once I went below ground into the subway for the first time. It was so strange, the energy, the feeling. All that had been lost to me since my release because I was a Jersey commuter: drive, park, walk into work, maybe walk a block or two from work to get the post shift drink, drive back home. Getting a MetroCard and finding my way brought me back to the days when I was working for my cousin in Soho as a production assistant and messenger. It was around the time my father had gotten so fed up with my drug dealing and decision making that he called my cousin, whom I admired, and had him step in. It

was the last-ditch attempt to save me from myself and the decisions I was making. He hired me and thrusted me into a world I
had only dreamed of: fast paced, highfalutin NYC.

It was the world I wanted to live in, but just didn't have a clue
how to get there. I dove right in, learning the city like the back of
my hand, experiencing everything it had to offer. Unfortunately,
I had gone back to dealing drugs and being a punk and my cousin
fired me for doing so and it ended about as quickly as it started.
But during those months, I really fell in love with New York. It
was one of the few things that kept me dreaming at night, in the
cold loneliness of my various cells. That one day, I would be back
and free and determined to set the record right. And there I was,
doing just that again, nearly five years later. The city had changed
so much by that time; it was in the post-9/11 world. No more
Giuliani. The feeling was not the same as that great slice of NY in
the late nineties, not as raw and real, but there was still something
there and I wanted to eat it up. As I made my way through the
subway traffic, I couldn't help but think it would soon be my life.
Each and every day; just as soon as I was off parole, which was
still a ways away.

I arrived at the base of a sleek, monstrous office tower. I was
instructed to take the elevator to the thirty-second floor. Soon,
I was off the elevator, surrounded by a large glass enclosed lobby
overlooking the city, with views from all sides. The receptionist
informed me that she would bring me back when Goldstein was
ready. I sat in a chair and watched the comings and goings of the
office. It felt good to be there, perched high in the sky and I
imagined it being my future. From the ground to the sky. My hope
held high. After some time, she rose and told me to follow her to
his office. We walked through a maze of cubicles, large conference
rooms, and smaller offices all overlooking some part of the city to
a small, windowless room at the back. I entered and she closed the

door. Behind the desk sat a man, mid-thirties, with long hippy-style hair, wearing glasses and a button-down shirt. He stood and we shook hands.

"Pleasure to meet you Nick, Goldstein. Sit."

"So, Max tells me you want to be an actor," he said, looking me over as he reclined in his chair.

"That's the plan. I know I gotta lot of work to do, but I'm confident I can figure it out."

"Have you done anything before, high school plays, regional theater, film, anything?"

"I was an extra in *Summer of Sam*," I gloated, as if that meant anything, one of a thousand people on a cold day, years back, on the steps of the Brooklyn courthouse.

"Well, that's something, but nothing all the same. Have you looked into schools? Training is very important."

At that point I took out my notebook and started rattling off the names of the places I had researched.

"I think Gina would be a good start for you. Eventually you'll need something more formal, but it will get your feet wet and give you a small taste of what the craft requires. And make no mistake, it's a craft, like any trade. So, tell me more about yourself, what have you been up to?"

I went on to tell him about my life and current position. Needless to say, it was not what he expected. We had a nice conversation and at the end he was very honest, as he had been throughout.

"Listen, you are at a place where I can't really help you. I deal with people with a lot more experience and training. However, there is something I can do that will give you a little start as you begin your journey into this career. I'm going to introduce you to my friend, Jenny, she's a commercial print agent at Abrams Artists Agency. I used to be an agent there for film and television. She should be able to get you out on some go-sees and from there, as you get training you can work your way to getting an agent in due time."

He wrote down her information, told me he would let her know I was calling and thanked me for my story. He wished me luck in my pursuit and told me to stay in touch as things progressed for me. As I left the building, I began to realize that it was no easy feat. That the amount of work I had before me was great. Far unlike the dreams I had that I would simply be discovered one day behind a bar and launched into a career in Hollywood. Instead, it would be years of training and struggle. And even with all the hard work I was to have to put in, I would need luck AND for the stars to align. I thought about it as I walked back to Ponte's.

Was I ready for this? Hadn't my life already been hard enough? Wasn't this exactly what Vinny warned me about? Why wouldn't I just go back to the comfy, small job with little growth opportunity and settle? That would be far easier. But as I walked and felt the energy of New York around me, running through me, I said no. *No fucking way.* I suffered through everything to have a shot at something more, or so I felt. I was not going to settle for anything, no matter how difficult the path ahead was for me. I was going to put my head down and work my fucking ass off at every turn and come hell or high water two things were going to ring true:

I would never return to prison AND I would succeed at something . . . eventually.

The first order of business would be to get into a class. I emailed the studio asking for a place in the fall classes and heard back a few days later about an interview. There was no preparation involved, the studio often taking people with little, or no, formal acting experience. I made an appointment for one afternoon and found myself in Chelsea, my old stomping grounds, remembering the venues that no longer existed where I first tended bar awaiting my fate while out on bail. I buzzed the third floor of a nondescript building. The buzzer rang back and the elevator opened, then was called to the floor. The doors opened to an apartment, vast in size, with large movie posters on the walls, an elaborate bookcase filled to the hilt, and large books strewn over the floor and tables. A short Jewish woman with red hair and the spunk of a child greeted me at the entrance.

"Nick, I presume?" I nodded.

"Gina, nice to meet you, welcome to my home, please sit."

She ushered me over to behind the bookcase into a vast living space with couches, a coffee table, and a large flat screen television on the wall.

"So, you wanna be an actor, huh?"

I answered yes and began to tell her my story. She sat intently listening, never breaking eye contact, not for a moment, until I had caught her up.

"Wow, that's an incredible story. It has depth. What a real actor needs! But . . . I can see, and feel, there is a lot of build up on you. A protection. Walls. Lots of walls that served you during your time, but won't do you any good as an actor. We will need to break those down. Shatter them! The best actors use their bodies as instruments. Vehicles. There are two methods, Meisner and Stanislovski. I teach Meisner, truth under the circumstances, we will get to that later. But you, you have gone through so much, maybe the method is what you seek. I am not sure. There is only one way to find out. Join my class. Let's dig into your soul, find out who you are, what drives you. From there, we will see the best path forward, whether that will be to continue with me or another. Only time and hard work will tell."

She went on to explain her fee, the class size, schedule, and place. I left thanking her and promising her a check by the following week to secure my place in her fall class. Next up, the agent.

I arrived a few weeks later to a large office building in Chelsea. There was no security in the lobby. I rode the elevator to the twenty-fourth floor and approached the receptionist, the gatekeeper to the walls of the anteroom; one that starving, desperate actors would do anything to get behind. I waited as people looked at papers before them and talked to themselves. These, I would later find out, are what we call "sides" in the business. The short form of scenes to be used for auditions. Though I did not know that on the day and instead thought that I was surrounded by crazy people talking to themselves. When I was called, I was greeted at the door by a very attractive young woman. We sat and spoke about my life, about hers, about the agency. She told me things about the business, the difference between modeling agencies (they were not) and her division, commercial print. They booked actors and less traditional models (not high fashion like the pages of *Vogue*) for jobs for clients as varied as fast food to cologne companies to shoes to resorts and hotels. There was a whole world of opportunity in advertising and people could do well and make a living off of it (back then, that is—no longer thanks to the rise of what I call "fodels," fake models who post airbrushed pictures on Instagram). The interview carried on for too long and eventually her assistant called and said she was late for another meeting.

She excused herself, told me we would begin working together and that her assistant would send all the onboarding contracts soon.

I found myself sitting before Carson the following week, having the same conversation I had with him every month for six months at that point.

"I'll see you before Christmas," he said, handing my pay stubs back.

"Really?" He shook his head and I got up, shook his hand and left.

I figured I must have been doing something right and took his latitude as a sign to continue on my journey. And I believed I was. I had no social life in which to cause trouble. I drank minimally, and most importantly, safely. I was worlds away from ANY form of criminality. I was "working the program," as they say. Abrams began sending me out on go-sees and I learned what the world of commercial print modeling was like. I had gone out for about a month, and it wasn't until late August, that I got a call from Jenny.

"Congratulations! *Maxim* wants to book you for a full-page spread!"

I was so ecstatic. I had never booked anything real before. I loved *Maxim*. In fact, it was one of the magazines I used to have delivered to me in prison. *Vanity Fair*, *Vogue*, *Maxim*, and *Details*. I could write another book about the comments made about that by everyone from guards to inmates over the years. I digress. I called my mother and she cried in happiness. I was so proud to finally have something achievable to relay to her. The shoot day was pure bliss. Fully catered food, people at my beck and call all day. It was a taste of what things could be like. When it was over, having taken the day off from work, I decided to call Jenny and thank her. She suggested we meet for a drink. I met her at Pastis in the Meatpacking District. She was sitting alone at the bar, sipping a martini when I arrived. We exchanged pleasantries and I ordered one for myself. I hadn't had a martini in some time and after a few sips I was feeling it in my head. I told her about the shoot and thanked her for believing in me. She demurred, saying it was her job, as she gulped the remaining contents of her glass and ordered another. I ordered a beer, finishing mine when the beer arrived. We ended up having dinner and speaking about the business. It was the most fun I had since I went out with Tony and I safely returned home later that night without incident.

I went to my first day of acting class full of hope for my future.

I entered the studio and took a seat amongst the other fifteen students, a lot of models; nearly the entire class actually. I found that strange, but who was I to judge? We introduced ourselves to the class and then partnered off to do some scene work. We were given scripts and told to read them, then think about the characters we were playing and what situations they found themselves in and react as if we, ourselves, were in that situation. It seemed easy enough. And as each group went up to perform in front of the group, watching, it felt that something was missing. Most of us were simply reading lines off a page, which is what, years later, I would come to find out was exactly what we were doing. But during that time, I didn't know anything, so I partook, and watched and listened to the feedback that Gina provided to each student. I assumed I was being trained in some great way; learning from the best and taking copious notes on her thoughts and musings.

Over the entirety of the fall season, I spent my days in class, my nights at Ponte's. I dove into my scene work and my classes and books. Prison had made me a student like never before with all the time I had on my hands, basically providing the time to give myself a faux degree in world literature and teaching myself how to write. Those months became no different. And when the holidays arrived, I found myself sitting across from Carson, for the first time since the summer, finding that he would no longer be my PO. He was retiring and I would be passed off to someone else.

"Does that mean I'm going to have to come here more often?" I asked, desperate with fear at the thought, as I hated going back. Everything in my being was about moving forward. Which I thought I had been doing.

"Not necessarily. My notes and recommendations mean a lot. I've had 'times in' as they say."

He completed my paperwork and walked me to a cubicle down

the way. A young man, not much older than me, wearing glasses and short hair parted to one side looked up.

"Becker."

He looked up, surprised almost, Carson's imposing frame over him.

"Wanted to introduce you to one of my finest. He's gonna be yours. Never been a problem, almost a year now, two left. Thought I should make the acquaintance myself, seeing as he's already on quarterly."

"Quarterly?" he asked, dumbfounded.

"Quarterly," Carson repeated. Becker took that as his note, nodded his head.

"Nice to meet you . . ."

"Marshall. Same to you sir," I stated as confidently as I could knowing my life rested in that young guy's hands.

"Guess I'll see you in . . ."

He took out his calendar.

"Early April."

"I'll be here sir."

"You'll probably see me before, have to check out your residence."

"There every night after midnight, sir, gone in the mornings early though, school then work."

"I'll review your chart," he said, putting the control back in his court, not mine.

"Like I said Becker, not a problem," Carson stated and nodded his head for me to follow him out.

As we approached the doorway he shook my hand.

"Good luck to you. I truly hope you find your way out of all this unscathed."

"Thanks Carson, enjoy retirement."

"Oh, I plan on it. Rum runners in the sun await."

I smiled and left. I would never see Carson again.

My time at Ponte's had become harder as the year turned and the months went by. Mario left and the younger manager was in charge. He had it out for all of us, felt that we were all too spoiled, made too much money, and left too much of the work to the back waiters. He began cleaning house. I survived, but knew it was a matter of time before I would be out, so I began to look for other opportunities. In the interim, I remained on my absolute best behavior. Never late, never complaining, always there when he needed me. It was my first lesson in work politics. Find out what drives someone, how you can fit into that drive, or simply stay away from what he hates about people in order to stay off the chopping block. Befriend them, become their confidant. Listen, don't talk. And take mental notes and then do your best to ride the wave until you can graciously get off and find another one. Always better to leave than be cut.

Acting school was nearing the end of the term. The entire first quarter of the year would be about our first stage performances in the spring. We were assigned partners and scenes consisting of seven pages, which seemed like a lot to me. I poured myself into the material, spending each day memorizing my lines, working on my character. Then we would watch one another rehearse in class, each class a different scene. The idea was that we would learn about the process from Gina's notes to each actor.

And during those first months of the new year, again, I spent my free time in isolation. Watching movies and taking notes; a practice I felt would help me in the future as a filmmaker. Three or four days of the week, I would watch classic movies, the "must-sees" that I would hear other actors speak about. I took a deep dive into cinema and started what would become another form of education for me. Before I knew it, the winter was behind me. The trees began to bloom, the sun shone brighter in the sky and the air warmed, the rebirth of spring. And I would soon find myself in the form of another rebirth, my first visit with Becker. I arrived, as usual, slightly early, only to find that the stunt dummy routine was on me. Not only did I have to piss, as it was my routine, but he was late, not even in the building. And since I was new to his caseload, they would not let another officer supervise my testing, some rule, bureaucratic no doubt, that again, was bullshit. And so, I sat, legs crossed. After forty minutes, he entered casually. I stood before him, hopping from foot to foot like a lunatic, he must have thought I was on something, nor did he recognize me at first which caused him to step back, defensively.

"Mr. Becker, I gotta go, please," he looked dumbfounded for a moment before realizing who I was.

"Oh, Marshall!" As if he finally put two and two together.

"I forgot I had you today. Come on back."

I rushed before him into the bathroom and swiped the cup from his outstretched hand, relieving myself, finally. I handed it back to him and he pulled the stick from the wrapper, showing his lack of experience versus his predecessor.

"Clean. You can dump it."

I did as I was told and went toward his desk. We sat and he pulled out my file. I held my pay stub in my hand.

"Look, I know you had a certain relationship with Carson. But you and I have to start fresh."

Here we go . . .

"Sure. Whatever you need from me," I stated, hoping that appealing to his ego would get me where I needed to be.

"First, I've never seen anyone on quarterly within the first year. So that's out. I'll give you monthly to start."

Prick.

"I'm not sure why I'm being punished for working my program and doing what is right and legal," I said.

"Because you're a fucking convict, that's why," he said out of the corner of his mouth. I was livid, the anger burning from within, if I hadn't made myself the promise not to be a criminal anymore, I might have jumped over the table and taken him out.

"Understood."

"And this back and forth into the city, I have to speak to my supervisor about it. I'm not sure it's legal," he added.

And with that I was seething.

"You want to take everything I've worked for from me?" I asked.

"It's about what's *legal*," he said, as if the law mattered there.

"Okay, so what would you have me do? Not go to work, lose my job over it? Not go to class? What is your remedy here?"

"As I said, I'll find out. No harm in continuing until I sort things out for you."

"And if there is an issue?" I asked.

"I'm sure you will find employment in the state. Shouldn't be that difficult," he said as he checked a few more boxes in my chart.

"Okay, I'll see you next month. Same day and time. I should have news before then, I'll give you a ring and let you know."

I rose and left the building. When I got outside, I kicked the garbage can over in anger. I was livid beyond all belief. I had been out for over a year at that point, did everything that was required, asked of me. And the little prick, out to make a name for himself no doubt, could decide the fate of my life! I was reeling. The next few days were miserable. I was a shell of myself. I couldn't pay attention. My mind was off in every permutation of losing the life I had built. *What would I do!?* I started shaking. My nerves were shot. I dropped a plate of food on the dining floor! I couldn't perform wine service. I was such a mess I was called into the manager's office at the end of the week.

"Is there something going on with you?" he asked.

"I'm sorry, I've been dealing with some family issues at home."

"Maybe you should take the next week off. Get some rest."

"No, I'll be—" he interjected.

"I wasn't asking. Take the week. We can revisit this next week. Give me a ring, we can discuss how you are feeling and take it from there.

I was excused. I got in my car and sped off. When I arrived home early, my father was concerned.

"What are you doing home so early?" he asked.

"Slow night," I lied.

"You hungry, some food in the fridge?"

"Nah, I'm gonna go get some school work done," I lied and left for my basement retreat.

I couldn't work on my lines. I couldn't read. I tried to sleep. No dice. I tossed and turned for hours. When I finally fell asleep, I woke up in a sweat from a nightmare about being back in prison. The night continued in that manner until the sun rose and I was still up, exhausted. I decided to go to the gym and sweat it out. I went crazy. I was like a lunatic on the bag, hitting it until I fell to the ground in exhaustion. I needed it.

Upon returning home I felt a small sense of relief. I began working on my lines and my mind settled. I focused on the work at hand and it freed me up. I even slept that night, shifting my focus from the anger I had to the fact that it was out of my control. That all I could do, could ever do, is focus on what I *could* control. All I could control was *how* I reacted to things. I went to class the next day and put my scene up in preparation for the big night which was around the corner. It was the best work I had ever done. It was as if that experience had allowed me to be set free. To live entirely in the moment of a scene, without pushing judgment upon myself. I was elated. I left the class and went with everyone to the bar and had a drink. As I was sitting there, basking in the feeling of having a breakthrough, my phone rang from a blocked number. My stomach dropped. *Was this him?* There was only one way to find out.

I excused myself and stepped out into the cool spring evening air.

"Hello?" I answered as confidently as possible.

"Mr. Marshall?" a voice on the other end spoke.

"This is he."

"This is your PO, Mr. Becker. I spoke to my supervisor and although not routine, it seems the program that Carson had you on and your allowance will remain intact, so long as your pay stubs remain consistent and you have proof of your class attendance."

A wash of relief overcame me.

"Thank you, sir."

"I'll see you in two weeks at your next scheduled visit."

The phone went dead.

I began to cry. I stepped aside and sat on the ground, my head in my hands, crying softly. After a moment, I wiped my tears and composed myself before returning inside. I realized many things at that moment. Notably, I had no control of the System and needed to get out of it as quickly as I could. And second, that it was, ironically, a good lesson. It taught me yet another way to deal with adversity and how to channel those feelings into something positive. Although I had wished the last two weeks had never happened, I would add them to the ever-growing list of things I had learned lessons from, always, albeit, the hard way. The following week I was on stage for the first time in my life. As I sat in the greenroom my palms began to sweat and my hands started to rattle. I had never had nerves like that before. Even when I stood before a judge, I was ice. But getting ready to bear my soul on stage and see if I had what it takes to make it in the biz, I couldn't get a hold of myself. I ran to the restroom and dry heaved. I threw cold water over my face and looked at myself in the mirror. I stared deep into my eyes and told myself I was being a wimp. That I had been through far worse in life. FAR WORSE. And even smacked myself, thinking that the shock would snap me out of that haze. Which worked. Calmer, I began to breathe. I took a long, hard breath and released it, counting to five, then repeated it five more times. Once my equilibrium returned, I made my way back to the greenroom, only as I went, I heard one of my classmates' voices, deep into character and had an urge to be nosy. I peeked my head through the door and noticed that there was no audience. The theater was empty save Gina, sitting and taking notes in a middle row close to the stage.

I laughed to myself and continued back to the greenroom where the other students paced, jumped up and down to release nerves, and performed vocal exercises. Content that no one was out there to judge me, I settled into a chair, closed my eyes, and thought about my scene. When our names were called, I jumped up, held my scene partner by the arms and looked into her eyes. It was a technique of trust between artists that we were taught, and after our quick powwow, we were off. I took my position in the low-lights of the stage. Ready. I waited until the lights were lowered to black, then LIGHT! ACTION! And I was there, I think, for it all happened so fast, I was unsure if I got my lines right, my blocking right, or did anything correct at all for within what seemed like a roller coaster ride it was over as quickly as it began and we were back in the greenroom high fiving and breathing heavily. When everyone was done, Gina called us out into the theater, one by one and spoke to us. When it was my turn, I rushed out.

"That was the most present you have ever been."

She went on to say some positive things before she gave me a laundry list of things I needed to work on: fidgeting, my arms, my hands, my gestures, my Jersey accent, my stillness, and my intentions. Pretty much everything that made a good actor good. Meaning, I had a lot of work to do. She suggested I take her summer course and bid me farewell for the semester. It was my first experience in the arts and I wasn't sure I liked it. I felt I had a lot of work to do, but I was not sure she was the right person to do it with. The reason was pretty simple, why only teach models how to act? I would have to do a pros and cons list and see what other programs were coming up in the fall, something more reputable maybe, or maybe I would just start auditioning and book work and not need any training? There were plenty of Hollywood folk tales about that, *right*? And I was ready to be discovered! I was putting the work in or so I became convinced in my mind. At least that's what I began to tell myself.

The minute I walked onto the dining floor I could feel the change. It was as if a ghost were in the building. Something was off, I just didn't know it yet, only felt it. Like when you arrive home after a break-in, you can feel the sense that someone, not yourself, has been in your space. Then you see it; the missing items, the disturbed scene. And when I went to the bar after preshift, someone I had never seen in my life was standing there. A young girl at that.

"Hey, did you see Edward?" I asked her, rudely not introducing myself.

"Who?" she replied. And right then I knew.

"Never mind," I said and retreated to the kitchen where the chef was cooking pigs tongue for the guys.

"Where's Edward?" I asked.

"You didn't hear Papi?" the chef shouted to me from behind the line as he made the sliced neck signal.

"Not possible."

"He got into it with you-know-who last night," he continued.

"No!"

"Yup, he almost tossed the little guy, but you know Edward, held his temper and walked out with his big round head held high."

The news crushed me. Edward was my mentor. My friend, even though we didn't socialize outside of work, but then again Edward didn't have a life outside of Ponte's. It seemed so unnatural, so unfair. And it also hit home. I had felt the change since the Indian Napoleon came to power. I knew I had to make my arrangements. And I had to do it swiftly, before I was caught without a pay stub for too long. Which, given my present PO circumstances, could be detrimental to everything I was building. I went through my shift, head down, silent. *Do not give him a reason.* I had been lackluster in looking for other options as I had so much going on and he was treating me nicely so I didn't think I needed to hit the gas. Until the news. The very next day I was pounding the pavement with my resume, beefed up with the three-year gap filled in to make myself more desirable than "the ex-con looking for work again." I went door to door, neighborhood after neighborhood, for the entire week before my shift. The only breaks were to eat and rehearse and go to class. I was relentless, though not desperate. I was offered many jobs, and most I couldn't accept. The pay cut and hour differential (not in my favor) would be stupid. And after nearly three weeks of searching, I found something that would work. I sat before Becker's desk as he went over my pay stub and returned it to me.

"I should change professions," he said, angrily.

"It was a busy few weeks, you should see it in January and August. It all evens out."

"See you in a month."

"About that," I said before rising.

He pushed his chair back and looked at me, his head tilted to the side, nonplussed.

"What's with the way you think you can speak to me?"

"Excuse me?"

He leaned in, elbows on his cheap little iron desk and asked, "Don't you realize I own you?"

"I do. I just assumed that since I was not a problem for you, that maybe you would see me as a person and, God forbid, maybe someone who needs your help," I said, attempting to play to his ego again.

"My help?"

"Of course. I don't want to be a problem to you. I want to be a nonissue."

"Out with it."

"I got another job offer with a salary and more responsibility at a restaurant in Midtown. It's a management position, a lot more hours, but a step towards a career in hospitality. Can I take it? There would be no lapse in pay stubs. Same rules. Same line towed by me. Only change is the hours and where the stubs are coming from," I pleaded.

"I don't care. Just keep having your stubs ready."

"Fair deal, thanks Becker, I appreciate your kindness," I lied and left his office.

The next day I gave my notice to Napoleon. He was surprised to see me go. He even tried to pick my brain as to why I was making the move and why I didn't want to continue. I put it on the opportunity for growth, a new place with new energy and shorter hours. He wished me well, shook my hand, and told me I didn't need to come back for any more shifts after the following night as he could move things around and have them covered by some of the newer, hungrier guys. Which was fine with me, it was another lesson about providing notice and leaving on good terms. It is our expected responsibility as employees to do so, however, employers rarely want you there for the time and often let you go sooner. But

I always provide it, as it is a reflection on my work ethic and thus, important as a "point" to everyone who works with and around you to know you are a stand-up person. It's a character thing at the end of the day. I learned so much from the experience at that restaurant. About people, relationships, food, wine, service, and customer service. It was truly invaluable to my growth in the hospitality business as I knew I would be stuck in it for a while as I pursued a life as an artist. I thank all those who crossed my path over those years as they began my process of boy to man.

CHAPTER 9

PAZZA NOTTE

New York, New York—2006

Pazza Notte was as far across the spectrum from Ponte's as a restaurant could be. Gone were my days of wearing suits to serve people overpriced, glutinous meals with expensive liquors and wines. Instead, I could wear a T-shirt, jeans, and boots and serve two-for-one happy hour martinis filled with rotgut booze from the well. It was a relief in many ways as I would feel more at home in that atmosphere than the stuffy, buttoned up world from which I had just come. Although the pomp and circumstance of Ponte's allowed me to grow and learn about food, wine, and service in a myriad of ways. I walked in knowing how to make a few standard cocktails and left knowing far more about service, food and wine than I had ever imagined. The experience I had there for those years was invaluable if I were to make a career in hospitality, as well as for my palette. Gone were the days of drinking a beer and having a burger or a medium well steak with no clue of its cut. Ushered in its place was a food snob; preferring lump crab meat, lobster, ribeye and strip steaks prepared medium rare. And let's not forget about the booze. I would only drink good wine from that point on, no Santa Margarita anymore. I had established a taste for the finer things in life, those that I couldn't afford, but would spend my paycheck on anyway, treating myself for all my hard work, as people in the service industry tend to do.

What I liked about the job before me was not just the change in atmosphere, but the opportunity. I had taken the bar manager position, yet instead of wearing a suit and being a dictator against my staff on behalf of ownership as many managers are, I would be tending the bar with my staff. I was in charge of ordering all the spirits, wine, and beer and creating cocktail and wine lists; something I had done briefly prior to my incarceration. Additionally, two things really sold me, besides the salary plus tips method of payment. One, that I could make my own schedule and I would have the first cut option on any night I worked. It allowed for the potential to start building a social circle, and dare I say it, friends. Second, I was allowed to dress however I wanted, so long as I could work in it.

I arrived early my first day and met with the owner. He was in his late forties, a very attractive man with a European sense of style. He was very kind, but I came to find, was unaware as to how to communicate what he wanted from his staff. He cared about money and looks, not necessarily in that order, yet when it came to actually running the business, that was left to his wife, who was his business partner, a kind and gracious person in every respect. We all spent that first part of the day seated in a booth on the dining floor, poring over menus, standard operating procedures, inventory sheets, and invoices. I made notes on all the changes they were requesting and explained the timeline I thought each could be accomplished within. The truth was, I had no idea what I was doing, not having had that level of responsibility in five years. Add to it that it was a far larger operation than the tiny bar I managed in Chelsea years prior, and you could say I was over my skis. So, like everything else to that point in my life and what I had done years earlier, I would fake it to make it and use other peoples' knowledge to help foster my own, especially the liquor reps and the other floor managers. It was a skill I had begun to master, listen and then ask intelligent questions that don't tip the other person's hat that you don't have a clue and are really asking them "how?" to do something. Instead, you empower them to tell you *how* they do it. Which people love doing. It uses their ego against them in a positive manner and it works nearly all the time, unless you are in a situation where people are out to get you, then you have a whole other rulebook to live by to survive.

After our meeting I took the owners through the bar and pointed out all the issues I saw: poor storage techniques, unkempt stations, missing tools, various bottles of the same spirit opened, lack of inventory control. There was a slew of things I saw that I actually knew what I was speaking of. I made a point that if we changed only those elements it would help stop all the money that was walking out of the door from his sloppy staff and mismanagement. Once the tour was over, I got to work in preparation for the impending busy happy hour. I got down and cleaned places that hadn't been cleaned in years. I married bottles together, I reorganized stations. And a few hours later, when the bartenders arrived, I was introduced to them and they were introduced to a whole new bar, with new systems in place. Let's just say they weren't pleased, but if they wanted to stay and keep their jobs, they had to get on board. Not that I was out to fire people, that wasn't my intent; everyone deserved a shot. But all the old habits had to go and I was put in that position to make sure that it didn't keep on the way it had been. And although I always hated a rat, have never and would never be one, being in that position didn't make me feel like one, for a few reasons. One, I didn't know any of those people (it was an all-male bar staff, girls on the floor—owner's rules). Two, it wasn't like we all came up together, worked together, did shady bartender things together (give free drinks, skim from the till, stuff like that), so I had no allegiance to anyone except the owner. I was there to make sure all those things stopped happening. Third, I told them all straight up I was watching their every move. And that if they wanted to buy someone a drink, there were going to be protocols in place. Everything must get rung into the system, no matter if they spill it or serve it, as I need to have an inventory match at the end of each week. And if it didn't, people would be fired and made examples of.

Honestly, it felt really good to be the boss. Something about finally being in a position of slight power after all the years of being told when to eat, sleep, stand, sit, workout, go outside; so many demands. Though I tried to be careful not to let it go to my head like I had so often seen and been a victim to. Though I am sure that it did and people that worked with me would absolutely have a different viewpoint than how I remember it. In fact, I believe they called me "Nick the Dick" behind my back, which I only found out a year later when I became friends with one of the bartenders I hired; such is life. Always three sides to a story.

And as we worked and set up the bar to begin to serve our happy hour customers, I looked up as the door opened from the street and was stopped dead in my tracks. For I couldn't continue what I was doing, the glare of beauty was so striking. As if the heavens opened up before me, the white light, illuminating a path to glory. Never before has love hit me so violently. I was locked and frozen the moment our eyes met. She was not very tall, a sprite of a woman, but her energy was that of a queen. Hazelnut eyes and auburn hair with a smile that could buckle knees. I could have sworn the moment lasted for an eternity, but I would be lying. For the moment, and all its impact, were as fleeting as the time it took her to walk up the ramp and speak to a hostess. And as I stared on, pouring the drinks I was shaking when we caught one another's eye, never letting my gaze leave her, I noticed that she was not a customer, but in fact, a new hire, like myself. Starting on the same day. Fate realized. As if God were sitting above, playing cupid with our hearts. Or at least mine.

She walked into the back to change and put her stuff away. I shook off my obsession while finishing the preparation of a martini I was making and poured it out into a glass before a customer and returned to work. I could not allow everyone to see the weakness she created in me. I had to continue on as if nothing had just occurred. Yet, to me, *everything* had just occurred. *How was I supposed to work like this? Concentrate on the tasks on hand, that's how! Focus!* I put my head down and moved from customers to bottles to the cash register and back again. I noticed floor tickets printing out and I tackled them too. As I set the drinks down onto the correct tickets, I looked up and there she was, before me, smiling. I was stuck on stupid.

"Are these the pear martinis?" she asked.

"Uh, no. Sorry, those are the kiwi, those are the pear," I pointed to the slightly pinker of the two, such was the way the mix looked after shaking it copiously with vodka.

"Okay, thanks. I'm Isabella by the way," she said, coyly as she placed the two drinks onto the tray.

"I'm Nick."

"Okay, Nick. Thanks." And with a wink she walked away.

What is she doing to me! Is this a game to her? This is my life she is messing with. My feelings!

The night went by far faster than any had at Ponte's. I was sweating by the time the bar started to thin out, most of the customers rushing off to whatever trains they took home to the suburbs. I finally had time to use the restroom where I cleaned myself up, washed my hands, and splashed water on my face. When I returned to the bar, Isabella was standing by the service station looking bored.

"That was fun," she said.

"Maybe for you," I replied.

"You were working harder, I noticed. Even broke a sweat," she teased, pointing to the underarms of my T-shirt.

Embarrassed, I looked down.

"Don't be such a tough guy. People sweat. It's natural. I sweat all the time when I work out, run, or . . ."

She was teasing me again.

We continued in that vein with intermittent breaks to do our respective jobs throughout the rest of the shift. Around 10:30 p.m. the manager let her go home. I approached him and told him I was going to leave for the night as well. He thanked me for what he thought was a successful first shift and told me he would see me the next day. As I came out from behind the bar, Isabella was approaching from the back with her coat.

"How about we have that drink now?" I asked.

"Sure, why not."

"Let me grab my things."

A few minutes later we were strolling down Sixth Avenue, a light snow falling upon us illuminated by the streetlamps.

"Where do you wanna go?" I asked, unfamiliar with the neighborhood, but sure that it was a bit late to find a decent place.

"I live in the East Village. I know a place if you don't mind coming down."

"Sure."

She walked towards the subway entrance.

"We can drive down. I have a car."

"That's right, Jersey," she smiled.

We walked to the garage where I parked, presented my ticket and waited for the attendant to return.

". . . so, NYU huh? I always dreamed of going to NYU." I said.

"It's pretty amazing. I've had a great time. I love New York."

"How long have you been here?"

"My third year."

"You haven't had to work yet?"

"Nope. My parents wanted me to focus on my studies."

"Why now then?"

"This city is expensive and I want to enjoy it! I'm not a girl anymore, I'm becoming a young woman."

"Makes sense," I said as the car pulled up.

"Nice wheels," she said as we entered.

"The benefits of not paying rent. Believe me, I would much rather live in the city."

"Why don't you?" she asked as she closed the door.

"Long story, but I can't right now," I covered.

And as I pulled off into traffic, my stomach dropped. If things worked out, how was I going to tell her about my situation? My past? *Fuck.* Those thoughts occupied the ride as we spoke. I think she could tell something shifted in me, but I would blame it on my need to concentrate while driving in the city if she asked. As we got down in the East Village, I began to look for parking. I found a spot that looked safe from tickets and pulled in.

"Nice work. I always hated parallel parking," she said.

"I've never had an issue with it, helps a lot in the city though."

We made our way to the bar where we sat at a table in the corner, away from people. We ordered a drink, then another, and another. We talked for hours. About life, family, school, goals, dreams; so many things. After we were some of the last people left in the bar, she noticed the time.

"Wow! It's 2:30 already!"

I was a bit tipsy, as was she. And I remembered I had to drive home. *Not again!*

"Let me grab the check."

I paid, even though she offered to split, and we left. Then, out on the street, on that cold winter night, the snow had stopped, and we kissed. A kiss like I had never had before. Soft, romantic, and filled with hope. Hope. *Shit. I wish I was normal!*

"Walk you home?"

"Sure, I'm just down the block."

We walked on in silence, holding hands. Only my mind wouldn't stop reeling. I really messed up. I got so lost in the moment, so enamored by her that I forgot how long a drive I had and consumed too many drinks to do it safely. I was not drunk, but far more tipsy than that night I had to sleep in my car. When we reached her doorstep, we kissed again, then stood holding each other, looking into one another's eyes on her stoop.

She looked at me sternly and said, "I don't want you to drive all the way home. Would you stay the night? We can cuddle. That's all!"

I didn't take a moment to weigh my options, considering neither were very good. Risk drunk driving and hurt someone or myself and go back to prison OR risk my PO showing up in the am for the first time, ever, and catching me having stayed out. Also, I could potentially get out of him catching me arriving home so early in the morning saying I went to get coffee. Hmmm . . . option two it was.

"I would love that, but I have to be up very early. I have things to do in Jersey tomorrow."

"That's fine. Come on."

She led me up a flight of stairs and into her apartment, where we quietly snuck through the living area and into her room. We took off our shoes and most of our clothes and jumped in bed. It was very PG as we laid together, looking into one another's souls and holding each other tight. I woke up to my alarm at 6 a.m. I grabbed my things, kissed her forehead and told her to go back to sleep and I would see her at work that night. I rushed out, found my car and sped off toward home. I arrived around seven, to my father sitting in the kitchen having coffee.

"You okay?"

"Yeah, I met someone, spent the night at her place in the city. I didn't think it safe to drive."

"Remember what you're playing with, son," he said. I nodded and left to go back to sleep for a bit.

When I woke with a crystal-clear head I got to thinking. I didn't feel the rules were very fair, nor that I could live with them for another year and change. It was one thing not to do drugs, commit crimes, and have to have steady employment. It was wholly another to have to continue to live in my father's basement and never stay out for the night. I decided that with my leash being lengthened, I would have to give myself a bit more freedom, even if it technically meant I was risking my freedom. I wasn't committing any crimes, only bending the rules. And the chances of me being caught bending them was very slim. So, I did what any dumb, twenty-five-year-old would do; I began to bend them to meet my needs. That night, after work, Isabella invited me for a drink and then to spend the night. Only that night was unlike the former. Two quick drinks and complete mental clarity led to our first love-making session. And I say that without judgment, for I was not in love yet, but our first time together was the most romantic time in my life. It was love; unspoken. And after we were done, I spent the night holding her in my arms without a care in the world. Almost asking God to come and get me if he thought what I was doing was wrong.

I became brazen as the days flew by off the calendar. I got a monthly parking spot as work was going great. Each day making money and pleasing my employer, most nights spent falling in love.

And as the days came and went, so did my conundrum. I had to find a way to tell Isabella the truth about me. And so, one night, I did. I stopped in front of her apartment and shut the engine. She knew something was wrong, as it was not the normal routine we had established over the past few weeks.

"We need to talk," I said. Looking into her eyes I'm sure she thought I was breaking things off, not that she would have EVER guessed what was about to be said.

"Look . . ." I said and buried my head in my hands, tears forming around my eyes. I breathed hard and could feel her watching me, careful not to console or touch me, unsure what was coming. I picked my head up and closed my eyes and took a very deep breath before looking at her. We sat suspended in time, silently.

"Isabella, this is probably the hardest thing I have ever had to say, but it's been weighing on me ever since we met and gets worse with each passing moment that I fall deeper for you. And knowing who you are and how you were raised, even saying this out loud is . . . Isabella. There is something about me, about my past, my present situation, that you need to know and that I need you to be okay with if we are going to move forward."

"You're married!" she guessed, disgusted.

"Oh no! Nothing like that. Not someone else, I don't have a kid or anything like that either. I don't have diseases, no, no, nothing like that!"

"Then what is it, Nick! Tell me!" she fumed.

"I was in prison and I'm currently out on parole with a little over a year left before I'm completely free," I blurted out with rapid fire.

The shock that went through her was unlike anything I had ever seen, or felt, in my life. Not even when I told my father (given it was over the phone in the county jail and I couldn't see his reaction) of what I had done to end up in jail with a very large bail number.

She remained silent for some time.

"Aren't you going to say anything?" I asked.

She began to gather her things.

"I'm sorry, this is . . . *this* is," she began waving her arms around like a butterfly, fleecing away all that we had shared together.

"I have to go," she opened the door.

"No! Wait," I reached out to grab her arm and she shook it from her.

"Please don't touch me," she said and shifted off the seat and halfway out of the car.

"Please, Isabella. I'm sorry I didn't lead with this, but how could I? I mean, it's embarrassing. How was I supposed to know that what we were feeling was, *IS*, real!"

"I'm sorry, I . . . I can't right now. I have to go."

She closed the door and rushed off into her apartment. I sat for a moment in silence watching the door of her building, only she was not coming back. I started the car and began to cry. I pulled off and down the road and by the time I hit the light I began to heave and cry and . . . I decided to pull over. I spent a few minutes digesting everything. When I felt good enough to drive, I continued on, in silence, replaying each and every moment we had briefly shared in those few weeks together. When I arrived home, I sat on the porch and took in the moonlight for a moment, then went inside and poured a nice two-finger pour of whiskey and returned to my seat. I remained there, thinking of so many things: her, my life, my failures, my road out of it all, the past nearly two years of life on the outside, the struggle, and my future. *Would anyone ever love me knowing what my past was?* I remained there for some time before I went inside and into the basement for the night where I curled up in my bed and cried some more. Realizing that the mistakes I made six years earlier not only still haunted me every single day, but would haunt me for the rest of my life. *The rest of my life.* She did not come to work for the next three days, or contact me, nor did I reach out to her. It was a difficult stretch. Head down, fake smiles, work, work, work. The irony was that prior to meeting her I was happier than I had been in some time with my new start. I could feel the opportunities that would manifest because of it. But at that moment, I felt nothing. I was mechanical. Wake. Commute. Work. Sleep. Eat. I returned to my routine of solitude. On the fourth day, I happened to be off, reading a book when she called.

"Hey," I answered, sitting up with my full attention.

"Hey . . ." she responded.

"So, I thought about everything and I would like to see you and talk."

"I would love that. When?"

"Today?" she asked.

"I can be there in an hour," I said, too excitedly.

"It's early. Can we say two?"

"That works, want me to pick you up?"

"No. Let's meet at Fiddler."

"Sure, that works. See you then."

"See you."

And the line went dead.

I was unsure of what it meant. She had some time to herself and I didn't push her. I was sure that helped. And she called me. Which showed she cared. But she didn't want me to pick her up (too personal). And wanted to meet in a public space (afraid of my reaction?). There were so many permutations running through my mind. I didn't have a clue what I was walking into. I arrived early and asked the hostess to be seated at the same table where we spent our first night. I ordered a beer to calm my nerves as I waited. She arrived on time, smiling bashfully as she made her way to me. I stood. We hugged; careful not to hold on too tight, lest I scare her. She sat across from me and I flagged the waitress. She ordered a beer and I another, as we sat in awkward silence waiting for them to come. When they arrived and the waitress had left earshot, she spoke.

"Listen Nick, I thought a lot over the last few days. About everything. And I don't know . . ." she trailed off and looked away. Then directly at me and into my eyes. "Why didn't you tell me right away?"

"I didn't think it mattered."

"You didn't think it mattered!" she exclaimed.

"No. Wait. What I meant was. I thought you would see me for me and that if you fell for ME, then you wouldn't care about the person I used to be. Does that explain it better?" I asked.

"I guess . . ."

I didn't push on. I was unsure what she was thinking and I felt it better to let her talk, then I would plead and beg if need be.

"It sucks, Nick. It really sucks. And I spoke to my roommates about it and . . ."

I leaned in, half off my chair, waiting for her to finish.

"Well, she's from the Bronx, so she didn't really think it was a big deal. But my parents . . ."

"You told your parents!" I sat back, angered.

"No way! I would NEVER!"

Relieved, I saw an opening and grabbed her hand and looked at her.

"Look. That was a long time ago. I cannot begin to tell you how different I am now. How what I went through, the hell . . . what I'm still going through. It has forever changed me. For the better."

She looked at me and squeezed my hand lovingly. As if she was seeing me again, like the beginning.

"Would you be able to see past all this? Allow us to continue on this journey, together? Isabella, one thing I realized over these past few days is that I can't imagine a life without you. I know that's crazy. I do. But I simply can't. I want to be with you. Grow with you."

She didn't let go of my hand. Instead, she rose and came across the table and sat on my lap and hugged me, then kissed me.

"I guess I have some growing up to do," she said.

"No. I do. I have. I am. Let's do it together," I said and we hugged.

"Now get off me, we're making a scene," I teased and she did, returning to her seat.

And then she asked. And I told. Everything. We sat there again, for hours, ordering food, more drinks. I told her about my life, all of it. And she listened and asked questions and listened some more. And when all had been told, we left and walked back to her place, arm in arm.

"Now that it's all out on the table, maybe I could learn about you?" I asked, sincerely and jokingly.

"I told you pretty much everything. I sure haven't lived as many lives as you. I'm just a normal girl from the suburbs."

"And that's what I love about you," I said and kissed her in the street.

And that was it. Game. Set. Match. I could get back to life. Life with her influence.

She was an actress and I sought her guidance within that sphere. She told me that I needed real training. That she had heard of Gina and the reviews weren't great. She taught models. She had no set technique. Ripping off Meisner. A cheap suit in the world of tailored cuts. She told me to go to William Esper. I did my research and found that he was the best nonscholastic acting coach in the city. He taught Larry David, Timothy Olyphant, Kathy Bates, Kim Basinger, and Kristin Davis, to name a few. I had watched all of those people and admired their work. I called the studio and got myself an interview to be considered for the program, which would begin in the fall. I entered the beat-down, nondescript building in the garment district and called the elevator. It took some time to make it down to the ground floor and what seemed like even longer to make it to the seventeenth floor. Outside the elevator I was met with a small corridor with four doors, advertising different businesses. I reached the one marked "Esper Studio," and entered it to find a small, barren room with a steel desk. Behind it sat a Middle Eastern man in his thirties, well built with a weathered face; a man with a story no doubt.

"Hi. I'm here for an interview?" I asked.

He stood and shook my hand as he said, "You must be Nick."

"Pleasure."

"Let's go sit in one of the studios and chat."

He led me down the hall, past a studio in session, where roughly thirty people of various ages sat enthralled as a woman in her sixties spoke before them. We entered a small space with makeshift risers and folding chairs spread out on them to reflect theater seating. He grabbed two chairs from the front row and placed them onto the stage area for us to sit.

"I didn't know your classes went through the summer," I stated.

"They don't. That is our summer session introduction class. It is for those who wish to get an understanding of the technique and what we teach here. I recommend it for people new to acting, which you stated you weren't, correct?"

"Well, yes and no, I guess. I studied with Gina."

"Don't say that name around here," he laughed.

"Really . . . ?"

I went on to tell him about my life up until that point. He listened intently and took notes. When I finished, he spoke.

"That's some story. Could make for a great actor if you learn to harness all that pain and anger."

"That's the goal."

"What about the schedule? We need a certain level of commitment. These aren't classes you dip into and out of, they are the basis for the work. And the work doesn't end here, it's only the start, the tool box. You have to work each day outside of class. Rehearsals, memorization, daydreaming. I also strongly recommend you take voice and speech, as you have a pretty wicked Jersey accent and movement, which will help you relax those shoulders, if you know what I mean."

I laughed to myself. They always say you can tell an ex-convict by the way he holds his shoulders. As if all that weight of doing time rests against the upper back, like Atlas. Seems this guy may have lived a similar life to me.

"I work five days a week, from four until midnight, roughly. The rest of my time is the studios and the craft," I stated.

"That's what I like to hear. Do you have any questions for me?"

"Will I be studying with Bill?"

"I don't know. Bill reviews all the applicants and then we all sit down and curate the classes as best we can. There are three people who you could teach you, all of which are great. No matter what, you will be in good hands."

It wasn't the answer I wanted to hear. I had hoped to study with the *best*. But the studio itself was the best, so I could put my trust in that and whatever my path would be, it would be. We shook hands and he said that he would be in touch, but that I should count on attending after Labor Day if I were accepted. Later that week I was back in front of Becker. When we were done with the normal formalities of urine and pay stubs, I told him about school.

"That's good for you. Happy to see you're sticking to the plan," he said, kinder than he had ever been.

"And I bring it up because I will be in the city even more."

"That's fine. No one is looking for you. In fact, I'm putting you back up to three months for the remainder of your time."

"Thank you, Becker! I can't tell you how much that means."

"Just keep on the right path and move on with your life. Sorry I was so hard in the beginning, but I needed to set a precedent."

I nodded and left from his office with hope that it would all, finally, be behind me before long. I continued with my daily commute, the occasional few nights spent at Isabella's and enjoyed what free time and falling in love in the summer in the city afforded me. The days flew by and as the summer came to an end, Tony and I found ourselves having a drink at a rooftop bar one evening after work when I had the night off.

"I've been thinking about your situation lately and how difficult it's been living so far from the city. Johnny and I just got an apartment in Edgewater that has a loft. Would you want to move into it? I'll charge you next to nothing and you can use it as a crash pad or live in it, whatever you want to do. I just figured it would be nice to be close to the city and I know you can't have your name on a lease of anything right now, but we wanted to offer it to you."

"Really? Like how much?"

"Four hundred?"

"I'll take it!" I said, not thinking at all about the issues surrounding my decision.

That Saturday morning, I asked my father to go to breakfast. We sat down at a local diner and ordered coffee and pancakes.

"Dad, we need to talk," I said.

"Figured it may have been something, not like you carve out time to have meals with me since you've been home."

"Here's the thing. I can't go on living in your basement."

"Why not? No rent. Free food. What are you complaining about?"

"I'm a twenty-six-year-old man. I want to be on my own. I need to be on my own."

"You only have nine months left on parole, why risk it?"

"Because I'm not really doing anything wrong," I said, knowing full well I was and was asking him for a lot.

"What do you want from me?"

"I want you to cover for me. If my PO ever comes by, just say I am at class, or work."

"At seven thirty in the morning like the last guy?"

"Dad, that was over two years ago at this point. You really think they're gonna lock me up for six months if they find out? And how would they ever? I don't have a lease, no paper trail. I am living in a friend's loft. In New Jersey. So technically, it's within the state."

"Why don't you ask for a transfer again?"

"They wouldn't do it last time and I don't want to subject Tony and Johnny to that."

My father sat eating his pancakes as he thought.

"I don't like it, but so long as I say you still live here, I don't see the issue. And so long as you keep on the right path. No bullshit," he said, staring dead into my eyes.

"No bullshit," I repeated, looking at him.

"And what about everyone else?" He asked, alluding to his wife and her children.

"I'm not asking them to lie, just not to answer the door."

"Hmmm," he grunted.

"I know it's a big ask Pop, but I need this, as a man, and it would make my life so much easier. I only have to go back there three more times. This shouldn't even be an issue."

"Alright. I'll speak to everyone."

"Thanks pal," I said and we finished our breakfast, and moved on to talk about the Yankees.

I showed up to the gate of a development and was allowed through after speaking with the doorman. I pulled the car into a spot and stepped out to a view of the city. The air felt different there, being on the Jersey side of the river. I took it in and smiled, thinking how nice my life would be with my commute shaved down to twenty minutes door to door (I had timed it prior) as well as the freedom to have Isabella sleep over my place for once. It wasn't as if I wanted to throw parties and afterparties and do dumb shit. My only wish was to get out of my father's basement and closer to work and school. And it had become such a drag on my daily life that I was willing to take the risk over the last nine months of my parole. I pulled my bags from the car, which included some clothes, (leaving others behind in case my PO came when I was not there and wanted to check my room) grooming supplies, towels, and shoes; really all I had to my name. Tony met me at the door and helped me up the stairs into the loft where he had set up an old queen size mattress on the floor and a night stand with some drawers. I would have to buy some sheets and a closet of sorts at Home Depot or wherever, but that was the extent of my move. I tossed my bags down and laid on the mattress, then looked up at the vaulted ceiling above me as I listened to the TV down in the living room. It would be my home for a few months. *My home.* Just thinking about it brought me so much joy and made me feel like an adult, finally.

The following week I had my first class at Esper. I did not get to study with Bill, instead getting an old, seemingly cantankerous man with bushy eyebrows who was missing part of his pointer finger. I sat in the back and participated begrudgingly, introduced myself to class, and found that I was so insecure that I regressed back to my high school wiseass. I thought I was being cheeky and entertaining, but truly I was embarrassing myself. I only realized as much when the teacher pulled me aside after and asked to speak to me. He asked what my intentions were for my work and told me that my behavior would not be tolerated; that it was the big leagues and if I wanted to be respected, I had to earn it. He spoke to me like a father does a stubborn son. I left, thanked him for the scolding, apologized profusely, and promised he would get the best of me moving forward.

I returned home that night after work with Isabella and a pair of sheets I grabbed at Kmart. It felt so nice to bring her there. To put those sheets on and lay down on *my* bed. I woke the next morning to silence, as Tony and Johnny had day jobs. Isabella and I cooked breakfast and watched a movie. It felt like adulthood: no roommates. I felt so proud and had neither a thought nor care in the world about my PO.

The next slew of weeks flew by as I began my routine of school, study, rehearsal, and work. I was so busy that the only time I saw Isabella was during and after work. And as I got deeper into my training as an actor, my moods began to fluctuate. The work we were doing was bringing up so much shit. I began to get nasty and short at work with customers, Isabella, and my other coworkers. I was changing, but unsure if it was for the better. I began to question everything about myself and the way I dealt with people, and thus, the world. It was as if I were in therapy, but instead of getting better, I felt worse off. Isabella and I started to hit the rocks during that period. She was in her last semester of school, getting ready for whatever her future held and I was struggling through finding myself in a myriad of ways. It was not ideal for a relationship. We were drifting apart and there was nothing I could do to save it. I needed to work on myself, my craft, and the changes I was experiencing while facing things about myself that I had buried for years. I was finally growing up, working through all the trauma that I had had, between prison and my family. I couldn't be responsible for another person's emotions. Looking back, I made the decision in haste. I wish there would have been another way, but I felt backed up against a wall. I should have tried to communicate; speak to someone about what I was going through and how much it hurt. Instead, I clammed up and kept it all inside, bubbling like molten lava, ready to explode. I began to feel the entire world was my enemy again and moved through judging everyone and everything about our interactions. All the while, it was inside me. None of it was really happening to me; I was manufacturing it. But with my mental illnesses that had gone undiagnosed for a lifetime, I couldn't escape it or the constant thoughts running through my mind; hurt, abandonment, anger, fear, insecurity, resentment, and too many others to list.

When the day came for me to go back to see Becker, the reality of what I had actually been doing came to the forefront. I was scared. I hadn't thought about it, or him, since I made the decision to move and spoke with my father about it. That was months prior. And although time was moving swiftly and I was nearing the end of parole, the visit weighed on me. I could feel my stomach turning and my nerves growing as I made my way to the office. From the moment I checked in, I felt like things were off. I was waiting too long. He was preparing to arrest me. I knew it. I could feel it. Only when he came to the door to get me, again, it was all in my head. He was the same as he always was. And I was in and out with another date scheduled for three months later. When I got outside, I laughed as I made my way to the car and told myself that I was being ridiculous about everything and that I needed to work on my relationship and continue on my path without losing my mind, or sense of self. Easier said than done.

CHAPTER 10

CRUMBLING

Shortly after, everything began to change. I didn't know just how drastic that change would be at the time, but each piece began to add up, creating a far larger structure of change and well, real life. Up until that point, of the years I had been out, each day brought a challenge that I felt I could handle: securing consistent work, furthering my education, saving money, establishing credit, paying bills, making friends, establishing relationships of all sorts, spending time with my now-fractured family (which I found to be a joy, considering all the holidays I spent on cold, hard steel surfaces without much food and no form of human touch or interaction), and most importantly, making it through parole so I could *actually* be free for the first time in over seven years.

I was learning to deal with the type of life most people have to face each day. My first true love was crumbling around me. Work was a challenge as ownership began to have issues with the way I was doing my job and I began to resent them and them me, but I couldn't quit, nor did I want to get fired, due to parole, so I had to learn how to survive in an uncomfortable environment. The holidays were also arriving and they presented other challenges: which parent to spend what days with, and lastly, acting was becoming tiresome and frustrating. I was finally affected by "the grind." And then more of life's challenges came my way.

I was at work when I felt a pang in my torso. At first, I thought I may have pulled something reaching for a bottle on the top shelf. Only when I took a seat on the edge of the storage fridge, I felt a sudden sharp pain in my side, cutting deep into my gut. Assuming it was a reaction to something I ate, I excused myself from the floor and attempted to use the restroom. Only nothing came, other than another shooting pain. I rose and went to the kitchen and as I was making my way there, I collapsed. The manager rushed over to grab me, helping me up onto the seat of a booth. I was told I looked as white as a ghost. I felt woozy. I was unsure what was happening, chalking it up to food poisoning. A busboy rushed to get me water. I drank and splashed some over my face, thanking everyone for their help, saying I was fine, that I just needed a minute. I attempted to rise and go back behind the bar, but another shooting pain came, one stronger than the others, which caused me to double over. At that point my manager told me to go home and get some rest, as my health was most important.

I thanked him and made my way from the restaurant to the garage, but as I walked, another pain shot through me. Rather than drive, I hailed a cab. As I sat in the back seat, more pains came and I found myself face down on the leather, the cabbie checking in on me throughout the ride back to New Jersey. I paid the fare, thanked him, and struggled up my stairs and into my apartment where Tony and Johnny sat playing video games on the couch.

"What are you doing back?"

"I don't know. I'm in pain," I said, making my way to the couch where I fell onto my side and writhed in pain.

"Go to the doctor," Tony said, not looking from the game he was playing.

"I don't have insurance. I'll be fine."

They continued to play and I continued to writhe. After what could have been ten minutes, maybe thirty, another shooting pain rang through me so swiftly I screamed out.

At that point Tony turned, looked at me and asked, "What does it feel like?"

"A knife through here," I said, pointing to my lower stomach.

"It's probably your appendix. Johnny, take him to the ER."

"No! I can't afford—"

"Dude, you can die. Go," he demanded and continued playing the game. Johnny dropped his controller and rose.

"All right Nickyboy, time to go," he said as he pulled me up and helped me to the door, down the stairs, and into the car.

The ER was ten minutes up the road in Englewood and once Johnny told the attending my symptoms, I was immediately admitted and rushed off on a stretcher, waving goodbye and thanking him. I woke hours after surgery in a room to Isabella holding me.

"How did you . . ." I said in my dream-like state.

"Tony called me. He came and got me and dropped me off so you wouldn't be alone."

"I'm sorry . . ." I said, a loaded attempt to apologize for our issues, maybe hope that it would bring us closer.

"Shhh. Let's not think about that now. You need to rest and get better. That's all that matters."

She remained with me, sleeping in a chair beside my bed, until they released me the following morning. Johnny picked us up and took us home. I called work and let them know what happened and that I would be out for a week or two as the recovery wouldn't allow for me to lift things for a bit. They were not pleased and told me that we could discuss "things" when I was able to return. I hung up the phone feeling hurt and angry. It was my first, though not my last, instance of dealing with the injustices of hospitality. A world unlike any other job. There was not only no security, insurance, paid time off, human resources, or any other protection most every job offered, but if you couldn't make it to work, they simply moved on. They would find another warm body needed to fill the space, lest they lose money from your absence and allow that to affect service. Nowadays that has changed. The same laws that govern employee rights from nearly every other profession have finally made it to the hospitality sector, for better or worse, depending who you ask. Shortly after hearing that, Isabella had to leave for work there herself, knowing how I had been treated and taking note of it; not that she cared a bit about being in the service industry, she was going to make a career in the arts and was already well on her way. She made sure I had everything and took off, leaving me alone on the couch, in and out of sleep from the drugs, to think about what I was going to do when they fired me.

The days turned to weeks and Isabella never came back, though she would check on me each day, calling and sending her regards. After I was healthy enough to move around and get back to work, I showed up and had an uncomfortable meeting with the owner, who basically said that he was giving me notice that things needed to change and that it may be time for me to move on. I assumed that it was his way of firing me, politely. With the stress of needing to find a new job, and quickly before I had to see Becker again, I returned home that night to my first piece of mail, stupidly having provided the address to the crash pad apartment, instead of my father's house. I cursed myself for being so sloppy as I opened it, my concern being with the material in hand, thinking it must be a mistake. I had received a bill from the hospital for twenty-seven thousand dollars! As I went through the charges I began to sweat. I had never received a bill of such weight. It was gut-wrenching and when I called the hospital claims department to speak to them, informing them of my situation, the bill totaling far more money that I had to my name, they offered what they called, "Charity Care." Which I came to find out is a pretty normal thing, as most Americans don't have health insurance.

The next day I was at the hospital, filling out loads of paperwork to be considered for that gift. And after reviewing my bank statement, pay stubs, and the like, I was granted a discount of 50 percent. Which still meant I owed them thirteen-thousand, five hundred dollars! To put things in perspective, I was taking home about eight hundred dollars a week after taxes. It was another slap in the face from real life. And it would only get worse. Worried on many levels on where I would go and what I would do next, I called one of the liquor reps that I had been purchasing from and told him about my situation. He was very kind and said that he would be able to find me something soon, as my skill set allowed for various positions and he would ask around on my behalf. I thanked him for his kindness and headed to work to start my shift. And as if that wasn't enough, an hour or so later I received a call from a strange number. I looked at it and did not answer. The phone rang again and my stomach dropped when I noticed a New Jersey area code that was part of the Elizabeth region. *Shit*. I rushed from the bar and off to the side.

"Hello?" I answered.

There was a pause, then a shuffle.

"Nicholas Marshall?" a female voice asked from the other side of the line.

"This is he," I answered.

"This is your new parole officer, Mrs. Stanley. Where the fuck do you live!?"

My mind began to reel. My stomach turned. Though I managed to answer on my feet.

"At my father's house, where I've been living. Why?"

"I was just there and that's not what your grandmother told me."

My father's wife's mother must have told her!?

"That's not my grandmother, first off. It's my father's wife's mother who is, sadly, getting old."

"Where are you now?" she asked, unsatisfied.

"At work in the city."

"I'll be at your house tomorrow. You better be there."

Click.

A wave of emotions swept over me: anger, frustration, FEAR. I had prepared for it, so I wasn't worried about not being able to prove where I lived. It was more so the pickle I found myself in, the arbitrary trip back to Westfield, my father's worry, and my having to meet a new PO in such an uncomfortable manner. All that, with less than four months left on parole. . . . I returned home that night and spoke to my father about what occurred. The night was uncomfortable as it became a blame game. After multiple discussions I retreated to my basement room. It felt awful having to be back there. I laid in bed, thinking about everything; especially what was occurring of late and decided that I had to make solid plans for my future, no matter what was coming my way. I had to be ready for my release. *What would need to be different? What would put me on my road to success? What did that success look like?* I fell asleep with those thoughts running tirelessly through my mind and woke at sunrise to the chime of the doorbell.

I made my way upstairs, my father already having let her inside, in my bedclothes, cleaning the crust from my eyes.

"Mr. Marshall?"

"Mrs. . . ."

"Stanley. Where's your room?" she asked unpleasantly.

I had her follow me down the stairs to the basement and into my room where she looked in the closet, drawers, and the bathroom. Having known that day may come, I was sure to leave everything that someone who lived there daily would need, including a toothbrush, facewash, and the like. When she was done, she stood, unsatisfied, almost perplexed, wishing she had more to go on.

"Why would she say you don't live here?" she asked.

"Because I'm never here when she is. I am gone between six and seven in the morning, and don't return until after midnight nearly every day."

"Why are you gone for so long?"

"I have school and work. Didn't you read my file?" I asked, knowing she probably was too lazy to have done so.

"Here's how this is going to go, Marshall. You're off quarterly. You're going to come see me every week now. And I'm going to show up here at all hours and days to make sure you're telling the truth."

"Don't you think that's a bit too much? I'm nearly three years in without incident, gone through two POs and I've never had an issue. I only have fourteen weeks left."

"I don't give a fuck. Every Tuesday evening from now till you're off," she said and began to walk away.

"I can't do Tuesdays. I work. Sunday or Monday," I said.

She turned back, one foot on my steps and stared through me.

"Monday it is. 4 p.m. Every week."

Then she left. I returned upstairs to the kitchen and brewed a coffee.

"Sorry pal," my father said as he entered the kitchen. He was seriously upset.

"Don't worry Pop, it's fine. I'll be living here again though, until

I'm done with this crazy lady and all the power she wields over me for the time being."

He nodded his head, put his hand on my shoulder, and left to get ready for work. I remained, furious, thinking of my next moves on the chessboard of life as the coffee brewed. After much thinking, changes had to be made. First, I would have to grab my stuff from the loft and let the guys know about the change. They were great about it, even forgiving the last month of rent. The next order of business would be to inform Isabella, unsure how she would take it, but if I had to guess, based on the past few weeks, it would probably be the final straw. When I met her for coffee to break the news, instead of the conversation being about me and my new-found lifestyle change for the next four months, she went on to tell me of her plans. She was moving to LA to live her dream. Although we had a beautiful start, things had gotten messy and it was time to cut the cord. The timing seemed to be right, and although I cried, I agreed. She shouldn't have to live with my mistakes, and change her life for a boyfriend who would have to move back in with his dad. Instead, we hugged, cried some more, and wished one another beautiful lives. I promised to help her move from her place and pack her car when she was ready to leave after the New Year.

And then I got to work and was fired. Yes. All of that on the same day. It had been a recurring theme in my life at that point. When things got bad, everything piled on at once. You know that law of threes? Well, I usually had the threes and more. I returned to get my car in the garage and spoke to the manager about discontinuing my spot. He was fine with it. I settled the balance owed, thanked him, and left. As I pulled onto the road I had traveled so often, I started to cry as I began the long drive back to Westfield. The ride seemed longer than it ever had as the tears ran down over my cheeks. I had loved truly for the first time in my life and lost it. I had been fired for the first time since my release, which stung my sense of pride. I had lost the first apartment I had, illegally as it may have technically been, but it was *mine* nonetheless and provided me a sense of self-worth that I'm sure people who work hard can understand. Acting and modeling was not maturing in the way I had hoped either. And then there was the thought of moving back to my father's basement. It seemed as if everything I had worked so hard for fell away in one swift swoop.

As all of those thoughts attacked me, my feelings switched from sadness and woe-is-me to anger and rage. I cursed the system. I cursed myself. I cursed my employer. My "fuck the world" mentality returned. It was not welcome, but it had found its way into my brain. It was my motto prior to prison and look where it had gotten me. And with it, the anger had returned. Hate filled my soul: for the system, my new parole officer, my boss, myself, my decisions, and my situation. Every. Single. Angle. I saw only the downside. I began to think dismissively about getting locked up again. It would be for less than thirteen weeks. I could do that standing on my head. Or so I told myself in my state of anger. When I arrived home, I went directly into the basement and retreated into myself. I laid on the floor and stared at the ceiling. The discomfort gave me a strange sense of comfort. As if being against the coldness of the basement floor reminded me of all the floors I had slept on; the sand-filled plastic mattresses, the bare steel. Eventually, I fell asleep.

I woke up in the middle of the night and sat up in the silence with an epiphany. *What was I thinking? Was I crazy?* I didn't want to have to go through any of that. I was *this* close. Meer weeks away from true freedom. I had worked so hard. I was moving towards my goals. I was on my path. I was doing well until that point. Life is hard. My life had been harder, mostly from my own mistakes. *Was I really going to let them win?* No. No I wasn't. And with that resolve I moved to my bed and laughed at myself for my childish, guttural reaction as I laid my head on a pillow and closed my eyes, trying to dream of the bright future I could have, despite those last set of challenges. Only I couldn't sleep. I thought of all the challenges life could bring. The normal ones. The ones like being sick, having an accident, debt, and death. Those things were so far off my radar, as I cared more about getting off parole, but they sat before me as another set of challenges I would have to face. The thought of them scared me. Yet, surprisingly, I felt another side of emotion wash over me that would drive me. I would simply have to overcome them as I had overcome everything else. Sure, it would be hard; miserable even, difficult, for sure, down-right impossible in some scenarios, but I would find a way. No matter what it took. I would face everything head-on and continue on the path I had built, despite whatever the next few months looked like. And as my mind raced, I thought of how important it is to stay focused on the course and only the things you can change. Let go of those you cannot control and move through each day, one moment at a time doing the tasks that can, and will, make you better.

I arrived at the parole office and was met at the door by a heavy-set man who stated he would be "peeing me," their choice of vernacular for drug testing me on each visit. It was new, but I also never had a female PO, so it made sense, as they had to watch over you to make sure the urine wasn't coming from a squeeze bottle or some other device. When I was done and marked clean, I was led to Stanley's desk, where I sat opposite her as she remained engrossed in something before her on the computer. I sat silently before her, and literally twiddled my thumbs.

"Pay stub," she reached out over the desk without looking at me.

I handed it to her. She wrote down the information in silence. I assumed I should tell her about work, not the truth (that I was fired) but that I was moving on, interviewing for new positions. Since I would have another pay stub, as checks were a week behind,

I thought it better than to provide her any ammunition that she could use against me at that moment.

"I need you to write the days and hours that you go to work and school. I need a detailed accounting of where you are at all times. Additionally, I want travel routes and times. Here," she handed me a notepad.

I did as I was told, leaving the free time before and after class as coffee/study time, added some for rehearsal, and made sure not to have any large gaps less she should have issue with me being in the city with "nothing productive" to do, as Becker once said to me in the beginning.

"Here you go," I handed it back to her. "And I want you to know that those are based on what I have been doing for the past year or so. I am not in school right now, as it's a break and I am looking for another job, interviewing as we speak."

"Why?" she asked, unconcerned, more so to satisfy herself.

"It's time to move on. I was thinking I wanted to manage, get a salary and health insurance. That sort of thing."

"But you get a salary," she countered and pointed to my pay stub.

"Yes, but the tips fluctuate each week and I can't really afford to pay for health insurance. So . . ."

"Okay, let me know how it goes."

Dismissed, I rose and left. I assumed that meeting had bought me a week or so, maybe more due to the holidays, to figure things out before having to address the issue. My friend at the liquor company managed to secure me two interviews set for the week before Christmas. I prepared by researching the establishments. What kind of food did they serve? What was their service style? How intricate were the drink menus and wine lists? I was confident I would be able to land one of them as restaurant manager was the toughest position in the business to fill. The hours were horrific and the pay, although consistent, was nothing compared to what bartenders make. The perks were being the boss, having a drink with friends or customers during your shift, eating off the menu, and having the ability to comp your friends' drinks. I was up for the challenge though, as I was tired of tending bar.

The first interview was brutal. I had never dealt with profit and loss statements, closing requisition reports, staff write-ups, or anything like that. My experience was in ordering, inventory, cocktail and wine list creation . . . "bar management." I was essentially laughed out of the place. But like everything else in life, I took it as a lesson and when I had that next interview, at a more relaxed restaurant (meaning not as high-end), I excelled in my embellishment. *P & Ls? Of course, show me what yours look like and I'm sure I'll be able to pick it up. Write-ups? I hate to have to do it, but if they are wrong, it's my job.* And on and on I went. When the interview was over, I knew I had it because he asked me to tour the back of the house and showed me where the clock-in, lockers, office, and everything else was. He told me he would be in touch as he shook my hand and bid me farewell. I was excited, but then I thought about school. How would I manage to keep up with everything I had committed to, something would have to give, and due to my circumstances with Stanley, I decided that the give would be in my rehearsal/out of class work. And like the seasons in the East Coast (when we actually had four seasons, that is) change came again. I received a call from Isabella taking me up on my offer to pack her car and see her off for a cross-country road trip to LA the very next day. Upon hanging up, I felt all of the feelings rush through me again, as it all became real.

I met her outside her apartment and spent the next few hours clearing her things out and packing her car. It was one of the hardest things I had ever done and reminded me of the last few days of freedom I had before my sentencing, where I cleaned out my apartment that I shared with my cousin and took stock of the few items I owned. Once the car was packed and the doors closed, we stood on the sidewalk of 24th Street and 9th Avenue and said our goodbyes. A long, soft, yet strong embrace. One I didn't want to let go of for fear of never getting it back. And when we did, I turned from her and walked down that street, my head lowered, fighting the urge to look back and when I finally did, she was gone, only the packed car remaining. And I cried. *Again.* The stark reality that our lives together were over and she was off to begin what would be the rest of her life, leaving me there to pick up the pieces in my city, *our* city; where I felt the most love I had ever felt, but was too young, too stupid, too much of a mess, and too imperfect to make it work. When I started work the following week, I needed it more than I knew. I craved something to dive into, something that wasn't my broken heart. I entered and was introduced to the staff and spent the shift training, side by side, with the GM, learning every aspect about a restaurant I didn't know. Each time something came up that I was out of my element with, I asked questions and took notes; careful not to ask rookie ones that would indicate that I was greener than I had let on.

I took for granted how much work these people actually did, having been on the server/bartender side for so long. Previously, I only saw them as thorns in my side, cogs in the wheel. When I left after the longest shift of my life, I had a whole new respect for them and their workload. I was becoming one of them, probably not for long, but at least long enough to learn all I could and make my way through the last eleven weeks of parole. Which was not easy. It was back to the years of Reliable and Ponte's all over again. Wake up, drive for an hour, work for ten to twelve hours, then back in the car for an hour ride home and try to get some sleep before having to do it all over again. On my days off I had acting class, rehearsals, books to read, and journals to write. And, most importantly, I had to continually appease Stanley; one less visit marked off my calendar as the days passed. It was a blessing in so many ways as I couldn't think about my life, or Isabella, who I hadn't spoken to. I didn't have to address how that made me feel, or the fact that I was about to be free from parole, or the stresses of how I would get an agent upon graduating or getting out of hospitality altogether and be an artist, full time. Each day was the same, yet slightly different. And each day the sun fell, the moon rose, and the sun rose again the next morning and then, before I knew it, *the day* was upon me.

I took off from work and slept in. Stanley had called the day prior and told me that she would be by my house with paperwork for me to sign at some point in the late morning or early afternoon. Her lack of consideration of my time, or if I had to be at work, was laughable, but at that point I couldn't care less. She, and the entire corrupt, bullshit, subjugating system would be out of my life forever in less than twenty-four hours. I was happy to provide her that last bit of power over me, as I could use the day off anyway and I would never be under her thumb for the rest of my years. When I woke up and went upstairs to make myself coffee, I noticed something right away. The sun was shining bright. The birds were out and spring had reached us early. Winter was behind us. The storm of life was soon to be behind me too. I took my coffee and stepped out onto the porch. The warm air engulfed me. The sun shone down on my face. There was not a cloud in the sky. I sat in an armchair and thought about what was to come. I had money saved. I had a job. I had a few friends from acting class who I had become close with. And soon, I would have the most important thing in the world: true freedom.

I had just finished eating lunch when she finally arrived. I met her on the porch, signed my paperwork, and just like that, she was gone and I was free. Free to succeed. Free to fail. Free to do whatever I wanted without the government telling me what I could and couldn't do. The first thing I did after she left was grab my laptop and started scouring Craigslist for an apartment. It was time for me to make my next move, the one I had dreamed of since I was sixteen years old. It was time for me to move to the city.

CHAPTER 11

NEW BEGINNINGS

New York City Bound—2008

I returned to the loft with all my belongings. I worked out a month-to-month term as I began to search for my first NYC place. I searched high and low for an apartment I could afford, without much luck. New York was so expensive. I simply couldn't find a place to live *alone*. I began to search for rooms and shares and found a few that warranted a look, so I did. The first was a tiny room with a full bed and a dresser (so small the bed and dresser filled the width of the room) with no closet and no window. I felt it was too similar to prison, so I passed on it. The second was in a beautiful high-rise building in the Village. I entered the apartment in awe, thinking I had hit the lottery. Instead, what I found was that it was a "share" apartment, unique to NYC as I would come to discover. A spinster in her sixties, with two cats and no job, who "traveled often," owned that prime piece of real estate. When she was home, I could have the couch. And when she was away, which she assured me was "often," the bed in the small bedroom. Besides the creepy nature of the arrangement, she was a hoarder; every belonging she had ever come across in her life stacked throughout the apartment. Needless to say, I passed on that one as well.

I contemplated deep Brooklyn, Harlem, Queens, and Washington Heights, but having lived in Edgewater (and knowing I could find something on that side of the river within my budget) I pressed on with the mindset that if I searched long and hard enough, was patient, and exhausted every option, I could find something in Manhattan. Each day was like a job. Wake up and peruse the various ways to find a NY apartment: the back of the *Village Voice*, Craigslist, buzz superintendents if they were listed on buildings; I tried everything. Then I found the hack: a luxury building. Now, I know what you are thinking: *how can you afford a lux building, but not any of the other places that were advertised?* Simple. I found out that in New York to live alone is the gold standard, and for that you will pay a heavy, heavy, premium. And in regular situations, roommates are not much cheaper since they are usually in two-, three-, or four-bedroom situations (true bedrooms, converted illegal lofts, etc.). But the hack is what they call "Flex." I came to find the term when my brother and his two roommates from college moved into a brand-new building on the far west side of Manhattan in Hell's Kitchen, which was being gentrified at the time. So, in what was normally a tough neighborhood with slummy rent controlled or stabilized or simply out-of-my-price range apartments, these luxury towers were offering concessions for people to come live there, such as a free month's rent which significantly lowered the monthly nut, as well as the opportunity to build walls to create additional bedrooms, hence the term "Flex".

I found out this hack after my brother and his friends took a two-bedroom apartment and built a wall for a third and then prorated the rooms out (master/junior/flex). The numbers dropped so significantly, it was as if they were living in an outer borough! So, I did what any other savvy person would do: I went to view them and price it all out. And upon touring I found that I could not only afford the place if I flexed the living room, but that I could afford the master bedroom myself if I charged accordingly for the flex. There were only two catches: One, I needed to find a roommate in place. And two, I needed a cosigner because I did not make enough money to qualify for the apartment (in NYC we have the lovely 40x rent rule, which means in order to be accepted for an apartment, you must earn an annual salary that equals *forty times* the monthly rent. And let's just say, I did *not* earn anything near that.) So, what is one to do but get creative?

First, I found a roommate through my brother's friend circle who was finishing college and needed a place; check. He didn't have anyone to cosign for us, but he was willing to put up six-months rent to secure the place. I also had enough in savings where I could put up my portion of the rent for six months as well, but then I would be cash strapped as that was my savings. I figured it was a risk worthwhile and went to the building management company and offered that permutation. They quickly shot me down, stating they didn't take those types of deals, and if we wanted the apartment, we would need to secure a guarantor. Stuck in a difficult position, having no one who earned that kind of money in my network, I was about to give up. But like everything else in life, where there is a will, there is often a way. It dawned on me to ask Vinny. We had kept in touch, having lunches and dinners throughout the years since I left Reliable and he always offered to help in any way he could. I decided I was going to try and take him up on it.

I reached out to him and set up a lunch. We met at his favorite restaurant on the Upper East Side. He congratulated me on finishing parole, on the progress I had made, and asked me what was next. Seeing it as my opportunity, I told him of the predicament and asked if he could help. He took a moment before answering, then stated that if we sent him the money for the first six months, he would be comfortable signing for us for the year, as he trusted me enough to know I wouldn't stick him with the bill. Ecstatic, I accepted the terms. I excused myself and called my potential roommate and told him the news, returned to the table, shook Vinny's hand, and thanked him for helping me, yet again. He explained that it was not only his pleasure, but that everyone needed help in life. He went on to ask that I pay it forward to someone else in need whenever I may have the chance; his only request. Eventually that became a motto for me; help those less fortunate than yourself when you can. It makes you feel good and helps balance the world out.

The next day I worked on selling my car. I needed the money for a bed, couch, television, and other moving expenses. I drove it up to the place where my father worked and offloaded it for less than market since I didn't have time to wait for a real buyer. Another life lesson, when you need money in a pinch, don't expect to get the value you want for an item you need to get rid of to survive. It's all part of the cycle. Armed with cashier's checks, I met Vinny at the building management's office the following week with my new roommate. I made introductions, signed the lease, and received our keys. After Vinny left, I entered the empty apartment and sat on the floor and cried tears of joy for once. For after all the years of dreaming of what it would be like to finally live in Manhattan, all the crap I had to go through to get there, I was finally going to be a *New Yorker*. Over the next few weeks, we moved and settled into our new abode. Roommate living was an adjustment; dishes in the sink, a dirty toilet, loud music at off hours, random guests coming and going. There were a lot of things I would have experienced had I gone to college and gotten a few years of that type of living under my belt. Instead, my obsessive-compulsive disorder and mindset conflicted with my roommate's at every crossing, often coming to bouts of arguing. But at the end of the day, despite those learning curves, I was finally on my own, building the roadmap to one day having my own place.

Shortly after that period, the semester was over and I decided to quit my job. I had had enough of the manager's life: the brutal hours, the thankless ownership, and the hate-filled staff I babysat. That life was not for me and since I no longer had anyone to answer to, I took the freedom to quit. It felt good handing over my keycards and walking out the door, no notice given, not a care in the world of what I would do next, but the comfort of not having a parole officer to answer to is what kept me driven. I simply wanted out from anything that I associated with my old life. A true fresh start on the horizon. But when I woke up the next day, I had a case of the "fears." *How much did I have saved? How much did I need to live?* Baseline. *Where would I go now? Could I find a comparable job in due time?* All those questions flooded my mind and I learned my first of many lessons in that regard: if you have the will to work, everything will work itself out. BUT, it's never a good idea to quit a job without another lined up. Unless you have ample savings and little to no debt, in which case, quitting a job that sucks your soul may be the best thing you ever did.

I graduated from Esper studio when the 2007–08 Writers Guild of America strike was still in effect. With the business we worked so hard to strive to be a part of in a shutdown, what could we do to provide ourselves a leg up; a home to hone our craft each week? One of my friends had an idea and recruited us all together. We all met at a Cosi sandwich shop one day and laid out what would become The Collective NY, a not-for-profit theater company, which still exists today. Our founding members were Amy Schumer, Kevin Kane, myself, and a few others whose names you may recognize in credits of films and television today. But back then, we were just a bunch of dreamers who worked our asses off trying to get into showbiz.

We had ambition and nowhere to put it. That was what we came up with. We set out to use the studio as our home base and began to write and produce things for ourselves, seeing as the monetary avenues of real work were not available for us. We decided to meet each week and put-up work, read plays, and develop projects. It became the place where I was able to test out the writing I was doing and act. We fought like dogs, week in and out as we tried to come up with a formula for the group, its goals, find plays to read and potentially produce, and the business side of things; how to get a 501(c)(3) from the State of New York and fundraise to help us put projects on. It was an amazing time in my life as I finally felt like an artist. I was working toward something. And feeling that way, not worrying about money and work as much as I used to (which would soon shift again when reality set in) became a relief.

I continued to write and soon I had put the finishing touches on a script for my first short film. Then I went about figuring out how to make it. I found a director who had done some things and was jazzed about the script, but I still had to figure out how to pay for it. With no real way forward to find where to get the money, I decided I had saved enough to invest in myself and my career. Seven thousand, five hundred dollars to be exact. I asked The Collective to produce it with me and donate a few thousand we had raised through events we did to round out the money I needed as it would provide roles for most all of us in the company. It would be my answer to not being able to attend NYU. I was going to put myself through real life film school at a fifteenth of the price.

Over the next few months, while unemployed, I put everything I had into making that film, on Kodak Super short ends I might add, (the leftover film stock studios used to shoot movies). And it nearly killed me, both personally and financially, as the budget ballooned to over thirty thousand dollars I didn't have, the balance of which I had to put on my credit card.

It was the third time I was unemployed since my release from parole and each time I learned something about steady employment; keep it no matter the cost as it is always easier to find a job when you have one. And life is expensive, it sneaks up on you. Before you know it, you have gone from having a little savings to heavy debt. And the one thing I had never had up until that point, was real, back-breaking debt.

A little lesson about credit, savings, and debt: I learned at a very young age, when I was dealing drugs and had a lot of cash coming in, that I would need to build credit in order to do anything in America, whether it be renting an apartment, buying any real estate, a car; anything. You needed credit and a credit score. I started at seventeen, maxing out my cards each month, paying them down in cash and building my limits (which I don't recommend as it was illegal, and what I know now was essentially like using it to "wash" drug money). Though I managed to build it quickly with this technique, from five-hundred-dollar limits to multiple thousands. This lesson comes with a warning: as much as credit is a great tool, it can cause serious trouble if you are not careful, as interest rates compound and paying the minimum will leave you under the cloud of debt for years, paying double, sometimes triple of the original amount owed. That is why it is imperative you always save money first. Don't make it and go buy the new jacket, gaming console, or whatever other stupid thing you want to waste money on to keep up with the people in your lives. Instead, save and do your best to carry no or little debt. As I was about to learn, the debt I had accumulated from the film, coupled with the few months of unemployment took me the next *seven years* to climb out of. It was one of the most stress-filled periods of my life (at the time) and I was responsible for it, so I had to pay it, lest I file for bankruptcy and lose any credit standing for the next seven years and have to start over again. The lesson here is don't do what I did. With the film in the can and the editing process about to begin, there couldn't have been a better time for me to get back to work.

CHAPTER 12

THE ROOFTOP

New York, New York—2010

Within a few weeks I had found a job at a popular rooftop bar through a colleague I had worked with who was managing the place. However, I was not used to being a bartender hidden away, in an alcove service bar. I thrived in front of customers, chatting them up and getting to know the people I served which kept them coming back. Unfortunately, at that establishment they had a rule: only girls worked on the floor in front-facing service positions except barbacks, back waiters, and managers, who were all men. I was the exception to the rule, hidden from the clients, tucked away into a two-hundred square foot hole in a service station because the manager knew I was a very fast bartender, which would help with service.

The job was a special kind of torture. First off, it was completely weather, event, or night-of-the-week-dependent. If it rained, was cold, or any other various issues out of one's control happened across the city, the guest count would either skyrocket or diminish with those passing whims. Simply put, it was feast or famine. Each day when there wasn't a rain forecast, and even on many when there was, I would have to pre-muddle one hundred mojitos and two other specialty drinks that were on the menu, then stack the glasses within one another so they were ready for service. The influx was so grand that not only would I run out of them during the busy shifts, but I would have to make more on the fly. It was back-breaking work. Twelve-hour shifts, standing in my box, no break, and fast food brought to me by a busboy that was taken out of my shift pay. There were no perks. No relationships to be had with clients, no growth potential, simply a workhorse, providing the girls with the drinks that made them rich. And make no mistake, these girls were cleaning up on most nights, tipping me out a small portion of their take.

I nearly quit on multiple occasions, so tough were the conditions. Yet whenever I was about to throw in the towel at the end of the night, when the tips were counted and it happened to be a big one, I was making more money than I ever had behind a bar; sometimes as much as $400 a shift! But those nights were few and far between and that level of financial fluctuation will weigh on you. I tried to embrace the freedom of working like that and really enjoy the fruits of a busy shift and the atmosphere in general, where people were kind to one another. Also, I didn't have to deal with customers, who are often the worst part of hospitality, as they can be snide, demanding, and absolutely awful in many cases. When it was slow I would read a book or work on my lines. I was really attempting to see the bright side and make it work.

Eventually I made it to the fall, where I learned the seasonal nature of the business more harshly than I ever had until that point, seeing as tips shrunk to fifty to seventy dollars per night. I continued on each night being told that the pendulum would shift again during the holidays which would be upon us in no time. I began to thank my lucky stars I didn't spend the money I made, instead, saved it, as I was never confident in how much I would make each week and I needed to replenish my savings account for "rainy days." It taught me how volatile a service industry job could be, never having worked at one that was so dependent on nature. The one really good thing that came from that job was that I found myself spending more time in rehearsal, really honing in on my craft. I was working so hard each night I relished in the freedom that acting provided me during the day. It became my social outlet. I would work all night, often desperately slow, long hours, where I would read for most of my shift, except for a few conversations in passing with the girls who came to pick up drinks or say hello because they were so bored on the floor and the next day, I would be brought back to life in class or rehearsals.

But as is with me, nothing lasts very long when my anxiety kicks in. I began to hate the down time which reminded me of prison, where all that I had to do was time itself. Those feelings and the resentment grew daily. Yet, each day I would arrive at work filled with hope that we would be busy and after a few hours, watch painfully as those hopes dashed into the night as the hours ticked by. My mind began to reel. The situation became unhealthy for me. It made me angry, testy, and quick to fly off the handle. I had still not learned how to handle or process my emotions. Acting had helped release some of the pent-up feelings I had, the resentments and angers from my childhood, and the experience of being locked up for so long, but nothing I did helped *fix* them. They always seemed to find a way to rear their ugly heads. I thought about therapy, but didn't have insurance and couldn't afford it.

I was feeling pretty down when the holidays approached and business didn't live up to the hype. The long fall months of making little money began to weigh on me with the realization of my financial situation. Pair that with the arrival of Christmas; New York City rent and bills, and the pressure of giving gifts and being cheerful got the best of me. I became Scrooge. I retreated into myself. I shunned people around me each day as the holidays came closer and I got more miserable. Gone was what Christmas actually meant: celebration of giving and love, family, and friendship. Replacing it were the bills I would be taking on to keep up with the gifts for my multiple Christmases, the resentment of having two families, and the endless hours of driving over the two days. It was as if I could no longer put myself back into the mindset of the past years filled with challenges and all that I had to be thankful for, it being my first Christmas as a truly free man. Simply put, I lost perspective and couldn't find it. Yet, as so often happens, the angel watching over me provided a glimmer of hope. She arrived filled with opportunity and suddenly gratefulness came to me again. Just in time, as the darkness was moving in.

At the holiday party for work everyone was given a plus one. I showed up with my friend Tony, figuring that there would be some single girls in attendance and I wanted to help make him a connection, being the eligible bachelor he was. As we stood at the bar, ordering drinks and chatting with people, I met one of the waitresses' boyfriends. He was a young Black guy with dreads and the most fashion-forward attire I had ever seen in person; the stuff usually reserved for the pages of magazines. We struck up a conversation and eventually I asked the dreaded "so, what do you *do*?" I have since come to hate that question and know how much it burns successful people to hear it, but I was young and naïve and I asked it with aplomb, fearing no offense. He responded that he was a bartender. I laughed out loud, thinking that he was joking, and when I realized he wasn't I had to apologize. I attempted to poke fun at myself, saying that I was and had been a bartender, bar manager, manager, and even a Captain on a dining floor and I could never afford such clothing. I even made a reference to the fact that he probably came from money; the entire conversation being a lesson on what NOT to say to people.

He laughed and said that he was from Jamaica, the island, *not* the borough. He went on to tell me his story. He had immigrated to America four years prior and began working in hospitality. He had worked his way up from a busboy, to a barback, then a waiter, eventually finding his way to the bar where he learned to perfect his craft and become a "star-tender," as he called it. When I asked where he currently worked, his answer was short and simple: "Cain," as if I was supposed to be in-the-know enough to have heard of it. When I told him I hadn't, he laughed and told me it wasn't just a nightclub, it was "the *hottest* nightclub in the city." I knew about Marquee and had been there with the model boys a few times when I was in Gina's class. But since then, I kept my head down, working and hustling my way through bars and restaurants, trying to make a living, not a scene, as they say. I was a nobody. I knew very few people and they were all basically like myself, not in any "scene." The most successful person I knew was Vinny. The rest were normal (broke) people, trying to be artists or writers or putting themselves through school for a career in something, but no one with any real success. I continued to pick his brain, asking about how much he made per shift (all of these questions were wildly inappropriate as I was without couth at that time and had no parameters). Though he answered me proudly, stating he usually made *between $800–$1,500 a night!* I wanted to call bullshit, as I had worked in various places over the years, including Ponte's, and had NEVER seen that kind of money in one night. A week? Sure, but even in a week not $1,500 take-home.

I asked him if he could get me a job and he told me that I would have to know someone. To which I brazenly replied that I knew him. He laughed at me and said, "you would have to know *some-body.*" Not a bartender apparently; they were at the *bottom* of the nightlife food chain, as I came to find. He politely excused himself at that point, having had enough of me and my inquiries. I returned to the party, had conversations and laughs, but always found myself clocking him in the background. And each time I saw him, I removed myself from the conversation, and tried to figure out how I could become him. A "star-tender" as he so confidently stated. It sounded like a different world than I was in. For there were no stars in my circle, only workaholics. *Who did I know that could help me?* I would have to find that out. *I would have to.* I told myself as I watched him work the room. It was the sign I needed to get out of the funk I found myself in. The inspiration for my next move. I was going to knock on the doors that could lead me into nightlife and once I found someone who would poke their head out and answer, I would kick the door down and enter like I owned the place. And that was just what I set out to do.

The next day I was extremely hungover. After the party the Jamaican took us out to a nightclub, where we were whisked past the doorman and the red velvet rope and brought to a table where the waitress delivered *free* bottles of vodka. I drank and danced like never before, relishing the mystery of the entire process. The door, the people in suits and earpieces running around behind the scenes like the Secret Service, and the girls, all the girls. It was unlike anything I had ever experienced and I was *hooked.* I spent the day making calls, asking everyone I had ever worked with about that world. And with each text sent or phone call made, they all came back with the same answers: "I don't," "That's a whole different world," "It's insular," "You have to know *someone.*"

Everyone in my network seemed to have the same viewpoint. Never one to give up, I was determined to change the narrative. I thought hard. I had to know someone who had an in. Then it hit me. The free bottles on the table were new to the Vodka market, and happened to be a brand that my friend, who was a liquor rep, sold. Epiphany! *Go through the back door.* Why didn't I think of that earlier? What does every single bar, restaurant, or nightclub

in the city need? Liquor! And who was the one person who sup-
plied liquor to nearly every large account in the city? My guy. The
same guy who got me interviews in the past. The one who taught
me the business of buying, and the power of brands. And guess
who I had seen only months back at the rooftop hocking his newest vodka that no one had ever heard of for us to put in the well?
You guessed it. I was on the phone with him in minutes, explaining the situation and what my angle was. He laughed at first then
repeated the same thing that everyone else told me. I continued to
press, refusing to take no for an answer. Could he introduce me?
No. Could he put me on email with a manager? No. Could he do
this and that and this? No. No. No. Well shit, there had to be a
way, just one way where he was left out of the equation and had
no responsibility for me and my attempt. As he explained, and I
was begging to know, all favors have an opportunity cost and he
wasn't willing to use the nightlife opportunity on me. Get me a
job at a restaurant? Sure. A bar, sure? Ask a favor of an almighty
nightlife person? Nope. Can't do it. It would end up "costing" him
too much.

I was demoralized by the conversation. I thought he would help
me without issue. And like anything else in life that you can't get
for one reason or another, it became my obsession. I was going to
find my way in, come hell or high water. I viewed it like Hollywood. I was working my way through school, shitty auditions for
college films, and cutting my teeth. I had more years than I knew
before I would get to where I was a working actor. I had accepted
that "discovery" was simply bullshit. It was a nice story, but never
the true story. The more I had gotten on the inside of the business,
I knew that the new, hot actor was in fact, not new at all. They
had studied, cut their teeth. Nothing happened overnight in any
business, especially show business. Nightlife was no different.
I continued to work in the service bar, counting the days until I

would break out of there and into the world of celebrity and most importantly, the money.

Until then, I needed to delve into the education of the world that was NYC nightlife. I read every periodical that supported celebrity sightings, public relations drops, and the like. I read up and researched the players and who owned what spots. I spent every day learning as much as I could find out about it, asking everyone that I met if they were familiar. Did they go out? Buy tables? Go to the bar? Know the doorman, the partners? I was in full education mode in preparation for when I had my chance. And then one day it happened. I was on my way to acting class when I got a call from my liquor friend who told me he had found the shot I had been waiting for. It wasn't an interview. It wasn't an introduction. It was a play. And it was the only real shot I would get. If I wanted it, I needed to show up to Aspen Social Club between six and nine that evening. He was hosting an event for one of the new brands he was representing and one of the invitees, who was guaranteed to attend, having just confirmed, was none other than the general manager of Marquee, Patrick Robertson.

I called out of work, crying bloody murder from sickness. They were suspicious, as I had never called out before, but thought I may be telling the truth, despite the short notice, as by that time it was nearly three in the afternoon. I went to class and couldn't stay present. I was on a cloud, dreaming of the world I would be entering. That, and thinking of the little time I had to go all the way back across town to shower and change, as I had to show up looking the part and get back to midtown in time so as not to miss him if he were to do a show and leave. I walked into Aspen at six fifteen, dressed in the best outfit I had in my closet, knowing full well that everything about your appearance mattered in nightlife. I charged up to my friend after providing my name to the woman at the door working guestlist.

"Where is he?" I asked, forgetting formalities.

"Hi to you too Nick, ya jerk," he said, in his usual ballbusting manner.

"I'm sorry buddy. How are you? Thank you again for inviting me," I said.

"Listen, he's not here yet, but calm down. You reek of desperation and guys like him, they can feel it. Have a drink and relax. Talk to some girls or something. I'll let you know when he's here."

I nodded and walked to the bar where I ordered a tequila straight, shot it back, and chased it with a cold beer. I chatted up the bartender, asking her my nightlife questions, finding that she had been in the scene for years and actually knew Patrick, had worked for him prior, and told me some points about his personality. Most notably the two questions he would ask in an interview: "What was in a Boulevardier?" and "How do you make a Vesper?"

As we continued speaking, I kept scanning the room to see what type of people went to those events. What made them different from the world in which I had spent the past few years of my life? Not much, it seemed. Yeah, maybe some were slightly more attractive, but most were like the goombahs I had been around at Ponte's. Not the real gangsters either, the fake ones, who talked tough and never actually had the balls to kill anybody. They all seemed like posers as I kept up my conversation, drinking with the bartender. My friend came up to the bar and sat next to me.

"He's here."

"Where?" I blurted, looking around searchingly.

"Relax!" he said and grabbed me by the arm, pulling me aside.

"Look at me, don't fuck this up. You act 'as if,' you hear me? Go be the Nick that I know. Confident; cocky, even. But personable and relatable. Someone he *wants* to talk to. Not some desperate shmuck. Go and leave it all on the floor."

He walked away. I remained for a moment, watching Patrick from afar. I noticed his outfit, a light puff jacket, jeans, and sneakers. He looked like a tourist about to go for a hike. He didn't look like everything I had heard about nightlife. He wasn't dressed with labels and brands. He seemed like a nice guy as he smiled ear to ear, tooth-filled, laughing at the person he was engaged with speaking. Maybe I had it all wrong. Maybe I didn't need to be so dressed up, so desperate looking. Or was I? I don't know. All I knew was that I was about to make my move.

I thanked the bartender and made a beeline to where he was standing.

"Patrick Robertson? Nick Marshall," I said, thrusting my hand out as he looked me over like I was a psycho, taking my hand, shaking it quizzically.

"Nick Marshall, huh? And do we know each other?" he asked, simply.

"No sir, but I know you," At that he laughed.

"You do, do you? And how is that, may I ask?" his strong accent which may have been Australian, or London or . . . I couldn't pin it down.

"Well, I follow you. Your club that is. I want to work for you," I said, sifting through the bullshit.

"Ah, I see," he said, pulling his hand back and sipping his beer.

"Look. I'm a bartender. Bar manager, even. I have paid my dues and now I want to come work for you," I stated.

"You and everyone else," he said, turning. I slid myself over, cutting him off from giving me his back.

"Look. I'm not fucking around. I think you are the best. I've done my research. I know everything about you guys, your club, your team, and I want in. I won't disappoint. You can ask him," I pointed to my friend across the room.

"I've been working with him for years. He taught me the

purchasing business. He's become a friend over the years. Ask him about me," I finished.

"All right . . . all right. This is a first. I'll give you that."

I nodded my head, as if there was more in my tank if he needed to hear it.

"Look. You seem nice enough, and maybe you can tend a bar, who knows. How about this? If you promise to leave me alone, you can come see me at Marquee for an open call. First Wednesday of every month," he said and my face dropped and he noticed.

"I thought you knew everything about us? I guess you failed to realize we have open calls every month. Helps us clean house and bring in new blood. So, come by if you want to have a chance. But for now, can you leave me alone as I'm not at work," he said.

"Ah, sure, yes. I'm sorry, yeah. Thank you for your time."

And I scurried away like the pestering rat I was. Cursing myself for missing such a big detail and returning to the bar to have a drink and regroup. My friend came up to me.

"You mess it up?" he asked.

"Probably. Why didn't you tell me there was an open call each month!" I blamed.

"Because it's bullshit. They do it for PR. The people who actually get hired know someone. And now you know Patrick. Go get 'em," he said as he tapped me on the shoulder.

I stood and watched everyone. I would have to learn the answer to those two questions if I were to survive. *What the fuck was a Boulevardier?* I had been bartending for years and never even heard of one. Though I knew the answer to the second question, it was simple, vodka and gin, which made it "perfect." The call was a few weeks away and I would be ready.

A few days later I got an audition for a commercial from my new agent. I had secured him prior to the New Year, a young guy who had little experience but enough of a reputation to get me into rooms. He worked hard and knew people, even if his client base was centered in what they called the non-union world. Which meant he didn't work on anything related to The Screen Actors Guild-American Federation of Television and Radio Artists. Those commercials were not dictated by a union and paid out differently because of it. I didn't know what a scab was at the time, so it didn't matter to me, so long as I had a chance to work. Even though those jobs paid a fraction of union work, I didn't know it at the time. The audition was for Mercedes-Benz and shot for four days in Vancouver if you got the part. It felt like the perfect job to get: free travel and paid work with a big, recognizable brand. I was in and out in a short time and left, forgetting I had ever gone out on it (a rule I was taught regarding auditions that I learned from more seasoned actors).

The next day I was called back. I was over the moon with the opportunity. I went and did my job and left the room feeling maybe, just maybe, they liked me enough to give me the role. I went to work, suffering through a brutally slow shift, money at the forefront of my mind as I was running out of it from underemployment, a new term I was learning to deal with. Though I was becoming confident everything would change once I made it to the open call in the short weeks to follow. Two days later, while walking to get my late morning coffee, my agent called. He wished me congratulations for booking my first job and applauded me for it being such a big brand. He told me he would follow up with all the details about flights and the itinerary. I hung up the phone and fell to the ground crying. I had finally accomplished something. My dreams were coming true. I called my mother and father and relayed the news. They were ecstatic. I had only been happier one time in my life, when I got into NYU for directing, only to learn I was to serve three years in prison later that same day. So, that day, the good news hit me hard. And it would hit me harder again over the next few hours.

When I arrived at class I was brimming with emotion. I spoke of my booking to my friends who all congratulated me. They were happy to see that I finally had some "steam" as they say, even if it were only a commercial. Then came the bad news. A friend pulled me aside and told me that he hated to be the one to tell me, but that since he was Canadian, he knew it to be true; with my prior crime, I would not be allowed into the country to work, or for any reason at that. The news crushed me. At first, I denied it. Then upon some Googling and a call to an attorney friend, I accepted it. The memory of being accepted to NYU only to have to turn it down resurfaced. I began to curse God and his foul tricks. How was it possible that the only two accomplishments I ever had in my life were not accomplished at all, but were simply unrealized dreams due to circumstances of my poor past decisions? I was so angry, hurt, and unaccepting.

I called my agent and told him the news. He was blown away. He didn't know about my past, and had to relay it to the casting director. A blemish on him as an agent. Then he thought better of ruining his reputation and told me that maybe there was a way around it. Maybe we could figure it out. His plan was for me to attempt to drive into Canada. If I got in, I could stay in Toronto for the night with a friend, and if that worked, I could fly to Vancouver. The idea seemed good at the time, though looking back it was rife with issues from the start. Although I was down to try anything. I took a flight to Buffalo and met my cousin who lived there. She drove me over the line, provided our IDs for entry without issue, and made our way into Toronto where she dropped me off at a hotel. I called my agent and told him the good news. He told me to wait until he had everything settled on his end and once it was good, I could take a flight to Vancouver. I waited for hours, going to the museum to keep me occupied as I waited, only to find that when he returned my call Germany had dropped me.

Instead of going along with his plan, he played both sides. He let the casting director know of my issue and had her try and figure it out while telling me to go. I was crushed. There I was in a foreign country which I most likely entered illegally and had just lost the biggest job of my career and upset a casting director in the process, as well as my shitty agent, all in one shot. I spent the next day on a train, heading back to the city, demoralized and depressed, wondering when the stain of my past would no longer be an issue for my life. The next few days were rough. I was angry and sad. And very unmotivated. I got into an argument with my manager and was fired *again*. I was losing everything. If I thought parole and prison were hard, life outside with the stain of my past was even harder. It was as if all the hope I carried toward getting better and changing my life meant nothing. No wonder people returned to prison. Why wouldn't you if the deck is stacked so far against you?

I didn't know how to go on. I felt trapped. Again, I felt like I had not made any progress since my release. I felt angry. Hatred. And most of all, fear. Fear that I may have no other choice than to become a criminal again to have some success, or face a life in hospitality, working for, what I had learned, were very often miserable people and wages that would make it difficult at best to support a family. *I would rather sell drugs and hurt people, right? I had done it before, why not do it now?* Those thoughts often came to me, as I was sure they do to other people who have walked in the shoes of the stigma of being an ex-con. Though they really made no sense. Wasn't I working, making a living? Wasn't I *free*? Weren't there other jobs I could have taken? Yes. Yes. Yes. But when you have a level of ambition like I do, and have paid dearly for the mistakes you have made, you feel that you deserve a slightly level playing field (even though NOTHING about the post incarceration field is leveled). I assume it is why so many people end up back in the system, because the level of injustices against those who are simply trying to make it honestly are often too harsh and become catalysts for people to regress. Even if those decisions make no logical sense. And I have suffered from it and these thoughts and feelings often over the past twenty years. But I have never acted upon them. And that is the key. Keep your head down, no matter how dark the storm and keep trying!

Which is what I did as I fought those thoughts that took over my mind. And eventually the day of the open call was suddenly upon me. And just like that I found myself standing in a line of fifty or more people at the door of Marquee on a cold, cloudy, light rain-filled February afternoon. When they opened the door at four, I followed everyone into the vast room with its thirty-foot ceilings. I had only been inside twice before. What I saw was eye-opening. The allure was gone. The room seemed cold, stale, and had the smell of an unwashed bar. There was a long queue of people standing by the bar area, résumés in hand. At two banquets in the middle of the dance floor, interviews were being conducted. A manager came up to greet each person in the queue as their turn arrived. I stood in the back, grabbed my resume from my bag, and watched as people came and went, emotionless for the most part; no golden tickets there. When it was my turn, I was greeted by a tall, skinny man with a receding hairline and a warm smile. He asked me for my résumé and told me to follow him to a banquet. I sat opposite him as he reviewed my résumé and looked for Patrick. I noticed him seated at the banquet across from me, going over a candidate's résumé.

"You've got a good amount of experience, but have you ever worked in a nightclub?" he asked.

"I haven't, but I've been making cocktails at a rapid pace for years. I can ring, just give me a shot to prove it."

He smiled and nodded his head.

"What brought you to us today? Seeing as you haven't been in and around nightlife."

"Patrick invited me to come," I said with confidence.

"Paddy?"

"Yup. Told me to bring my résumé and come by for the next open call. Here I am."

"How do you know Paddy?" he asked.

"We have a mutual friend in the liquor business."

"Oh, yeah? Give me a second."

He rose and walked across the room to the other banquet where Patrick was interviewing someone new. I watched as he interrupted him politely, then leaned in and whispered something into his ear. Patrick smiled, laughed, and looked over at me. He shook his head as if I would become his problem, then said something else to the man who I was interviewing with who stood up and made his way back to me.

"He's going to come over and join us when he's done. He wanted me to start, if that's okay."

"Whatever works," I said.

"What's in a Boulevardier?" he asked and I answered, confidently.

"You're the first person who's gotten that right all day."

"I'm hired! That was easy," I joked with all the seriousness I could muster.

"Not just yet. What about a Vesper."

"At least throw me something difficult," I said and rattled off the answer. "Not like anyone orders those in a club, or at all for the most part."

"You may be right, but we have high standards here for our staff. It's one of the ways we weed out the beer and shot 'tenders.'"

At that point Patrick made his way over to the table and sat.

"How'd he do?" he asked.

"Flying colors."

"No shit. Maybe you can back up the talk," Patrick said to me.

"All I have is my word."

"When'd you guys meet?" the man asked.

"Two weeks ago. This guy accosted me at an event," Patrick said.

"Accosted?" I asked.

"What would you call it?"

"Persistence. And knowing what I want. You guys gonna give me a shot or what?"

That gave them both a laugh. Then they looked at one another.

"You know what Moose, you're in. Let's see if you can hack it."

"Really!?" I said, not hiding my elation.

"Thanks so much! You won't regret it, no sir! When do I start? Will I be at that bar or the back one? What should I wear? What time—" They cut me off.

"Love the enthusiasm, but you won't be working *here*."

Immediately I was deflated. And they could tell.

"We're fully staffed here, but we are opening a new venue in two months down the block, it'll be called Avenue. And you're going to be a part of our opening team. So, get ready, because we overstaff openings and only keep the crème."

"Challenge accepted," I said.

They stood. I followed suit.

"Thank you for the opportunity, guys, you won't be sorry," I placed my hand out and we all shook.

The tall man walked away.

"Thanks again Patrick, truly, you won't be sorry."

"I don't think I will Moose," he said and shook my hand again.

I left the club containing my excitement and when I got outside, I did a little dance. I thanked God for the opportunity, the same God I had cursed weeks prior over the debacle of my first commercial and the way the outcome had left me feeling like life would always hold me down, based on my poor decisions as a kid. Then I apologized to him for my reaction, lack of faith, and the volatility in my emotions. I had to be better. At everything. If I ever was truly going to succeed, I had to shake the prison monkey from my back. It was time to change the narrative from "woe is me" to "I got this." And that carrot of a job opportunity was just what I needed to do it. The first thing I did was try and get another job to hold me over since I was unemployed again. Truth was, I had been floundering financially for months, ever since the pre-Christmas holiday parties. The money simply wasn't there, so getting fired wasn't the worst thing to happen. Always a saver, I had enough to skate by and survive if I had to, so long as I didn't buy anything and kept my eating and drinking habits to a minimum, but I still needed something to help the months pass.

After a week of dropping résumés and shaking hands, I had no bites. I decided to accept it as the universe sending me a sign. I had a job starting in the near future, one that I believed would change the course of my life. I had enough to survive. Why not spend my free time concentrating on my career considering I had secured my next night job to provide me a living? So, that's what I did. Over the next few months I dove headfirst back into acting, and more so, writing. I had an incessant need to express myself and writing was something I had taught myself how to do while in prison, but life had caught up and my focus in the real world was on work, money, parole, and a social life. I was never in the mind frame to spend the few free hours I had in my head, writing (other than the short film I had done).

That all changed with so much free time. I quickly fell back in love with writing because I could control it. It didn't cost me anything. I could do it wherever and whenever I wanted and there was no partner needed, no instrument; nothing but me and a notepad or a computer. In many ways, I preferred it over acting as it allowed me to be alone with my thoughts, the complete opposite of being behind a bar and having to be "on" all the time, or the mental exhaustion of living through feelings on stage that came with acting. Then it dawned on me, maybe I should start to write about my life, both as a catharsis and, potentially, with the goal of completing a book that I could try and get published. And that, as well, set me off on a journey that would forever change my trajectory in life. Each day I wrote and wrote and wrote some more, alone with my thoughts. I spent my mornings writing for a few hours, went to the gym, then into rehearsals, and back to writing. A social life, once again, took the back seat. Plus, I didn't have the disposable income, so it was a wonderful confluence of events that forced me to work.

CHAPTER 13

AVENUE

Before I knew it, I received an email that my training at Avenue was to begin. The first few weeks were unlike anything I had experienced in the restaurant/bar world from which I came. In truth, the closest was Ponte's, but even that paled in comparison to the operation of a nightclub of that magnitude. We spent the first two weeks learning everything about their style of service and expectations. We organized the back bar, the storage rooms, and the computer systems for inventory. It was all-hands-on-deck. There were mock service runs. There were cocktail tests and tasting trials. There were lessons on how to pour drinks, place them on trays, open bottles, how to deal with comp drink tickets, comp bottles, promoters; everything. And I excelled, mostly from my many years of management experience. I was battle-proven and ready to lead those troops into war. And troops were a-many, and a different style of troop at that. The closest experience I had to it was the rooftop, where many young, attractive girls worked. I had been around that industry for years and had never seen a staff like it. It was like a model casting for a music video. Everyone that was client-facing was beautiful. Even our busboys and barbacks had a presentable look to them. Our managers wore fitted suits, looking like mini-James Bonds with earpieces to boot. Everyone looked the part.

On the first night we opened, everything we learned, all we had trained on, got tossed out the window, and it was complete chaos; unlike anything I had ever experienced. I was ready for war, face paint on and all (metaphorically). And as we opened the doors at 10 p.m., far later than I had ever started a shift, people trickled in, slowly. It was basically dead until midnight. And during that time, there were only promoters to deal with. I had never heard of such a thing, nor had to deal with the egos of who they thought they were, but I learned quickly to appease them, as they were the backbone of the nightclub, carrying a similar weight to the clients, who purchased ridiculously expensive bottles of overpriced liquor for their tables. A promoter's sole job was to bring women to a nightclub. There were many of them and they all brought ten to twenty young women. I stood and watched as those beautiful women were paraded into the club and sat at tables, strategically. Though the first thing I noticed was that none of them seemed to be enjoying themselves. It was as if they were indentured servants, which I would come to find, most were.

For my first three hours, all I did was give them free drinks, to which they did not tip, and provided the waitresses their comp bottles at the service station. I was starting to think I had been duped. It was nearly midnight and there were no paying customers. And then things changed. The music got louder, and the crowd began to trickle in. The service bar started printing bottle tickets; Dom Pérignon, Grey Goose, Patrón, and the like. There were bodies at the bar, men dropping their platinum and black Amex cards to buy drinks for themselves, their friends, and whichever girls were around to impress. And as we pumped the bottles and drinks, the register rang, and so did we. And before I knew it, the night was winding down, people were leaving, the music slowed, the lights rose, and the night was over. It was like a concert, or a play. Preparation, rehearsal, curtain, lights on, the show, the grand finale, and then the lights go up and everyone leaves.

When the lights had fully risen and the doors were locked, security stood around as we counted our banks and the waitresses did their paperwork in booths. Soon we were downstairs in the office providing our paperwork, the girls massaging their feet from working in heels all night, the bartenders having beers or left over liquor from tables, as we all waited for our managers to close us out. It was surreal. The juxtaposition of the "show" versus "behind the curtain." The stark contrast of glamor vs. reality. *Exhausted.* The clock was past four thirty, the sun was about to rise, and I was still waiting to be called to close out. After another thirty minutes or so, the bartenders were called and we presented our paperwork and banks, one by one. Then we got our numbers. I made five hundred dollars and was perplexed as to how. I never felt very busy, and if I was, it was only for two hours throughout the entire shift. *Was this the life?* I had so many questions and concerns, but after knowing I was making that kind of money, the only thing I thought about at that moment was my bed.

I returned home, unable to go to sleep, and smoked a bowl of weed to force myself and as the sun rose, my eyes closed, carrying me into a slumber, finally. The next morning, I woke up in the afternoon, later than I had in years. I had my coffee and attempted to write for a bit, then headed off to class to keep me fresh. I was a shell of myself that day, and thank God I didn't have to perform, only watch. I had some adjusting to do. I was going to be a vampire, working three nights a week, sometimes four. I would have to regulate my schedule as best as I could, lest I become a nightlife person with no future. The next few weeks were rough as I adjusted to my schedule.

Avenue was unlike anything in the world, or anything that I had experienced until that point. Each night women would throw themselves at us bartenders. It was as if we were on a stage. The lights, the money, the clientele, the music; everything about it was different. I would serve celebrities, whose work I loved, no different than the regular joes I had over the years. I would get numbers from girls, some top models, who came with promoters and date them. I was hit on by older women with status and made myself a sugar baby for a night. Every night was a different party with different people trying to escape their real lives, living under the veil of nightlife. I was making more money than ever, and I was getting caught in all the honey traps that lay themselves bare before me. With my personality, in that sphere, it was caustic. I was becoming *someone*, or so I thought. People knew me and those who didn't, wanted to, such was the electricity within the venue and the world; it surely wasn't me. To some, I told my story. To others I spoke of my dreams. I met some of the most influential people in the world and I was just a bartender! A bartender who experienced some crazy nights, though. The craziest, maybe ever, was the night Jho Low, the now-disgraced financier, made his mark on nightlife, and the world.

I was posted up at the bar, flirting with a model who had come to say hello, one I had a thing for, when the ticket machine started going wild behind me. I heard it rattling off, but was far more interested in what was before me than actual work. Until Patrick came running towards me, charged, and I knew I had to get to it before he had words with me at the end of the night.

"One hundred bottles of Cristal! One *hundred*.!" he bellowed at the top of his lungs as he ran past the bar into the storage area with all the busboys in tow.

I took his cue and rushed to the ticket machine and sure enough, they were rung in. I began pulling every bottle from our fridge under the bar as the busboys were bringing crates filled with them from the storage fridges downstairs. We began lining them up onto the service bar as Patrick screamed at us not to open any of them until they were all accounted for. Every single waitress, bartender, busboy, barback, manager, and host were lined up at the side service bar, ready to move on command. Once they were accounted for, Patrick had all the girls and busboys put sparklers on each bottle. When that was done, he called the DJ over the radio. The music stopped and the lights were lowered to near darkness. And then, on command, the sparklers were lit as the Superman theme song played and the bottles were whisked off and delivered to every single table in the club. I watched on as *two hundred and fifty thousand dollars* of product left the bar and went out onto the floor. And as the waitresses, busboys, bartenders, and managers high fived, I cursed the person who did it. Not because we all weren't going to make a small fortune that night, far more than I had, or will, ever as a bartender. But because of all the artists who could have made a film for that amount of money, or the many, many people in the world who could have fed their families or paid off their debt or . . . or . . . or . . . It was the most egregious waste of money I had ever witnessed. And that was only the beginning of my foray into the dark underworld of extreme wealth and nightlife.

With months under my belt and many experiences to boot, I arrived at work to find Patrick was gone. Off to travel the world for three months. I was devastated. Patrick had not only given me an opportunity I could never repay him for, but he was my mentor, and had become my friend. I was called into the office by the new manager, a Napoleon of a man, with the complete opposite energy and management style of Patrick. He was out to make a name for himself and prove he had some sense of worth, aside from being a lucky sperm.

"I hear you're the best bartender we have" he opened, a heavy lisp on the "best."

"I'm flattered," I said, waiting to see where it was going.

"We've been talking and we would like to offer you the bar manager position," he snarled.

"Wow, that's . . . wow . . ." I answered, actually surprised by the conversation.

"We think you would excel in the position," the tall manger standing by his side added.

"This is great. I mean, as I said, wow. So, what's next? Do I get a suit and an earpiece like you guys?"

They chuckled to themselves.

"Oh no, not like that. We think, well, we need you to stay where you are. It would be in title and a little bump in salary, but not a real manager, per se," he lisped.

"So . . . no suit then?"

"No suit. Still bartending. We would just ask that you inform us what's happening behind the bar," he spat.

You want me to be a rat? Work with people in the trenches and snitch on them, to you?

"So, to clarify, you want me to give up the people I've been working with for months now? That it?" I asked.

"No, just let us know who's stealing and we'll take care of the rest."

I had a problem with it, many problems actually. One, I hated fucking rats. HATED. And it would be one thing if I were new, told the staff I would be working with them and provided fair warning that I would be the house's eyes and ears as I had done before. But to put me in that position with people I had been in the trenches with for the past few months? It wasn't right.

"I'm sorry guys, but I'm not your guy. I can't rat on people I work with. Thank you though."

I got up and left.

And when I did, I knew I wasn't going to escape that rebuff cleanly.

A little over a month later I was making my way home from a rehearsal when I had a call from an unknown number. I answered it.

"Hello?"

"Nick, this is your manager from Avenue," he said.

"Hey man, what's up?" I asked, casually.

"Uh, well, well, you see, we think it's best if we part ways," he said.

I was so stunned, I didn't know what to say or think, I just reacted.

"Are you fucking serious? You just tried to promote me a month ago. Now you're firing me?"

"We just feel it's time to move on, fresh blood."

"Fresh blood! Are you kidding me!" I screamed.

"This isn't your personal pussy palace! It's a workplace!" he shouted.

And then I knew. The argument was arbitrary. I had slept with someone who was off-limits. And for that, they were giving me the ax. Kicking me out of the exclusive club. That's how things work in the real world. Piss off someone with money, you're out on your ass. Back to the bread line.

"Fine. When can I pick up my check?" I asked calmly.

"We'll mail you your check."

I hung up, seething. I was back on the unemployment line, albeit a bit more well off than when I began, but back on the line no less. My time in nightlife lasted only half a year, which was more than most. Only I had a taste and I couldn't *not* be in it. The money and perks were far too good.

CHAPTER 14

THE DARBY

New York, New York—2010–2012

Y ou believe this prick?!" I shouted at Patrick to tell him the news as he traveled off in some far away land.

"I'm sorry Moose. But, all things happen for a reason. I'm cutting my trip short to come back and open a new venue for Scott and Richie. I'll bring you over. Be in touch in a few weeks when I get back."

My savior, good 'ol Paddy to the rescue

Patrick called me down to a pre-opening meeting at The Darby, a brand-new supper club inside the old Nell's space on 14th Street. The Darby was a new concept from nightlife impresario's Scott Sartiano and Richie Akiva. It was a throwback to yesteryear. The Copacabana in *Goodfellas* was probably an inspiration. The ground floor was a restaurant, led by Food Network Chef Alex Guarnaschelli, serving steak, seafood, and chops. The main draw, besides the food, was a house band performing various sets nightly. The downstairs was reserved for what those guys did best, super VIP nightclubs. Only that one was slated to be incredibly intimate as it was very small. The Darby was set to be both a throwback and a new concept, fusing the restaurant with performances and the basement lounge/club, accessible from the street or a VIP staircase within where they could swoop their large list of celebrity clientele from one room to the next without subjecting them to paparazzi.

We met in the basement lounge, a room that resembled a beehive. Once again, the staff was stunning, something about nightlife that I was finding was part of the allure. Patrick introduced me as the bar manager, in title, not pay, and had me lead a team to begin devising a cocktail list based on certain parameters (spirit, suggested fruits/flavors). I went off to the bar with the other bartenders and set to work. The opening was far different from Avenue's. Less corporate and far more independent, meaning our opinions mattered to Patrick and he would take or throw away what served him and the venue as we went. Our training period lasted two weeks, learning the food, flow of service, cocktails, and bottle offerings. Overall, it was similar to most every opening I had been a part of, save Avenue's, which was very intricate and belabored. And quite honestly, ahead of its time.

Darby's hours were also going to be an adjustment. Gone were the days of arriving at 9 p.m. It was part-restaurant and they split shifts for the bartenders. Which meant two people opened at 4 p.m. in the restaurant, serving until ten when it slowed, then another arrived to open the lounge at nine and one of the bartenders from the restaurant would move downstairs for the night. That allowed for an even cut of the pie, as the restaurant was our main focus, the lounge more of a den of iniquity for ownership, as I would come to find. That first night the stars were out. Jay-Z, Beyoncé, and many more turned out to support their friend in his newest venture. I had never seen star power like that at Avenue. Occasionally a celebrity would sneak in, sit with Noah Tepperberg, (its main partner, the brains and probably the most successful *business* nightlife impresario in nightlife history), and have a night. I had always heard the ramblings that Strategic Group (as they were called, now known as Tao Group after some corporate purchases and shuffling over the years) was corporate and mainstream, whereas Richie Akiva and Scott Sartiano were *celebrities*.

I saw the difference that first night, completely starstruck, as I served Gisele Bündchen and her supermodel friends drinks. No different than the "regular" folks who made it past the doorman at Avenue. I was in awe. Until the end of the night, that is, when we counted tips. After working from 4 p.m. to 2 a.m. I made $82 dollars on the books. I was immediately concerned as to how I would make ends meet. I needed the cash flow of Avenue. The large nights, packed with bottles flying and clients three-deep at the bar. Short and sweet, but lucrative. I spoke to Patrick about it and he told me to relax, that in the beginning hot clubs take time before people make money. It was the nature of the beast. When you had so many celebrities in a room, everything was comped (meaning free). And no one tipped. But once they opened the doors a bit and let regular people in, the money would get better. I trusted his wisdom, and really had no choice, lest I look for another job, which I wasn't about to do.

As the days and weeks went by, the money slowly got better, so long as you were upstairs in the restaurant. It was by no means "club money," but it was enough to survive. Though, without it, I would have had to find another job because any shift I had downstairs during the first two months, was sickening. I would average *seventy* dollars per shift. Five hours at $5.25 minimum wage and tips of forty-ninety dollars. However, the "perks" of working there were unbounded. Not only did I serve models and actresses, society girls and all areas of fashion, finance, and every titan of industry you could think of, I was able to meet them, chat them up, and angle for my acting and film career. In addition to that, there were the surprise performances all the time from the owners' friends. I'll remind you that the ground floor was all of three thousand square feet, including the kitchen and back of house. More than half the size of Avenue. Add that to the layout, which was intimate and then the star power who showed up? It was like being at Oscar parties nearly every night of the week. Prince, Taylor Swift, John Mayer, Gary Clark Jr., Kanye West, and many more would be dining and decide to jump on stage and do a set. I would stand in awe, watching, mere feet away as I tended bar, to some of my favorite artists with impromptu sets. It is where Kanye name dropped Richie in the song "Diamond," and where Jay-Z spit lines about extravagant partying at The Darby and 1Oak in "Beach is Better."

Then there were the after parties downstairs. From Leonardo DiCaprio to Cher to Naomi Campbell, the list went on and on. And each night, though I made no money, I was introduced to a starship of power and influence; always remembering what they drank and always had it ready for them. A thank you and a smile was usually all I got. Each night was so unique and you never knew what would happen next that it was a joy to come to work, despite the lack of "nightclub" money. After a few months they opened the doors a bit more and the money began to flow. I asked to stop working in the restaurant, so good it was. And so short. In order not to cannibalize their main club 1Oak, the parties went early, from ten at night to two in the morning. And in those four hours, I was out the door by two thirty after my closeout and on my way to Oak to catch a glimpse of what it was like not to be the help.

And then one day Patrick told me his job was done. He was leaving for another jaunt in some third-world land, where he would hike, backpack, and learn the culture; his way of balancing his life out after having to deal with the stressors of nightlife at that level. I thanked him for everything he had done, again, and promised to keep in touch. Shortly after our conversation, he introduced me to Evan, the new boss. He was a few years my senior, a New Yorker tried and true, having been born there; a street kid with an edge to boot. We had taken to one another seamlessly. After my first shift, I learned he respected my anal retentiveness behind the bar (clean station, product placement, systems) and would leave me be while he aimed his proverbial gun at other, sloppier, staff members who he would need to get rid of. We hadn't been working together for more than two weeks when he would forever change the trajectory of my life in the business. It was a slower night, mostly bottles at the tables, very few people at, or around, the bar. Though the room itself was filled with the who's who of New York. Evan came up to chat with me, as he had been accustomed to doing, and asked me who some of the people in the room were. I rattled off the fashion magazine editors, the titan of real estate's sons, a famous photographer, a filmmaker, and some off-beat character actors who peppered the room that night.

"How do you know all these people?" he asked, seriously impressed.

"I read everything I can get my hands on. I study life. If I have to spend as many hours doing this shit in order to be an actor, I might as well be the best I can be at it. And knowing who these people are could help the career I'm really chasing."

"Interesting. You're fired," he said and walked away.

"What?" I complained as he left from behind the bar. "What do you mean? Are you serious?!" I asked, anger growing inside me.

"Yeah, your days of bartending are done. You'll be rehired tomorrow as a Host at 1Oak."

"A host! I'm a star-tender! I'm not a fucking host!" I screamed at him.

"Calm down, alright. This is happening and your life just changed. You'll thank me later. And don't ever fucking yell at me again or I'll rip your fucking trachea out," he said and walked away, confidently.

1Oak of New York, New York—the world-famous nightclub.

Prior to working at The Darby, I had never been inside the club. Instead, I was one of many whose only experience with it was out-side the velvet rope, never seeing past the wood paneled doors, being told by the doorman "private party" as he disappeared back into the room. Here are the few things I learned: one, it didn't matter that I worked for the company, I was still subject to door-man approval every time I attempted to go after work, and let's just say I was rejected a few times, which didn't sit well with my ego. Two, the place was a cesspool of characters. Yes, celebrities came frequently, but so did drug dealers, hustlers, pimps, rappers, mod-els, fashionistas, filmmakers, producers, executives, billionaires, and con men, who spent money like they were billionaires off the backs of other people. Three, it was known as the "late night spot." Oak opened at 11 p.m. each night, Tuesday through Sunday, six nights a week. And each night was different, yet the same. Mainly, the place was empty until two-thirty in the morning. In fairness, it was in its sixth year of business. For any nightclub to remain hot after one year, took boatloads of work: PR, promotions, *Page Six* drops, etc. etc. And Oak managed to do it with flying colors.

Then there was the process to my hiring. If I thought getting a service job in nightlife was insular, having a title (doorman/host) was next to impossible during that time. (Nowadays it's such a joke and so different that any Tom, Dick, or Harry is courted to come put a suit on and work a door or be a host or manager or promoter— the business is *nothing* like it used to be.) The first step was a meeting in the office that sat above the club, in which I had never been. Evan told me to be there at three that afternoon for a meeting to discuss my new position. I arrived and waited outside a conference room for a meeting between the owners and managers to end. When it did, Evan came out to grab me and a young girl I did not know, a very beautiful woman in her twenties who was polite, sweet, and very kind to me on that first day.

We entered the room and were formally introduced to Richie, Scott, and Ronnie; the main partners and faces of the club. All of whom I had made drinks for, said hello to, but never once had any of them introduced themselves or said so much as "hi" before demanding a drink or some other duty for them or their guests. We sat across the table from them, being introduced as the new hosts of 1Oak. They were immediately skeptical and held nothing back. I had no clients, knew nobody, and was a fucking bartender, according to them. As they argued over my position in front of me, I listened, and didn't disagree with any of their points. I was happy to go back to the bar and continue on the road I had made for myself. But Evan wouldn't take no for an answer. He flexed his muscle as Director of Operations and stated that not only did I know everyone, they knew me. I had the respect of people who respect no one. And he had not only seen it first hand, but inquired as to my manner directly with many of those people, the ones whose opinions mattered in the nightlife world. The regulars.

After what was a grueling forty minutes of back and forth about my lack of qualifications for the position, Richie got a call and left the room. Scott decided he no longer needed to be at the meeting and told Evan to figure it out. Whatever he decided he would be fine with in the end, then he said goodbye, shook my hand, and left. Ronnie remained behind to give his two cents, which I later found held no real weight as he was the wicked stepson of the partners operation, a distant third party in name and salary; not an equity shareholder with Scott and Richie. After Evan shut him and his thoughts and ideas down, he left the meeting too.

"As you see, this is going to be an uphill battle. But I know you can do this. You two are going to have to lean on one another and learn. This won't be an easy transition. This isn't a job, it's a lifestyle. Say goodbye to your lives. You will now live and breathe Oak," he said.

I nodded, but felt a tremor inside me. I didn't want to *live* nightlife. I wanted to live acting and writing; just like my friends who were succeeding. That job was supposed to be a pit stop to make some cash and go on to the next one. Instead, I was about to be installed on the front lines of arguably the world's most famous nightclub; and I couldn't just show up for a shift. No, no. There was work during the day, "outreach," as they called it. Promotion. I didn't just stand outside a club. I had to bring people. And not just any people, money. And when I say I knew one person with money at the time I wasn't lying. I felt daunted by the task before me, but had no choice. I had to learn and excel. That would be my only way out, so I set out to succeed.

After the meeting Evan took me to H & M and showed me some styles to try. I didn't have the money to buy expensive suits, but I had to invest in myself to look the part. I had no choice. It was part of the job. I bought two suits, a gray and a blue, and a pair of sharp black shoes that fit the mold. Grabbed a few dress shirts and ties. And nearly eight hundred dollars later, I was ready. Evan promised me that I would make it back in two shifts, maybe less, depending on the night. I rolled my eyes, as I figured he was playing me, but took my medicine nonetheless. That night I left my apartment looking sharper than I ever had. I may not have had a clue what I was doing, but I looked the part. I laughed at myself as I made my way on the subway downtown, receiving looks by passengers that I had never gotten before. If for nothing else, I was feeling myself as I walked out from underground and walked the block over to 1Oak, where various security guards stood chatting out front.

"Is Ralph here?" I asked a large guard who seemed to be in charge.

"We're not open yet. Text him," he said.

"I'm supposed to train with him tonight but I don't have his number," I stated.

"Ah, that's you? Nice to meet you," he smiled, putting forth his hand.

"Nice to meet you too."

He opened the rope and let me in, introducing me to the other guards as I made my way inside. The house lights were on. A group of waitresses sat at booths, as they did their hair and makeup and chatted. My counterpart was standing by the bar, where I joined her.

"Hey," I said.

"Hiya," she replied and kissed my cheek and gave me a fake hug.

"You meet Ralph yet?" I asked.

"Yeah, he'll be up in a moment."

I stood and studied the room for a moment, I never noticed all the tables on my past visits, mostly because I never made it past the bar. I simply wasn't cool enough.

As I began to count them, Ralph, a tall man with short hair, who had to either be a model or once was, greeted us. He was very kind and invited us to sit at a booth to go over the seating chart; which was basically another language to me.

"Here is the room. Each table has a number. You have to memorize them, maybe take a pad for the first few nights and give yourself a cheat sheet. We start the night by strategically placing our promoters throughout the room based on who they are and what they bring. Image promoters go by Richie and the DJ booth."

"What's an image promoter?" I asked.

"They bring models, ten to fifteen a night. Best girls. Sometimes they have clients sit with them and spend."

"Mid-grade promos here and here," he pointed to two tables that were within the middle of the room, and somewhat close to the DJ.

"And fillers go back here," he said, pointing to tables in the very back and side entrance of the club; no man's land.

I took the titles of the last two as pretty straight forward. I would learn more as I watched and worked each night.

"Your job is to seat these tables and clients around them. All the tables have minimum spends. DJ tables are three and a half to five thousand, these over here, two and a half to four thousand, these back here, two to three thousand and the smaller ones in the front by the bar, one to one and a half thousand. You good?" he asked, knowing that I had no idea what he was saying.

"I'll get it," I said, completely confused.

"He'll be fine, I'll walk him through," my counterpart said, flexing her experience.

"Alright, so here is what we have tonight," he pulled out his phone and began rattling off reservations. Names, number of people in the party, and the guy to girl ratio. I quickly learned that everything was subjective. He would read off one name and state that the person has a shit crew, but they spend a lot, but we couldn't put "those people" near Richie or anywhere that was high profile. Then you had sons of real estate scions who would only buy a bottle, but because they had a great crew (guys/girls that looked the part) they would be in the DJ area for next to nothing. Those were just a few of the things I learned during that first preshift.

After some time, we had the room sat, in theory, as everything was subject to change on the fly, lest Richie walk in with Rihanna and the entire floor plan got thrown away and we'd have to improvise, which I would come to find, happened all the time. After we were done, the manager came to introduce himself. A short, little sprite of a man with a perfectly tailored suit and a bald head. He had been in charge since the beginning and was not thrilled that two new, inexperienced hosts had been thrust upon him at the same time. He did not mask those feelings during our first meeting. *Yet another challenge, check.*

Ralph went on to explain how things worked. He was the doorman. His job was to sort through the people outside and decide who to let in, who to charge (a bar tab or table), and who to deny. He was the first, and only, decision maker. We did nothing until he had a potential table on the hook, or a pre-reserved reservation. When that happened, he would call one of us either to negotiate a minimum based on the party size and look of the group before us, or get a credit card and ID for the person with a reservation. He went on to explain that everything was even further subjective outside during the "show." Just because someone made a reservation for a certain minimum for a certain number of people with a certain ratio didn't mean they got in. If they showed up and were unattractive, overweight, poorly styled, looking like they came from Jersey or The Islands (Staten or Long), all bets were off. Either they were denied entry or we upped the minimum to what they called a "fuck you" number. And if they agreed to pay that grossly egregious amount, then we would let them in and hide them in the back with the fillers where the "good people" couldn't see them. That was another phrase that came to me during my education. "Good people" was code for the following: good-looking, rich, stylish, or important to someone (in which case you could be a fat, disgustingly dressed pauper, and you were not only in, but treated like a king). The business was completely discriminatory, and they had every right to be. It was their place. They paid the astronomical rent (which I believe was close to eighty thousand dollars a month). They could run their spot however they wanted. Again, that was before social media destroyed our world and the nonsense of "equality" and "fairness" came into the social zeitgeist. No such thing as equality back then in nightclubs. Either you were in, or you were out. No explanations needed. These were the rules and needed to be followed.

That was what Ralph instructed us to do on our first night as we sat in a booth doing our internal preshift. At eleven, the lights went down, the stations were ready, the servers and bus staff and bartenders stood in place and . . . waited. For hours. As I said, the amount of people in the club before two-thirty was next to nothing: filler promoters, some corporate post-dinner sales or finance groups, basically a depressing place to be. And then, once two-thirty hit, things got interesting. Messages started coming over phones. SUVs began rolling up and before you could look up, the line stretched down the block and around the corner. Avenue lost its crowd around that time, a large swath of their guests coming over to party with us. I stood and watched as it all unfolded, mesmerized. It was organized chaos. People yelling to get the doorman's attention. People crying and throwing fits when they were denied entry. Cursing Ralph. Some people tried to fight him, feeling disrespected in front of their friends or girls. Security tried to diffuse situations. Ralph had no other choice but to stand back and take the verbal abuse and attempts to lunge at him. It was madness. And I loved it! I suddenly felt alive! As if that had been what I needed. It was to be my stage!

The night began to fly by. I would meet a client outside, get his card, shake his hand, walk him through the packed, bustlingly loud club to his table where I would, very often, be palmed fifty or a hundred dollars. I smiled as I got the hang of it. It was like being a maître d' in a restaurant, only much, much higher stakes and exponential amounts more money being spent. I watched as a parade of bottles went over to a table who gave me a tip and went and looked at the menu. I added up the order I saw going out. It was more than eight thousand dollars! Evan didn't lie, I was going to make a killing! As the night turned into 4 a.m., I was exhausted and couldn't wait to leave and get some sleep. I approached Ralph and he told me that only the door left at four. The hosts would be required to stay until all the tables were done. I was about to ask him how that was even possible, considering 4 a.m. was the absolute latest a bar could remain open in NYC. But again, I was not in a normal bar. We wouldn't kick our clients out at four. Instead, we would lower the music, close the front door, remove the ropes and barricades, leave a few security guards outside to direct exiting traffic, not allow any more entries, and we would continue going until roughly 4:30 a.m. Around that time, the lights began to rise. We were officially done for the night. Hosts didn't have closing paperwork, a nice perk, and I was finally allowed to leave as the bartenders and waitresses went about their closing duties, which would take another hour or so, ending their shifts at roughly five thirty to six each morning. At Avenue, we were out the door by 4 a.m. every night. It was my first shift and I was already struggling leaving the club at four thirty in the morning, I felt for those staff members.

That first week was one of the most difficult I had experienced in my career. Between the long hours, the high stress levels and demand, as well as the fact that Evan called me every morning at eleven and pushed me to think about the upcoming night and to reach out to potential clients all day. I was told to text, call, or email every person whose card or number I got the previous night and try to build relationships to get them back into the club and spend money. The outreach took up large swaths of my day. They were not lying about it being a lifestyle, and it was only the beginning. But already, after only a few weeks, I was feeling the schedule. Sleeping four or five hours a night and up and working each day. It became another challenge to shift focus to my career, as I wasn't in a place, mentally, to write, and I was auditioning more frequently during the days, having secured a new, union agent. It was a grind to keep the candle burning on both ends, but I did it, and soon both jobs started to gather steam.

I had been paying my dues in the nonunion world for some time. From the first booking that never was (Mercedes), to many small, shitty commercials that paid next to nothing and owned my image for years, Grey Goose being one of them, I was finally gaining a little momentum. It came hot and fast. I became a regular at the top commercial casting offices in town. And as each day went by, the auditions piled on and my biggest struggle wasn't the material or the craft, but the lack of sleep. I would get home at 5 a.m. and have to be at an audition somewhere below 57th Street by as early as 9 a.m. sometimes. Most were after ten in the morning, but some were before and it was taking a toll. Between that and the demands of the job during the day: texts, emails, phone calls, visits to concierges of each and every hotel with an ADR (average daily rate) above two hundred and fifty dollars a night as I was a one-man marketing team; it was draining my energy and mind.

Soon I started booking work and the multiple nights I had two hours of sleep and had to be on set for eight to twelve hours a day, answering emails and texts for the club throughout, and then had to be at work at 10 p.m. and do it all over again. It finally broke my body down and I got the flu for the first time in years. I was told I could take two nights off to recover, then needed to be back by the third. I accepted all of that, as I was finally making real money as a host. Add in the commercials and I was almost out of all the debt from the film and began to save money. I had no time to spend it as all I did was work. And being a host, when I did go out on Sunday or Monday nights, I didn't pay for a thing. Dinners at restaurants: free. Drinks at lounges and clubs: gratis. I was bribed with clothing, sneakers, and cash handshakes. You name a plug and I had it. The perks were great and the money was flowing, but I began to hate it.

Not every night was busy. Most were dead. Walking around, standing around, having banal conversations all reminded me of the doldrums of dead time. Then, like the flip of a switch, the club would be jammed and we would have two big nights and they would pay so much that the entire week became palatable. Though it was a cycle I didn't want to be in for much longer and with acting finally working out and my savings building, I started praying that my big break would come soon and get me out of the "life." It was around that time that I heard Ralph was leaving to open 1Oak Los Angeles. I seized the opportunity. The way I viewed it, the doorman made a substantial nightly rate, far more than a host, and they had only to show up each night and curate the room. No marketing, no clients, nothing at all to do during the day. I thought about the money I would be "losing" from the big spender nights, but more about my time and how valuable that had become. Acting was moving and I could taste the change I had spent so many years working toward and if I had more free time I could get to writing again. In my head I had it all figured out when I walked into Evan's office.

I sat down and asked him to move me to the door. He had an issue with it immediately. First off, they liked the job I was doing as a host. Second, I had never done a door. Did I know who was who, really? Could I do it well? There were many questions. And I fought to answer them all. I stuck my feet in the ground and politicked Richie, Ronnie, and Scott at every turn. I would get them alone at night in the club, in the office, call them during the day; I was relentless. Finally, it worked. They decided to move me and let my counterpart handle the floor alone. She was elated because it meant more money for her. And so was I. No more promo, no more marketing, no more begging people to come spend their money. My days would be mine to cultivate my craft. To build on the small opportunities I had gotten in the rough world of acting.

My first night at the door couldn't have gone worse. When Richie arrived, he laid in the cut and watched me, er, should I say overrode me, and did my job for me. He berated me like a child in front of a line of a hundred people, not to mention our staff. I simply didn't know what I was doing and the nuance was so subtle and subjective I didn't understand it. The next night, after taking my lumps, I set out to change the narrative. I decided I would do the door my way, not try to be Ralph. His style was his alone, which is what I would come to learn in life about doing doors, there is no exact science; it's fluid. I had read about Studio 54 and the way Steve Rubell had done it. Let people wait and come outside and pick them out from the crowd. So that's what I did. And it seemed to work well. At the end of the night I had no complaints, in fact I was encouraged by security that I did a great job. Only as the weeks went on, as the club lagged and dragged from night to night and attendance and spending began to be affected, I was brought into a firing squad during our weekly meeting. I was verbally eviscerated by Richie for thinking it was Studio 54. The club was seven years old! He screamed. How the fuck do you think we are going to make it to eight? The yelling continued until I was thrown out of the room.

My ego destroyed, I returned to work that night like a dog with its tail between its legs. I didn't know what to do. I couldn't do the door the way I had been, I couldn't do it the way I was taught, what could I do? So, I did what anyone would do to play it safe,

I let most everyone in. The club was packed. And then Richie arrived. He took one look at the room and rushed to the front, surely ready to choke me with his bare hands until security stepped in front of him. He settled by kicking me off the door and telling me to get off the property for the night, as he couldn't stand to look at me. I left, deciding to take a walk home, upset, my ego crushed, and thought about my life. *What was I doing? Why was this world so important to me?* It was more than money; it was *ego*. And my ego had been destroyed by the biggest person in the industry. I was so upset, I decided that the only way forward would be to quit and focus on acting and writing. I had money saved, I had residuals coming in, it was time to make the plunge.

The next day I heard from my counterpart that they were moving me from the door and putting me back to being a host. I felt it such an affront, not that they were removing me, that much was clear from the prior night, but that they felt I was their property to move around as they saw fit for what suited them. I still didn't understand power dynamics and the fact that I simply didn't have any. I was lucky to be given those shots. I should shut my mouth and take whatever they gave me. But that is not my personality. Nor is it my ego. I called Scott, whom I had a better relationship with and asked to meet him. He was kind enough to give me five minutes on his walk from the office across the street to his apartment. As we entered the elevator I finished my speech.

When it opened on his floor he stopped and said, "I get it. I do. And if that's how you feel I can't force you to stay. But acting is hard buddy. And you're going to need some kind of money coming in. You sure you don't want to bartend again if it's the pressure of the job that's eating into your schedule?"

"No. I'll be fine. I have money to get through a year or so."

He shrugged and extended his hand.

"Thanks for everything," I said.

"Good luck to you, buddy," he said and entered his apartment. I left that building feeling I had made the best decision in a long time. That I was finally free of hospitality. That my yellow brick road lay out before me. That I would finally be an artist. That after all these years, my dreams were finally coming true. Or so I thought.

CHAPTER 15

A WANNABE ARTIST'S LIFE

New York, New York—2012–2014

Sleep schedules are a real thing and they affect your performance more than you can imagine. Mine had been turned upside down years back. From my teenage years of dealing and partying, never having a bedtime and rising whenever I felt like it, to the daily regimen of prison, 6 a.m. breakfast, lest you sleep through it and miss one of the three subpar, lack-of-nutrition-filled meals they served, followed by dinner at 5 p.m., and lights out at ten. My time at Reliable had me arriving at the office by 7:30 a.m., and staying up until nearly one or two am each night, depending on the commute, which determined my ability to go to sleep upon getting home. Then going to work in bars from four to midnight and finally into clubs where I would learn to take disco naps at 7 or 8 p.m., waking at 9 p.m. And then, suddenly, I had all the time in the world to set myself on what most people call a "regular" schedule. Only I had trouble doing it.

At first, I felt free not having to punch in anymore. I woke, wrote, had calls about projects I was trying to get off the ground, worked on and attended auditions, and had a social life, daily. It was as if I was living life for the first time, ever. I could suddenly attend birthday parties and dinner with friends, weddings, and the like. I had previously sacrificed nearly every night of the week and holidays for the money that provided me a small piece of lifestyle comfort in the city; all with the hope that my "career" would kick off and afford me simply the amount of money hospitality had provided me. Though it didn't. I booked a few commercials, but only made the session fee, which, suffice it to say, you can't live on because none of them ran (residuals are how you make the real money). I did some odd jobs here and there for cash; moving, day labor, light construction, Taskrabbit; I even cleaned some friends' apartments to get some extra cash as each day, week, and month, I watched as the savings I had drained away from rent, debt, food, and fun.

During the first few months I was confident things would turn. That it was an expected step in the transition away from hospitality into the arts. But with each month coming and going far quicker than it ever had previously, it seemed like something was going to have to give. And by give, I mean, either I was going to finally move to LA and try to make it in that cesspool of wannabes called Hollywood, or I was going to have to go back to the comfort that hospitality provided me: stability. Which I needed more than ever as my life of "freedom" had become chaotic. I had no schedule, nowhere to be, no paycheck coming in each week, and nothing but the lonely stress of wishing the phone would ring, the email would ping, or someone would respond to the various inquiries over scripts I had written to try and get produced. I was experiencing failure at every turn. Stubborn as I am, I plowed on, praying each day that all would change in my favor. Then I began to experience the mental toll that not working and wanting more than anything to work has on you. What it was doing to me was unlike anything I had ever dealt with prior. In prison, there was always hope that things would be different when I was "out on the street" again. I was out, had been for years, and had experienced the struggle that is life. Nothing had been easy and at every turn I felt stymied. I admit, I made poor decisions, but they were made with *hope*. The hope that those jobs were stairs in the ladder of my journey, though instead of climbing consistently, I often tried to jump to another ladder that had less steps and usually found myself back on the ground, looking up, cursing myself.

Things got as bad as they could. I was nearing down to my last thousand. Literally, I remember having nine hundred and eighty dollars to my name at that point, and my rent of $1,580 was due in two weeks. I came to the reality that life had gotten the best of me. That my dreams of being an artist were just that, *dreams*. If I was ever going to make it in the world of film, I would have to take a step back, tend to my lumps, and start over, *yet again*.

My first call was to Evan.

"To what do I owe this? Been a long time, Marshall," he said as he answered.

"Sure has. So, listen, I hear you're opening something new in the old Darby space. Could you use a stellar host?" I asked.

"Now you wanna host?" he laughed.

"That train's left the station buddy. I already brought someone in as lead. Not really room for you."

"Who is it?"

"Simon."

"What? I can sweep him under the rug with my eyes closed," I said, my ego fully involved.

"Not sure Richie will go for it, maybe Scott will. He likes you. Call him."

"Would you broach it for me?" I asked.

"I'm not your agent. I gave you the keys, you handed them back."

"Listen. You're right. I'm wrong. I thought I was going to be a working actor. I wasn't. I'm not. And now I'm desperate Evan, like fucking down to the wire desperate. I need this, I'm begging."

"Call Scott and I'll see what I can do. No promises."

Click.

If I were to make it happen, I would have to suck it up and call Scott. Tail between my legs. *Fuck.*

"I heard you might be calling," he answered.

"I'm desperate and I'm calling in a favor."

"I don't know that we have room for you. How's your acting career going?" he asked, his dry sense of humor not amusing to me.

"I failed Scott. Like you said, it's tough out there. I should have never left, or at least kept a foot in the door."

"I'm just not sure we have anything."

"Scott. If you give me a chance, I promise I will be the best fucking host in the business. Full stop. No more complaining. No more being a pain in your ass. No more infighting. Just give me the opportunity and let me ride with Evan. I promise you won't regret it. Please," I plead my case.

"Let me speak to Richie," he said, and I knew I had a little more lobbying to get through, but things were potentially looking up.

I called Evan after and further plead my case, making my promises and basically sold my soul for the opportunity. I got the call the next day.

"You're in. Not the lead, though. An opportunity. That's all," he said.

I thanked him and promised him I wouldn't mess it up.

The following night I arrived for my first shift. Technically it was supposed to be a trial, but as soon as I stepped foot onto that floor, into the room I knew so well when it was The Darby, it was as if all the years of my hospitality training, coupled with my new-found sense of desperation from being dead broke, ran through me, and transformed me into a super host. I had been reluctant to be a host at 1Oak, despite the opportunity, as it wasn't for me. The later start, the later release, there was no chance I would have a career during the day if I had to work those hours. Only at Up&Down, as it was now called, things were different. It was slated to be the preparty spot. A club, full on, opening at ten and clearing out by two-thirty, shifting the party to Oak, so as not to cannibalize the brand. The opportunity not only suited my schedule better, it was a different beast in every respect. First, the club was huge. Spread over two floors, twenty-six tables to sell, nearly four-hundred-person occupancy; it was a larger undertaking than Oak. Coupled with the fact that it was the newest brainchild of Scott and Richie, the crowd was set to be top notch, nothing like what Oak had become. It was their chance to bring back all the A-listers in their rolodex and give them something new and fresh. I sat in the preshift meeting run by Evan and was introduced as an old face that some may have known. I did, in fact, know some of the staff that was retained for that venue; either having worked with them at Darby, Oak, or Avenue. It was commonplace for the venues to steal staff from one another.

After the preshift, I watched as Simon led us to the host stand and went over the seating chart for the night. I watched as he stumbled along, fully out of his league, yet in charge nonetheless. And he had survived the grand opening, where I was left to stand outside in the cold by the new doorman, Bedar, days earlier when I came to scope out the scene. I was on staff, on his team, everyone's team; a new free agent or an old pick up off waivers, whichever way you prefer to view it. I remained silent as I noted the mistakes he was making, having the experience of working with Richie at Oak and dealing with his whims and constant audibles. I also recognized most of the clients who were coming in for tables that night. Another piece of back pocket knowledge I would keep when shit hit the fan later, as I am sure it would, no chance of it not, as Simon simply wasn't prepared to lead the room; I was and would after the night was over.

The night began faster than anything I had ever experienced. The line outside was made up of hundreds of people, the chaos palatable and it wasn't even midnight. The promoters flooded in; some I had worked with prior, others I was being introduced to, and their egos, as they complained about the tables they were assigned to sit at. I laughed to myself as Simon began to appease them. Mistake number one. He started moving the floor seating around to coddle their egos and it would come to haunt him when the clients, and eventually Richie, would show up and start flipping out as the room wasn't seated correctly and all hell was about to break loose. I waited, and worked as I watched it unfold. By the time Richie arrived, with various A-listers in tow, he began barking his demands, and flipped out on Simon for seating promoters at his table.

"Where is Rihanna going to sit?!" he bellowed.

I watched as Simon crumbled. Seeing my opportunity, I slid right in and up to Richie, whispering in his ear the moves I could make and him nodding to me, furious with Simon, then telling me to go get it done. With his blessing I swept through the room like a crook. I came upon promoters and told them in no uncertain terms they had to get up and move and when they barked, I bit. I was the pit bull in the room, nearly coming to blows with a few of them, security by my side, pulling them from the tables they had no right to be at and moving them to where the room needed them. My thought process was that we paid them to be there and they should simply do as we asked, not fight because their girls wanted to be closer to Richie, Justin Bieber, Bradley Cooper, and Leonardo DiCaprio.

And after, I returned to the cluttered and completely distraught host stand to find angry clients I had known ever so briefly while at Oak. Who upon seeing me, lit up at the sight of a friendly face. They came with hugs and handshakes filled with cash and told me to let Simon know who they were and provide them with the tables they deserved. And then I took charge, pushing Simon aside, and began to orchestrate the room like I was Leonard Bernstein; the tables my symphony orchestra. The other junior hosts and runners all took to me as I became the decision maker. No longer even listening to Simon as I sent them away, credit cards and commitment envelopes in hand to the desired tables and the waitresses and busboys ready to serve and gauge. That night we were going to break records and, in the end, I would not only establish myself as the top lieutenant, but Simon would be no more going forward. For it was my ship and I was to be its captain, guiding it through the storm into safe, calm waters.

By 2:30 a.m., as Richie called me to his table and told me to prepare the Oak staff for his arrival and what his guests needed, he patted me on the shoulder and asked me to walk him and his crew from the club into their waiting SUV. Which, for him, is the highest of compliments. And so, I did it, leading the trail of A-listers through the room and off into the car, then returning to the host stand, reviewing the current situation on the floor and then returned into the club, touching tables and checking with our clients if they needed anything, handing my cards out like chicklets to children in the school yard. By 3 a.m., the club was nearly empty. The waitresses and bar were beginning their closeouts as Evan and Simon were having it out in the service area. I took it upon myself to close out the host stand, cut the runners, and get the paperwork ready to provide to Evan when he was done with Simon. I waited like a good soldier, a stiff drink and paperwork in my hand at the host station, ready to be anointed as the man in charge. Which I wasn't. Instead,

I was thanked, told that I would need to get along with Simon and that we would discuss things more tomorrow. I left for home, disgruntled at the thought that I would have to work under someone who couldn't keep up with me.

The next night, upon arriving for my shift, Evan was sitting with Simon and told me to join. He gave us both a talking down, stating that the night prior had gotten out of control, but that it was ultimately saved by some on-the-fly thinking and that moving forward we would need to learn to work together, to be a team and we would be stronger for it. Neither of us were happy with the arrangement, and said as much. Simon was concerned about me and my ambition; I simply thought he was an idiot and had no place on the team. But we shook hands and lied through our teeth that things would be different that night. Let's just say they were not. I was even more emboldened the second shift as I came into my own. It was like I had never left Oak nearly a year earlier. It was mostly the same people; other than the onslaught of A-listers who came in like it was Studio 54. Again, I pushed Simon from the podium and took over, making decisions he couldn't possibly fathom as he simply didn't know the crowd, Richie's crowd, or what to do with it. I did. And by the end of that shift, things were different.

Simon quit. And I felt no remorse taking his place. I cared only about myself and my success. I had been through my own wringer for the past year. And, given the chance to excel there, I decided that it was going to be my life. I would have to "live it" as Evan once told me. No more half in. I was all in and I was going to take it for all it could provide me. And that was the beginning of what marked my trajectory into the highest levels of nightlife. The next few months were a whirlwind unlike anything I had ever experienced, or would ever experience. I was focused. I was on top of my game. And I came to win, and win I did. I was quickly making a small fortune. Money unlike ever before. Each night, I built my Rolodex. And each morning I followed up, creating spreadsheets and client databases. Following up with each individual I met. Gathering the contacts of celebrities, billionaires, titans of industry, models (for personal reasons), and everyone in between. If I thought the gifts at Oak were good, they had nothing on what people would try and bribe me with, nightly. Hottest new Nike drops? Got them delivered in fresh boxes during my shift. Invites from dentists to clean and whiten my teeth. Complimentary meals for me and a guest whenever I wanted to come to the various restaurants I was invited to. Complimentary hotel rooms. Drivers of car services offered me rides home each night, or whenever I went to the airport. Jackets and shirts from top designers, er, the store managers that is, or brand ambassadors. Courtside seats at sporting events, backstage passes to concerts. Private jet trips. Vegas vacations. I was offered, and took advantage of nearly every perk you could think of. And all of it was *free*!

I was saving more money than I knew what to do with as everything I did outside work was gratis, save my rent. Anything I wanted I had access to. And the best part was that while all those perks were coming my way, I would run into all of our clients, because why wouldn't I? That's who ran New York, *right*? Mostly they did. Though as I was learning, nightlife people ran a good chunk of New York. They were your ticket to any and every social setting you could imagine. Art openings, massive parties in the Hamptons, in hotel suites you couldn't imagine existed, every level of debauchery on display through wealth I couldn't fathom, for nothing prepares you for it. The irony I always laughed at was my apartment was the size of most of the bathrooms I visited while at those events and parties. I was in the scene of all scenes, but I was not *a part of* the scene; not from a financial perspective and I accepted that. I became the go-to host, rivaling the greatest host in NYC at the time, maybe ever, Andrew Goldberg of Tao Group. And I didn't only have fans. I had enemies. Many enemies, never spoken to my face of course, but I knew who they were. Why would they like me? I was not only their competition; I was a dick. I ran things like a military general. You sat someone at the wrong table? You would hear my wrath. You gave my billionaire client the wrong liquor bottle?! Wrath. You came to the door and begged for me to let you in for free? Fuck you, you're not my friend, and it is a business, come correct.

I was a loose cannon. The power went to my head. And I became so caught up, as they say, that I fell off as an actor and writer. I simply didn't have the time. I was always working. Always. If I went out, it was with clients on my nights off. I set up dinners with girls and clients before work to help get them to the club after so they would spend money. When their jets landed at Teterboro, I was their first call: "line up some girls for dinner at Tao, private room, then Up&Down."

I was booking so much it became laughable. I was on pace to book two point five million dollars in table sales between Up&Down and Oak alone! I played dirty. Any promoter who sent a table, I stole the client by the end of the night, in fact, anyone who sent a table, I set out to own that client. And I usually succeeded. It was all about money, ego, and lifestyle. I was living the celebrity life, dating some stars you have heard of, having sex with others. It was like I cut the line of Hollywood, nightlife being my way in. And then came the pop-ups. The first time I was told I was going to Art Basel I had no idea what it was. They informed me that I was leaving in a day and would be in charge of running the two events we had for brand recognition (which I came to find out was big business in nightlife). The pop-up: a takeover of another club in another city. But really only in cities that have the jet setting crowd for the weekend: Sundance, Basel, Coachella, and Formula One to name a few. Those spots were where we found the whales, the spenders who would drop twenty or thirty thousand in a night on bottles. The gold standard of clients. And I had managed to get a few. I had been to Miami a few times, but never like that. Our flights were paid for, we each got our own hotel room in a nice hotel on the beach and were allowed to expense our meals (within limits) each day. I was in heaven. I was being paid to go to Miami, hang out at Soho House and other venues during the day, and meet people whom we would invite to our events over the weekend. My only "job" was to show up to the club, have a preshift with the staff that worked there, tell them how the night was going to go (as they were our clients and thus, our venue for the night) and execute for three hours, then party with our clients, end up at Eleven with them and a slew of the strippers, and get back to the hotel as the sun was rising, maybe after, then get some sleep and do it all again. It was my first experience doing a pop-up and it felt like something I could get used to. After returning, I was focused on lobbying for our next event; Coachella.

In the interim, it was the best Christmas I had in years. I was flush with money for the first time in a long time. My debt was no longer a concern. I showed up to my parents' houses like Santa Claus, with gifts and wine. I was happier than I had been in some time; even though I was very far from doing what I loved. I was highly compensated and it put me in a better mood than I had been in some time, but at the end of the day, alone with my family it reminded me of the old adage, money can't make you happy. Then I laughed and thought, *well, try not ever having any and living under the cloud of debt for years on end, then get some and tell me you aren't happier.* Because you are. Even if you are not doing what you love. I took New Year's Eve off for the first time in my career. I learned that my skill set would no longer be needed that night as the one percent of whom I serviced, was not in town. What was, for most people, the biggest party night of the year was not for them. Not in NYC at least. They all went to Saint-Barthélemy or some other tropical, or winter, wonderland. And I took advantage of booking my own tropical escape for a few days to clear my mind and enjoy the fruits of my labor.

The month of January brought with it the usual bitter cold and post-holiday slowdown. I took advantage of my position, leaving early each night, finally working smarter, not harder, as my skill set was not needed on nights where there was little to no money in the room. I was built for the Big Show, having proved I could handle the most difficult of nights. It was time to let the juniors run the room while I went out and saw what other clubs were doing and combed their rooms for any clients spending money, introduce myself, and try to befriend them so they would feel comfortable coming to our venues.

One night I was checking back in with my staff and standing outside talking to security and up walked my friend Kevin. I hadn't seen him in over a year, having taken a hiatus from The Collective due to burnout from work and my frustration with the group and my own shortcomings as an artist. And there he stood, before me, at the velvet rope.

"Hey man, what are you doing out?" I asked.

"Ah, just coming from an event around the corner, thought you may be here, so I popped by," he said.

"Nice, what event?"

"We got nominated for an Emmy today," he demurred, and my heart sank. I was happy for him, no doubt, but the news ran through me. There I was, standing there in the world of money and celebrity I fought so hard to get into and become a part of, with the thought that it would somehow springboard my career, but reality stared me in the face. He never cared about money, success, celebrity, or anything of the sort. He only cared about the work. And he struggled for years bartending or doing whatever shit shift jobs he could muster to survive, not excel as I did. And for that, he spent the rest of his days and each and every hour he had honing his craft. And nearly ten years later, he was being rewarded for it at one of the highest levels. And there I was, standing in a suit, smoking a cigarette, saying my hellos and goodbyes to a bunch of people I couldn't care less about.

"That's great man! You wanna come in for a drink?" I asked.

"Nah, you know I don't like that scene. And I got an audition early tomorrow. But I wanted to say hi and that we should find time to have lunch and catch back up," he replied.

"Yeah, that would be great. Let's find some time. It was great seeing you," I said, and meant it.

As I watched him walk away, one of the security guards came up to me and recognized him from his show and asked him how we knew one another.

"From the club?" he asked.

I shook my head, said no, and told him I was wrapping it up for the night.

I left and walked past the few raucous bars I would usually frequent for a nightcap but suddenly had no interest in going. Instead, I walked home, my head in the clouds, feeling bad about myself and my choices, *yet again*. When I arrived home, I sat on the couch and thought about my decisions and which ones I could have made to garner a different result. After replaying all the permutations in my head, I decided to stop beating myself up. His path was his and mine would be mine. There was no guarantee that had I never stepped foot into this nightlife world that I would be a working artist already. So, instead of trying to think my way out of this life and into one I could be proud of, I decided to stick with my motto of accepting the things I cannot control.

When I got the news that I was attending Coachella, I was over the moon. I hadn't been to a music festival, ever, in my life and I loved some of the acts that were headlining that year's festival. Add in the fact that we got VIP passes from the organizers of the festival, for free, and I couldn't help but count the days. The only issue would be, I was going alone. It wouldn't be the normal team of operations that went to Basel. That was more about the brand and the party would not be like the usual takeovers of nightclubs, but instead, a house party, to be held at a mansion we rented with some other famous brands. It was my first foray into event cobranding.

We partnered with Bumble (a new dating app at the time), a fashion brand, and a liquor company. All of which sponsored the party and had their PR teams handle nearly everything. My job would simply be to make sure the right people, our people, had no issues getting into the party and those of our VIP's spenders (as our whales were called) had tables and bottle set ups, gratis, for our event. Again, tickets and transfers were booked, though there were no hotel rooms. Instead, I was to get a room in a house that the promotional director was renting for us to house girls for the party. The issues were numerous. Operations and promotions/marketing were two very different worlds. The operations team was in the trenches each night, dealing with clients, money, seating, promoters, and celebrities, as *the help*. Promotions and marketing *were the party*. They brought the girls, the brands, the influencers (not social media ones, *real* ones). We did not always see eye to eye as our agendas were different—theirs to "take care" of people, ours to gouge people with smiles on our faces and our outstretched hands. We were the ass-kissers concerned with money. They were the sycophants concerned with image and status.

When I landed in LA, I was presented with my first issue. There was no transportation set up for me and Palm Springs was nearly a three-hour drive from LA. There I was, with no way to get there. Why? Because I wasn't a person in the world of the promotional director, and thus, even though I was to be given a room in the house and treated like the family we pretended to be, I was an afterthought. I rang Evan, bitching about the disrespect and had to wait at the airport for a few hours while they sorted out a ride for me. Which meant having the assistant rent me a car, for everyone was already on their respective ways. Once I was in the car, my worries dissipated as I popped some tunes on, dropped the windows, and set my GPS toward the desert. I enjoyed the four-hour drive, stuck in traffic with some of the most entertaining caravans of Los Angelenos headed out to party on the sand for the weekend.

I arrived at the house, impressed, wanting to start fresh after the (possibly intentional) mix-up. The promotional director was smoking weed in the living room, and having cocktails with four models. *I could get used to this,* I thought to myself. I said hello, he apologized about the confusion, and told me to pick a room that didn't have any bags in it. I left to tour the house, opened doors, and saw luggage on the beds and floors of each one. I opened the last door at the end of the long hallway to the laundry room with a single blow-up mattress on the floor. It couldn't be . . . I returned to the living room, pulled the director aside, and made him aware of my discovery. He shrugged his shoulders and said, "At least you don't have roommates like everyone else," and walked outside to the pool area where the girls were taking off their clothes to swim. Although the scene was what I had come for, the housing was not. I called Evan, furious. He was unmoved and laughed at the thought of me and my ego being stuck on a blow-up mattress in a laundry room.

"It's only for two nights. Suck it up. You're there to work," he said.

I hung up the phone fuming, and attempted to sort out the small room I had. I opened my luggage and used it as a makeshift dresser, taking out some clothes and putting them on loose hangers over the dryer. As I sat on the mattress and assessed my situation, I sank into it, and immediately experienced back pain from the awkward position of having my legs pushed above my shoulders. Sure, I could bitch and be upset at the stunt dummy treatment, or I could be thankful that I was there, with the same badge all the other VIPs had and pretend I wasn't sleeping in a makeshift bedroom.

I decided to go mingle with everyone by the pool for a bit and quickly realized why I didn't hang out with promoters. They had no substance. I was chatting with grown men in their late thirties and young women in their early twenties and the difference between them was . . . well, there wasn't any. All they did was scroll through Instagram and post pictures of themselves by the pool. It was not my scene. I liked the glitterati of nightlife, but I spent my time with the real movers and shakers of the world, not these children. Luckily, I had planned to meet up with plenty of them over the weekend. I excused myself after a short time, found a shower I could use, and got ready for the night's festivities. I donned my badge, a summer scarf for the sand showers that often plagued the festival, and met some clients in the VIP area. I walked a few football fields worth of backyards before I arrived at the festival grounds where I was taken to the VIP via golf cart. I was met with clients and more models than one could ask for. Seriously, it was on another level. My head was on a swivel as I was introduced to model after model by LA clients whom I hadn't seen since their last visit to NYC.

I quickly forgot about my laundry "room" and delved into the party. Hours later I was dumping ecstasy with one of the girls I had met, running off like kids into the festival, getting lost as the sun went down, the drugs taking hold of our euphoria. As the sun fell and the moon took over, the drugs began to wane and we watched from the front row as the headliner, The Weeknd, performed his latest hits. As the first night came to an end, the crowds dispersed to the various afterparties. I had invites for many, each house marking a different client's den of iniquity. And each one a few hundred-dollar Uber trip away. I scoffed at having to pay that much just to travel to a party. So, when I saw party vans being loaded in the parking lot with people whom I worked for, I dove into one as the doors closed, unaware of the destination. When they stopped, I found myself in the mountains at a mansion the likes of which I had only seen in movies. It was a colossal house in the middle of nowhere and the party had begun. A DJ spun tracks in the living room, as some of the biggest celebrities in the world sat and chatted one another up as they drank and smoked. I made my way around, ran into people I knew, and networked my way through the party.

Before long the sun was making its way up and people began to leave. I found a car going toward the grounds where my house was and hitched a ride. In the back of the SUV, I listened to the conversations of those coming down from their highs; it was like a soundtrack to the lifestyle I was living at that time. I had sat in so many of those cars, in various cities, and had the same conversations with different people; I thought that the allure of all of that was better than anything outside our bubble had to offer. I thanked the client for the ride, turned down the invite to their after-afterparty and returned to my house, where people were already home and asleep and made my way to the little flat mattress in the one-hundred-square-foot-room and closed my eyes. When I woke the sun was beating down on me from the shadeless window facing the backyard. I looked at my phone; it was nearly noon. I would have to get moving as our party started at three and I needed to be there early to go over the setup and the operation with the PR team. I showered, got myself together, and met my hired driver for my ride . . . I sat in the car, going over emails and any instructions that I might have missed, seeing as I was on one the night before experiencing the festival like a concertgoer. The ride lasted nearly thirty minutes and left me outside another mansion nestled within a complex of similar houses, all built onto a fake lake. It reminded me of Disneyland. *Who in the world would buy a house here?* It was all so manufactured, yet there we were, renting it to throw a rager.

I met the PR team and those in charge of the waitstaff. They walked me through the house, the setups, and the tables. It was simple enough. Nothing was very put together, all very makeshift, from the bottle packages we were to present to the allotted tables and celebrities appearing for us. My job was to stand outside and make sure the right people got in. Seemed easy enough. That was, until it began. The line outside was so large the police were called and my first duty of the evening was dealing with a local cop and a fire inspector who told me in no uncertain terms that they would be the ones enforcing order all day. I listened to them and shook my head, agreeing with any and everything they were asking, even though I knew Richie would flip out about most of it when he arrived. The next hour was miserable. I had the PR girl with an iPad telling me who should be let in even though I knew who needed to be let in, but with the lawmen breathing down my neck, it was all a lost cause. There must have been more than five hundred people outside the gates and I did my best to get the people who were supposed to be inside, in.

All hell broke loose when Richie arrived with DiCaprio and their crew. The cops nearly took me into custody as I opened a small chain that they had used to cordon off the crowd and control traffic for Richie's SUV. It took him getting out and speaking to them to calm the situation and then return me to the dogs out-side. If you have never been to a sponsored PR event, then you can't imagine the chaos that was occurring. If you have, then you know: people are horrid. When you mix celebrity and free, all bets are off. People become the worst versions of themselves. There were grown women (girls really) who cried because they weren't allowed in. Tough guys tried to fight me. Fashion-forward men cursed at me; I was getting it from all angles. After about two hours of it, with Richie and most of the important people we expected inside, I said fuck it and left the door to the cops and the PR girl, who had by that point began crying for fear of losing her job. I left Rome to burn and made my way inside to enjoy myself. Work was done for the weekend, so far as I was concerned. From that point on, I was a patron. I partook and enjoyed, and ignored whatever fires were burning outside the gates, and soon I found myself with a new group of strangers, with whom I drank and eventually rode with to the festival. I wish I could tell you more about the night, but it would simply bore you as it wasn't any different than the previous, except for the NYLON party, which was and still is, the best thing about Coachella. That year it was in an old amusement park, replete with roller coasters and other small fair rides, DJs, drugs, and weed. It ended with a large swath of people heading to another afterparty at some guy's mansion. Where it was the same people as the night before and I drank and danced until the sun rose. *Again*.

And *again*, I found myself a ride home and, *again*, did not attend the after-afterparty, instead choosing to go to sleep and skip the last day of the festival. I drove back to LA where I got a nice hotel, washed the stain of Coachella and all the wannabes that haunted me all day from my being, and met a local girlfriend for a night of casual dinner and drinks. I landed at JFK around ten at night the next day, exhausted from travel and "work." I had to get a car home, drop my luggage, shower, change, and head to work later that night.

When I arrived, it was slow. We had begun a new Monday night party, Blackout (as it was aptly named). I assumed that meant the night would be slow and reminiscent of the NYC Blackout where the city shut down, though I was not in marketing or promotions, so who was I to provide my two cents as to the name of a party? Its attempt was to rival Avenue's dominance of Monday's (their best, non-commercial night—as when Up&Down opened, Avenue was in year three and had gone completely "commercial," which means no more models and celebrities, just regular folks who couldn't get in the first two years) and it was hell. Especially that night, as all the "good people were still in LA" as the verbiage goes, except for some promoters who were filling in for the normal ones (who were in LA) there was not much activity. I grinded through, counting the hours until 2 a.m., when I was able to leave. And once I did, I returned home to my bed and passed out like a child.

During the weekly meeting after all the staff returned from Coachella, we spoke about the successes and failures of the event; mostly successes (except for the door debacle, which I was scape-goated for). I accepted it, and when the meeting ended, went to Evan and told him I couldn't do Mondays anymore. It was time to return to Tuesday-Saturday, as I needed two days off in a row to rest. He granted it and I remember actually cheering as if I had won some type of lottery, pathetic as that was. The next few weeks came and went, status quo. The club became like Groundhog Day for me. Each night arriving at the same time, doing a preshift with the floor and door staff, then out to the front to wait until midnight, when the majority of people began to arrive. Then sell and seat the tables and hopefully look down and see by the flow of the room, that two thirty was upon me and I could go home, or to Oak, if I needed, or wanted to. Then came another of those nights you just can't fathom as a little boy from New Jersey. I thought myself to be pretty in-the-know about events and happenings in high society (thank you Graydon Carter) only I had never heard about the Met Gala, for some ungodly reason. *Was I living in a cave?*

It was Richie's biggest night of the year, as he was known to throw one of the two best afterparties (the other being André Balazs in the Boom Boom Room). There was no shortage of high-wattage superstar power to go around, and Richie captured a large swath of the crème-de-la crème of the night. The event would be controlled by his consigliere, Shayna; no one else. She selected the best team to assemble for the night and ran it her way. I was told that I did not need to work the event, instead, that I could use my network to offer three tables to our top clients at twenty thousand dollars each. I reached out to a few clients, not many of whom were willing to pay that amount. The ones who were needed to be screened by Richie, as he didn't want celebrity gawkers or fat, rich losers with their Vegas-style hookers in tow in the room with the A-list. Two of the tables I had managed to sell were both denied for various reasons, leaving me pissed as I would have also collected a four grand bonus based on my commission structure for the night and I felt robbed of that. Undeterred, I set out to do what fit my personality and my wallet. I went to my biggest clients who lived in Paris and offered them the opportunity. They jumped immediately and because they ran in the same circles as Richie, (they were African royalty), they were accepted. And because those guys were like my little brothers from another mother, I was slated to join them, as their guest. Win/win!

It was a black-tie affair, so I set about procuring an outfit. I figured I was living in a world where every man should own a good tux and shoes. When the night arrived, they planned dinner at Carbone for us, four guys and three of their female cousins. We started the meal with Cristal and caviar, then drank Puligny-Montrachet with dinner as we ate Dover sole and spicy rigatoni. We skipped dessert. The check came and I was kicking myself for having come, until they pushed my credit card back to me and said it was on them. Relief! As that bill would have been more than two thousand dollars just for my share! Nice life, if you can live it; tough life if you're trying to keep up with it. We got into the SUV waiting outside and headed to the club. That was the extent of my workload. I began to text Shayna and gave her real time updates for our arrival. By the time we arrived, we were one of many SUVs in line dropping very important people off. Not the type to wait outside, for fear of being seen as "waiting," we sat in the car until Shayna gave me the okay. I jumped out, grabbed the head of security and he opened the rope and escorted us in as people in line yelled for my attention, to which I ignored, as that was not a battle I was about to fight. We went inside and were brought to our table where our first order lit up the room with ten bottles of Cristal.

The room was insane. It was the best party I had EVER been to. It was, what I assume, the *Vanity Fair* Oscar afterparty would look like: DiCaprio, Rihanna, Jim Carrey, Naomi Campbell, Madonna, Cher, John Legend; the list went on, and on, and on! I was careful to keep to myself and kept socializing to a minimum, lest Richie saw me out of the corner of his eye trying to talk to Kate Hudson, or some other single starlet. I knew my place, I was the *help*, even though I was there as a guest, I was not *there*. Nor should I have been. I was no different than the scores of people standing outside in line thinking they may get in and get a chance to be a part of it; nope. Not tonight. Private event. My handling of that night got me some street credit with Richie. I was well-mannered, didn't make a spectacle of myself, and didn't talk to anyone who I didn't happen to rub elbows with at the bar or walking through the floor. And for that, he decided to reward me. I was told by Evan that I had been selected by Richie to work the DiCaprio event in Saint-Tropez, yet another event I was unaware existed. I was over the moon, as I had never been to France, nevertheless the South of France and it would be paid for by the company. And, I would be attending the event as a guest. *A guest.*

And you know how that went. . . .

When I returned to New York I found that 1Oak was closed, having been shuttered by the New York State Liquor Authority for 311 issues (these are complaints by city residents about noise, trash, crime, etc.). It was a late-night club and unfortunately, things happened both inside and outside. The reason it was such an issue was that apparently the SLA wanted the names of every employee of the company, for some reason or other. I knew full well that my name run through a government agency would reveal my crimes and prison time, and I was worried.

I approached Evan in his office.

"Can I have a minute?" I asked.

"What's up Marshall, I'm in the middle of something," he barked.

I entered and closed the door.

"What's going on?" he sat up, stopped what he was doing as I have never closed his office door behind me.

"This Oak shit."

"What about it?"

"You know . . ." I said.

"I don't."

"My past . . ."

And the bell went off in his head.

"I remember you saying something about that."

"I don't want Oak to lose their liquor license due to me, I barely even work there anyway."

He sat and thought for a moment.

"Leah knows. Go speak to her and ask her what to do."

"Okay," I said and left for Leah's office.

Leah was the head of human resources, not that there was such a thing back then and especially within The Butter Group, but she held that as one of her many titles nonetheless. I knocked and entered. She motioned me in as she put her finger up, finishing a phone call with her headset on.

As I rarely visited her office, she asked, perplexed, "What's up?"

"Can you speak for a second?"

"We are speaking."

I turned and closed the door.

"Rather this be between us, if you don't mind," I said as I sat in a chair before her.

"Go ahead," she said, studying me.

"Do you remember me telling you about my past a while back, like in the Darby days?"

"I think so . . . some arrest? Or . . ."

"I did three years in prison. And I don't know much, but I know what I am NOT allowed to do and when it comes to my name being anywhere around the SLA, I'm not sure that is a good thing, for you and this company."

"I didn't realize that you had all that on your back," she said and sat back, thinking.

"Let me talk to our attorney and I'll let you know what they say."

"Thanks, Leah."

I left the office and went about my day.

A few hours later she called.

"Hello?"

"Hey Nick, I have our attorney on the line with us."

"Hey," I said.

"Look, there is no easy way to say this, but we are going to have to let you go. We appreciate your honesty and all your hard work, but this has to be dealt with accordingly. Once we sort everything out, maybe there is a path back, we don't know yet."

"Have you considered an expungement?" the attorney asked

"I don't know what that is."

"It is asking the court to wipe your records. It's been how many years?"

"Eleven since I was out, eight since parole ended."

"Oh, you would qualify. Let's talk offline and I can help you look into it."

"Thank you!"

I hung up the phone both completely demoralized and curiously hopeful. I had worked so hard for so many years to get rid of the stain, the scarlet letter of my past and, in the grandest sense of irony, I was up-front and honest and I was being punished for it; go figure—such is life. I had lost a job making nearly two hundred thousand dollars a year. I was dumbstruck, angry, and hate-filled; there were too many emotions running through me. So, I called Evan.

"She fired me!" I screamed when he answered, not giving him time to say anything.

"What!? What do you mean?"

"I mean she and the attorney just called me and let me go."

"What! Hold on," he replied just before he hung up on me.

Three hours later, he called me back.

"You're rehired, only you aren't allowed to work in any venues. We are creating a position for you. We are going to call it Head of Client Relations. Come in and we can discuss the compensation package."

Yes! A win . . . or was it?

I entered the office within an hour and waited for Evan to see me.

"Sit down," he said, and I did.

"Here you go. I told Leah we can't lose you. I had to point out that you booked nearly two point five million in sales alone last year. Money talks."

He pushed a contract across the table. I read it, but had to read it again; it was such a swing.

"Fifty grand? Evan I was making two hundred!" I stated emphatically.

"You weren't making two hundred. Your tips allowed you to make that and we can't tip you out from floors you are no longer allowed to work on. This is good for you. You will keep your health insurance, which we will pay, and you'll get one thousand dollars a week plus 10 percent of all your commissions. This is good. And fair. And the best I could do."

"After taxes that's not enough to live on."

"You won't be taxed the same. You have to start your own business. Like the promoters. You have to be an independent contractor. I think it will work in your favor. Just keep the bookings coming and you'll make money and will just have to show up to the clubs for an hour or two each night to shake hands and kiss babies."

The sound of it seemed interesting. No clock to punch, no hours, and not many deliverables. I would have a lot of free time to write and act, something I had let fall by the wayside. Plus, what other choice did I have? There was a very slim selection of other venues I could have gone to, none of which were as exclusive, and even if I got hired, could I get my clientele to go to a shitty club? Maybe once, not consistently. So, I did what any rational person would, I accepted the offer and signed on the dotted line. What turned out to be the beginning of the end for me in many respects.

CHAPTER 16

THE FALL

New York, New York—2016–2019

Free time is a funny thing. When you don't have any, you feel like your life is too hard, that you need an escape; some time for yourself, your family, and friends. When you have nothing but time, life can be challenging in a myriad of other ways. For me, the latter reminded me of prison, so mentally, that's where I was: back in prison. I had no schedule, nothing to keep me grounded anymore. And money was coming in, so long as I booked, or even if I didn't, as I had saved so much by that time, the money I was receiving paid my bills, so long as I didn't go crazy.

Being in the world of money, status, and influence is often a trap. And without the solid structure of a job, things began to get out of control, *quickly*. At first it wasn't an issue. I woke up, wrote, went to yoga, had a jog, hit the gym, then spent my afternoons texting clients to get bookings. It was a relatively easy life. I would show up to the club, say hello to my old coworkers, and then act as if I still ran the place; especially when my clients were involved. My word was everything and I never broke it before losing my position and title. If I told a client he was getting a certain table or minimum, he got it. But I was subject to a few things: my junior host who reveled in being the top gun, and the rest of the staff gunning to steal my clients. *Nothing in nightlife is sacred, especially clients.* I had stolen half of my book simply from being in charge. If someone else booked you and then I met you, I would stick you with a higher minimum, or sit you at a shitty table, whatever I had to do to let you know I was the decision maker and thus, if you wanted to be taken care of, you called me, not John Doe.

It was around that time that I thought my luck was finally going to change, for my career, not nightlife, but film. A client of mine with whom I had been spending a lot of time with owned a movie studio. He had passed along a script my writing partner and I wrote months prior, but we never heard anything. Then one day, I got a call, asking to set up a conference between myself, my partner, and the head of development for the studio. I was elated. It was the perfect time to shift my focus from the changes happening to me with work and focus my energy on what I loved. With my newfound zeal, I decided to try my luck. With hopes of getting an expungement, I reached out to the attorney who I had spoken with when I was being let go months back. She explained the difficulties (it was extremely rare for anyone with a gun charge and violent crime to get one), and proceeded to inform me of the cost (about five grand). She told me that she focused on New York, not New Jersey where I did my time and committed my crime, but she knew people who could help. Then she asked who my attorney was, when I told her she lit up.

"He's the best! I know him well. I'll put us all on email."

And yes, he was the best, one of the greatest criminal defense attorneys in the state.

He responded immediately, remembered everything from the years prior, and set up a call. Over the next few months, while I was juggling everything else, I put together a submission package with over fifteen letters of recommendation from family, friends, and people who mattered (attorneys, a CEO, a COO, a very well-connected individual, and a highly-ranked New Jersey State Trooper—whose letter I will never forget. For the rest of my life, I will be indebted to all of those people—but mostly him, as within it he said he had three daughters and that he knew me before, during, and after the crime period and that he would trust me baby-sitting his kids). And then I left it all in God's hands. Which sometimes takes time. . . .

Over the next nine months, we wrote three drafts for the studio; the last being the one they decided to make. I negotiated a small role and headed to Atlanta to film for two weeks. My first real movie. And I was one of the writers! I was over the moon, my partner, not so much, as they had completely torn apart the fabric of what we wrote and used it to create the biggest piece of shit to ever hit the screen. But unlike my partner, I would take a piece of shit if it meant I finally had some real street credit in the biz. I went to Atlanta with high hopes and worked my ass off for two weeks. But as the days clicked by, I knew that my performance was shit and the movie even worse. Maybe my partner had the right mindset, removing himself from the process, after all.

When I got home, the hope I held for that opportunity being my ticket out, quickly materialized into nothing. I was depressed. I had my first opportunity with a studio and I was run over by a freight train in every respect. It took the wind out of my sails. And with that, I was home, to further experience what had been occurring to me incrementally over those months of writing, but having been gone for two weeks, it was as if I had been *gone*. And like everything in life, the pendulum was swinging against me. I was the victim to all that I had done to others over the years. The only difference was that I was still working for the company and it was my coworkers, not random people. And each night, as I stood and argued with the other hosts, pleading my case, my power waning vastly with each passing day, I eventually said "screw it." I fell heavily into depression. It was a sad time. At first, I felt I had something to fight for, all the work I had done, all the money I had made these people and myself, then I realized life is never fair (not that I hadn't had many examples of it prior) only then, I turned to the bottle and drugs. I became a shell of myself; and everyone noticed.

I took off with a client to Vegas and Miami for three weeks. Private jets, yachts, hookers, blow, you name it. I indulged. The wheels were falling off the bus. I was walking throughout the Wynn in my robe and slippers, watching him win and lose hundreds of thousands of dollars each day. It became the saddest moment of my life. Talk about vapidity. I buried myself in every substance I could grab. And when it was all said and done, I left back home on a first-class ticket, a shell of a human. When I got back it was as if I didn't have a job anymore. My bookings had dropped more than 70 percent and I could feel the ax coming. Evan left to start a company. New faces were brought in and half of the company was sold to a billionaire who brought in some people to clean house. I knew I would be on the chopping block so I did what I had always done: I lobbied for a new job. And surprisingly, they gave it to me; what I would later find was their sending me out to pasture.

I opened the Mondrian hotel lounge and rooftop for the group, only I had no help. I did everything myself and failed miserably at every step. For a variety of reasons. I was becoming a functioning alcoholic and my mind was not right. I was depressed. I was suicidal. I was a happy-go-lucky man about town. But alone and inside my mind, I was a mess. Then a silver lining came. I received my expungement. It felt like the dark world I was once again living in and staring down had opened before me into a world of light and opportunity. It was around that time that I received a call from an old client who happened to own a very large hospitality company out of Los Angeles. He asked if I could find spaces for them as they were trying to move into the New York market. I said yes, not having a clue what I was getting myself into, or how I would do it. I called a friend who was in commercial real estate and told him of the opportunity. Immediately, he wanted to help me and I was about to let him do it, but first, I ran his offer by my little brother of sorts who comes from a developer family in New Jersey. He told me not to do it, and explained that my "friend," (really a nightlife acquaintance) was trying to take advantage of me. He used the metaphor of having a huge fish on the line and fighting it for hours, then coming over to reel it in and instead of sharing the catch equally, I would be given a filet to take home. So, as I always did, I taught myself how to reel in the fish.

I would first have to obtain a real estate license from the state. Thank God for the expungement as I would finally be able to put it to use. I Googled real estate schools, what I would need, and set off to register for class. The fee was nominal, less than five hundred dollars. I signed up and began my seventy-seven-hour course. At first, I thought it was a joke. The learning was so remedial. The courses were online, where the teachers laid things out, then you were tested after the class, and if you got a 70 percent score or higher, you'd pass and could move on. Let's just say I graduated in three weeks, mostly due to my schedule. When you pass is when it gets interesting. They immediately push you off to offers for an exam class, for another two-three hundred bucks. Being frugal, and sensible, I figured based on what I learned, I didn't need the class. I scheduled my test in some government hellhole, reminiscent of prison. My PTSD and anxiety came to life as soon as I walked in and sat with another hundred people with aspirations of being the next real estate mogul like Ryan Serhant. Let's just say every walk of life was there, and like me, many of whom had no other skill sets in the real world; no wonder real estate brokers get a bad rap.

They handed out the good 'ol number two pencils (which I love and am currently using for my notes to outline this book) and the standardized testing templates. A proctor stood at the front to read the rules and remind us that a calculator, not a phone, was acceptable. If anything else was seen on your person, you were out. Try next time and pay the state the fee again (which was nominal, fifty dollars I think). And then they hit the timer and it's off to the races. As soon as I opened the test, I knew I wasn't in Kansas anymore. From the first question, I realized the test was not based on the material learned in the online class. So, I did what any SAT taker would do and started to eliminate the answers I knew to be false and guessed based on what was left. I was done before anyone, as usual (or at least "usual" for when I was in school), but left feeling uneasy about it. A few weeks later I found out I failed, by three points and had to take it again. I sucked it up, paid the fee, and bought the study program. And of course, true to any government agency bureaucracy in line with the private sector (they do the schooling) the test was exactly the study guide material. I was done in twenty minutes, confident I had passed. Which I did. Then I set out to learn *how* to do the job, which of course, they did not teach us in school.

I was introduced to a gentleman who let me hang my license for a ninety/ten split in my favor. But with no resources. No learning tools. Just a place to hang my license for when I rolled my fish into the boat. I set out to Google my education. I read everything I could about commercial real estate and how to find it in New York. I began using LoopNet, the equivalent of StreetEasy, and started cold-emailing top brokers from my Gmail. Red flag! Some would respond, some would not, but each time I held a trump card, and when they asked who I represented, I told them (first and usually biggest mistake in business, *never give away your hand*). But I was green as fuck, what else would I do? And from that, I started showing spaces, more than ninety of them over the two years we looked. Eventually we narrowed things down and they came to town for a day packed with tours. And having the group in person changed things for me. People who had been playing in the big leagues started asking: "who the hell is this guy!?" I had no other clients, nor did I work for a reputable firm, and though I got close, I never closed a deal.

As I ran around attempting a new career in real estate, the Mondrian fell apart so swiftly I didn't know what hit me. And before I knew it, I was getting calls from my inner circle telling me I was about to get axed. And within weeks, I was back on the unemployment line, with very little money to my name. And not many options, or ideas, of what to do next. But I had relationships. Someone would hire me, for sure. And so, I set out to find work and did. I was given a host job at a new club and after about a month, I was fired for underperformance. And so, I fell off the wagon again. And it repeated itself on multiple occasions, so much so that my friends would get me an interview and look me straight in the eye and say, "You gotta be sober." My depression and self-medicating had taken a hold over me. I lost a few more jobs and soured my reputation further, falling deeper into depression and alcohol. And as I went through that period of hopelessness, addiction, and struggle, I was alone. I told no one how bad it had gotten. I slapped on a smile and pretended to work and be fine, yet all the while I was falling apart, going broke, and sinking into debt, slowly at first, then more rapidly.

I decided it was time to get away from nightlife and the fast-paced world in which I had built my career. But what would I do to make a living if it weren't in any form of hospitality? Real estate could work, but it was commission only. I needed a paycheck. I felt sales could be an option for me with my experience, so I began to doctor my résumé a bit, making it look and sound more professional, then set out to apply. I applied for every single sales job I could find on every job website from Indeed to LinkedIn, day in and out for months on end. And when I tell you that I applied to more than one hundred jobs and only got two interviews, over forty responses of "no," and the rest crickets, I wish I were lying. Talk about demoralizing. I was applying for everything, and at that point even hospitality jobs, using my overqualified résumé in that sector. What restaurant manager in his right mind is going to hire me to be a server or bartender with such a large amount of experience? None. And they didn't. It was torture. Finally, I sucked it up and asked Evan for a job at his construction company as a laborer. I needed to make ends meet somehow and there seemed to be no other choice. I found an old pair of Timberland boots buried in my closet, probably from before I went to prison, and got to work. Six a.m. wake up, onsite by seven. I worked vigorously sweeping the floors, removing garbage in giant metal bins, swinging a sledgehammer to knock down walls during demo, and sanding and painting (a task from which I was removed because I was awful at it). My work partner was a sixty-year-old man who outworked me every single day and made me feel even more inferior. Perhaps the most demoralizing, (humbling?) experience of that work time was when I was assigned to Zero Bond for the week. I was atop a ladder, eighteen feet in the air, wearing a mask and goggles, sanding brick, when I was told to stop as Evan was walking Scott through the venue to show him the progress. I was covered in sweat and soot and had pulled my mask and goggles from my face to wipe the sweat away when Scott looked up, did a double take, and stood below me.

"Hey buddy, are you okay?" he asked with genuine concern of how far I had fallen.

"Yeah, just earning an honest days' pay" I said

"You know you can bartend for me when we open, right? I mean I'll always give you a job if you need it."

"Thanks Scott, I appreciate it. But I think I'm done with that life."

"Up to you buddy." He said, shrugged, and continued on his tour.

I lasted for another three months before I threw out my back and couldn't physically perform the work.

I was back to submitting online applications; a special kind of torture when you have never held a corporate job. During the first few days I held out hope, again, that maybe I would get some positive responses and a chance at securing a career somewhere. I scoured the job opportunities, again, applying for anything that I felt fit my skill set: sales, brand ambassadors, management, and production. At each turn I filled out countless redundant HR forms, uploaded various résumés (by that time I had three I used) and even changed my hospitality résumé to look like I had very little experience. I spent hours on the phone each day making calls, reaching out to everyone in my network under the guise of "catching up," but in reality, I was seeking employment, opportunity, anything. I was desperate. Lonely. Depressed beyond all belief and watching my debt begin to multiply.

I fell into an even worse routine. I couldn't write, my head and emotions were so out of whack. My anxiety was through the roof and the depression really set in and then I began to do something I never had before: drink alone, at home. No more leaving the house and potentially embarrassing myself. Oh no, I just bought cheap bottles and drank myself to sleep, hoping I wouldn't wake up the next day and have to face the debt, depression, failure, and lack of opportunity and hope. Then I would repeat the process upon waking up the next morning. At first, I would curse the foul God who allowed me to wake again. Then I would have coffee and attempt to call Hope and see if she would come back to me. Somedays she did, briefly, as I toiled away, trying to find work, then, with no responses and feeling hopeless about my prospects for my future, or any future for that matter, I would start drinking again.

I would sit on my couch, listen to music, think, cry, and drink. Then I would smoke weed and eventually pass out again, waking up at some ungodly hour of the night, and look at my phone to find no text messages; feeling even more alone, I would smoke again and go back to sleep. And each day and week passed with that routine. And each afternoon or evening the same result would occur: I would begin to drink alone, then smoke and pass out again. I was simply trying to die a slow death. Take no responsibility for my life, or those that I loved. It was heart-wrenching as I managed to hide it from everyone under the excuse that "unemployment had taken its toll." Then one day I got a job interview. I was over the moon! I got up, showered, and tidied myself up. I looked the part, résumé in hand, and set out like so many years before when I was young and pounding the pavement of New York when I knew no one. I entered a small restaurant on the Upper West Side and sat at a table, awaiting the manager to greet me. When he did, I stood, shook hands firmly, looked him in the eye and chatted about my experience. I lied through my teeth as if I was relatively new to the city, to the business and was looking for full time work, as many shifts as possible. I knew what he wanted to hear from all my years on both sides of that trade. And when I was done, he stood, shook my hand, and told me he would be in touch soon.

I left with Hope. She came back to my side and I even went to a museum that day, and experienced culture and art to pass the all too overshadowing hours that I had been facing each day. I returned home, watched a movie, and went to bed, like a normally functioning person might, without the substances to punish me. The next day, I woke up and waited. When no calls, texts, or emails came, I fell back into the cycle. And it followed again, for days on end. And then, miraculously the manager called, offering me the job. I was through the roof. When I hung up, I laughed. It was as if all the worries went away. With that little piece of stability, I could put the building blocks of my life back together. All I needed was work, as I knew it begot more work. And I was up for the challenge. I was counting down the days until my first training shift. And then, like so many things that had happened to me over the past few years, the COVID-19 pandemic broke out. And with that, I received a phone call that due to the unforeseen circumstance, we would have to hold off on training and see what was to come. But sadly, as the pandemic swept across the world, I saw an opportunity for a fresh start. I called my mother and asked her if she would mind her forty-year-old son moving in with her for a bit, just until things settled, seeing as the city had just shut down. She told me she actually preferred that, as she was watching the news each day and NYC was no place to be. Having just moved to Florida, she asked if I would drive her car down since it was still in New Jersey. I decided to throw in the towel and leave New York, the city I loved and had dreams of succeeding in all my life, for the wide-open state of Florida. If ever there was a time, it was then.

I broke my lease and stored whatever belongings I had left in my father's garage and set off. I drove for two days in what seemed like the apocalypse prior to getting to Florida. While I drove, I listened to music and thought about what had gotten me to that horrible point. I decided it best to see if I could stop drinking, lest

I have to really begin to worry and check myself into a facility. Those thoughts were solidified as I spent the night in a Motel 6 off I-95 in some shoddy town in South Carolina, sleeping on plastic over a mattress to protect against Covid. I tossed and turned that first night, sweating out the booze, and decided to stop drinking. The next morning, up at the crack of dawn, I felt a new leaf was turning as I jumped back into the car and began the second leg of my trip. I sped through ghost town after ghost town, nary a car on the road, until I crossed the border into Florida.

It was as if nothing was happening throughout the country. Traffic everywhere. Hours later, as I got off I-95, the inlaying towns were packed. People dining, shopping; the complete antithesis of every other state I had passed through. I pulled into my mother's complex and watched as people swam in the pool, and laid out in the sun. It was as if I had entered a surreal sci-fi novel; and I would happily join its company. When I arrived, I unpacked the one suitcase I had and relaxed for the first time in quite some time. The sun, the openness of the city and state, and the feeling of being back in the nest, so to speak, calmed my soul. Up until that point, I had not lived with my mother since she moved out when I was seventeen. I had never asked her or my father for money, no matter how hard it got for me; it never crossed my mind. But I had swallowed my pride and asked my father for free storage and my mother for a temporary free room. And it further deflated my ego that at my age, I was resting on my parents' responsible lives of being homeowners. I had nothing, (and it seemed), no opportunity. Until another small stroke of luck hit me.

I had received a phone call from a director I knew, who was producing a movie to be shot entirely over Zoom. They didn't have money, but they would provide back payment and small equity for writing the script. I told him I loved the idea and I went to work on spec. I toiled in a small anteroom, looking out at geckos and palm trees as I spent eight to ten hours a day, writing and conversing with the producers and director via Zoom. I would take long runs, work out, tan, read, and swim. I hadn't felt that alive in years. After a month, Florida started to shut many things down. No more swimming, though I could run, walk, think, write, and eat three meals a day with my mother; the best part of the experiment; living with my mother. It was an absolute gift, in that respect, especially as you watched and read daily about the atrocities of death and despair so many people were facing. It made me feel thankful for the first time in a long time. Made me forget about the debt, hopelessness, despair, and uncertainty that I would face when it was all over. I was living in the moment and didn't touch booze, nor crave it. I ate my fair share of chocolate chip cookies and ice cream each night, but they were a far better vice in comparison.

Around that time the government began getting involved with people who couldn't work remotely. It was that stroke of luck that enabled me to rebuild. I applied for unemployment based on a very short (one month stint) at a club. Due to the new rules, I was able to do so, receiving two hundred dollars a week from unemployment and emergency Medicaid health insurance benefits. I didn't think I was fleecing the system because I had only had to file once before for a few months in my life, and I had paid taxes for so many years, (well in excess of what I was taking) that I felt no guilt. Only thankfulness. After nearly three months of that, the script was done and so was I. It was time for me to leave and start over again. I had a friend who was living in Mexico at the time and found a room for me by the beach. I moved there and spent the next four months living like the writer I had always dreamed I could become. I would wake and write, then go for a swim in the Sea of Cortez, then come back, write some more, and then read as the sun set. It was a slightly perfect life.

I began drinking again, but responsibly, and sporadically. I truly enjoyed that time, as I worked on a new script and thought of nothing else. No future plans. No stress. No worries. I just paid my very small bills with the government assistance (make no mistake I would not have been able to live anywhere in the US on what I was receiving each week) and enjoyed the fact that they lived as if the pandemic didn't exist down there. Only after the months came and went, I became homesick and lonely. I needed to be around some friends, enjoy a social life. Miami had reopened and quite a few friends had moved down from NYC. I began to put a plan together on how to get back to work. I moved to a rooming house in Miami and began to live again, not excessively by any means, but live nonetheless. And as I did so, the debt began to pile again. Only I discovered how to take on zero-interest loans to avoid the ballooning interest. Always thinking that I had money owed to me coming from the script and once I got it, I would wipe it out and start fresh. Best laid plans . . . After a few months, New York reopened and I wanted, *needed,* to get back and start over. I hopped on a flight, stayed with a friend, and got a job in nightlife. It was not ideal, nor what I wanted, but I needed it to pay off the debt, especially since the film was never bought and I never got paid for my work.

Although it would end up being more money than I had ever made in nightlife, it came with a huge cost; my soul—once and for all. For I wasn't at just any nightclub, I was working at a strip club, hocking tables and private rooms for dancers. And as anyone who has ever been in that world will tell you, it is shady beyond your wildest imagination. I pressed on, with the clock counting down until debt was paid and there was money in the bank again. It was arduous. The schedule, the work, and the sheer desperation of the place. But each day, each week, as I was able to pay down large chunks of debt, I told myself it would all be over soon, as I would stand in the back of the room, watching on as if out of my body. And as the debt load was nearing clearing, I decided to focus on a way out and joined a commercial real estate firm to cut my teeth. I would work full time each day and again, each night. Sleep was a gift again. It was as if I was back at Ponte's and Reliable. I kept my head down and fought hard to keep it going.

Over the next year, when it was all said and done, I had paid off nearly all my debt, put a little bit away, and had come to the end of my rope with the daily strip club grind. I couldn't stomach any of it anymore. The long hours. The people. And most importantly, what I was facilitating. It was not my bag. I left on good terms (in case my life ever fell apart again) and said adieu. Then this book opportunity came. A bucket list dream, from all those nights, sleeping on concrete floors, cold steel, and sand filled mattresses. I ran with it. I stopped everything to write; to help tell a story for anyone who has been through the system, depression, or fallen on hard times and struggle. To help someone have hope. To put something out there in the universe for anyone looking for inspiration when they are going through the bad times. For all those who suffer from the same mental health issues of PTSD, ADHD, OCD, depression, and anxiety that have plagued me, and of course, to all the addicts out there who are still trying to put it together, or have it together and are, like me, trying to hold on and not fall back: this is for you. I pray that you all find happiness and contentment, employment and love, family and friends; not in any particular order. And that one day, like me, you may finally find peace, and dare I say it, true *happiness*. (Which I'm still working on myself—all of them!)

SPECIAL THANKS

First and foremost, before I get to everyone in my life for all these years, I want to thank the two people who are the most important in reference to this book: my Agent Scott Kaufman at Buchwald and my editor Ashley Calvano, at Start Publishing, for without either, this book would have never been. I will start with Ashley, as if it weren't for her, Scott would probably still be shopping my original manuscript (not the book you just read). She shaped it, cleaned it, and kept me away from myself. Ashley, thank you for everything. First off, thank you for loving my OG manuscript so much that you offered to take me on as your "project" to write this book, which I would have never written without you and this opportunity. Your kind words about my writing and your belief in me and my work, has carried me through this process and I am so incredibly grateful to have had you by my side throughout. Words truly aren't enough to express my gratitude for your going to bat for me and reading my first draft, or whatever that was that I delivered, to see if I even knew what you wanted me to write or how to do it.

Scott. Man, oh man. You signed me twenty years ago as an actor. You pushed me to other agencies when I got dropped. You read the OG manuscript for *Going Down* in its infancy fifteen years ago and said "this is a book!" You always gave it to me straight, no matter how brutal. And to think that we just reconnected two years ago, and we have already done *this*? You believed in me throughout and I thank you for that. And I thank you for this opportunity. I think it is finally time for all of our hard work to start paying off. . . .

Mom and Dad. I am so sorry to have put you through all that I have. The kicking and punching through walls, the temper tantrums, getting kicked out of schools, getting all those detention hours, getting in fights and brawls, and for never walking the aisle of high school graduation because I thought I was "too good" to do it. I'm sorry I never went to college and made something of myself and I'm even more sorry that my college fund went to a criminal defense attorney. I never thought that selling drugs and the behavior that I exhibited during those teenage years would ruin my life, and in many ways, yours. I was too young, stupid, egotistical, and ignorant to realize what I was doing and how it was affecting you. And despite all that (and lots more I assure you) you stuck by me. You knew that at my core I was not what the system painted me to be, but a kid who made a mistake. Thank you for that, for visiting me, keeping money in my commissary, and finally, for believing in me all these years after the fact when the running family joke was "does Nick have a job today?" as your other son went further and further into the heights of success as I faltered by.

And for you Chris, I am sorry for the shame I brought upon our family and for every comment you had to endure because of it. I am sorry for the way I treated you as a kid, my intention was to make you tough, not to treat you unkindly. That is why I have made it my life's work to be a good brother to you as an adult, despite how hard you have made it at times.

I love the three of you with all my heart and, hopefully, this serves as something that you all can finally be proud of me for, because as we all know, there really hasn't been anything tangible prior.

I have one special thank you for someone who doesn't know it, but if she reads it, I think she will know who she is. Thank you for breaking my heart and moving away to pursue your dreams. It was the catalyst for my beginning to write my memoirs. After you left, I decided to pour my heart and soul into exploring my life and the decisions I had made. It was my therapy. And I thank you and know that you are doing so very well and have a beautiful family that you so very much deserve.

Here we go . . . Tony, you are truly my brother. You were my only friend when I got out and have remained so much more through the past twenty-five years. There is simply no way I can repay you for all you have done, including making me an uncle to those three little rascals!

Johnny, who would have thought your brother going to get sushi on that fateful day twenty-five years ago would have reunited our childhood friendship? It's been a pleasure to watch your girls grow and to be there as you found your wife!

KK—brother, from the day we met in Esper, it's been a journey, man. We have been through quite a bit over the last twenty years and we are still at it! It's been fun getting to know your little one as she gets older, and it has been an honor to watch your life change for the better that day at City Hall. Lots more life and work together to be done!

Jordan—thanks for sticking by me, I know it's just repayment for keeping all the bullies away from you growing up when you were a little mute kid with coke-bottle glasses, but I'll take it none-theless. Half-kidding. I can't wait to be a great uncle and watch Julian grow.

Mo—dude, who would have thought this is where we would be after you handed me your card and ordered a parade of Dom? The shit we have been through could be a movie. I really can't thank you enough for all that you have done for me (you know), your continued friendship and support, and allowing me to be a fake uncle to your kids.

X—what's the word, what's the word? You have been one of my rocks and I can never thank you enough for all that you have done and the friend you have been to me.

Craig Cohen—you believe this shit man! Thank you for always believing in me and being by my side. This is only the beginning! Let's go make some movies!

Evan Frost—thank you for giving me the job that changed my life and seeing it in me. And thank you for then going on to become one of my closest friends. Look forward to a lot of golf as we get older.

Ioannis Pappos—thank you for listening and thinking I had a story. Thank you for reading it and believing in my work enough to edit it. Your work and words helped get me here. Thank you!

And for everyone else, you know who you are. There are far too many to name. I cannot thank you all enough for your sup-port and friendship throughout the years. I owe so many dinners, golf rounds, vacations, clothes, shit, everything to you all as you have been my lifeline and support system as I struggled to find my way as an artist. I may not be a wealthy man in dollars (yet), but what I have in friendship, I am rich beyond my wildest dreams!

To my sister-in-law, Amanda, thank you for all your support and kindness! And thank you for making me a real uncle, can't wait to spoil those little ones.

To all the wives of all my friends whom I have had the luxury of being around and their kids and the great conversations and the wedding invites and the overall good times!

For everyone I have ever worked with or for. You know who you are. Specifically, Patrick Robertson for allowing me to get in the door and Scott Sartiano for giving me a chance and believing I could do the job. And Richie Romero, for giving me more jobs than I could hold over the years, thank you!

To my aunts, cousins, and "steps": Mark, Tim, Colleen. Jen and Stacey. Carrie and Elizabeth. Gary and June.

For those no longer with us: Grandpa Tony and Grandmas Helen and Claire, and Aunt Marie, and Sue. May you rest in peace, I know this would have been your proudest moment and for that I am finally proud of an achievement.

And finally, for Julia Tchen. Thank you for sticking by me through an otherwise miserable period in my life. I love you from the bottom of my heart and only wish and want the best for you, no matter where life takes us.

SPECIAL DEDICATION
TO MY DEAR FRIEND,
SCOTT KENYON 1985–2024

It brought me great sadness to write these words as I sat at my desk, even though I had done so for nearly two months, daily, trying to come up with something hopeful and celebratory of him, yet touching to all those he left behind. I feel it best to simply tell the story of what would, sadly, be our last interaction together, in this life, to give you an understanding of his personality, his friendship, his love for family and friends, and how much fun he was as a person. . . .

Having just submitted a rough-rough, throw-shit-at-the-wall version of what I thought this book was, or could be, to my editor, I received a phone call from my friend, jovial as always.

"Sup doggie! Guess who's coming to town next weekend?"

And that was all it took to set my spirits high and stop worrying about work and money and the grind that often buries my mental state and causes me massive anxiety. One of my best friends was on his way to town. We hadn't seen each other in nearly six months, which for us, was an eternity, as I had to bail out of our New Year's trip to Mexico due to a variety of factors in my life.

He arrived a few days later. As we were on the phone deciding where to do dinner, I told him I would wait in line to get us bar seats at L'Artusi (one of his favorites) for his homecoming while he settled into his hotel.

I secured a reservation and we met for a predinner cocktail around the corner at Dante as we waited to be called. I arrived first and ordered a martini, one of our usual ways to start the evening. I called to ask him what he wanted, but he explained he was running late from a work call and was just about to hop on a Citi Bike (his favorite mode of transportation around the city he loved). I took his order and told him to text me when he was close so his drink would be waiting for him upon his arrival.

As I sat and sipped, a text from the restaurant came through that our seats were ready, earlier than expected. We had ten minutes to make it over to secure them, or else they would be released. I picked up the phone and rang him. I could hear the sirens and sounds of New York around him as he explained he was on the bike, making his way. I told him of the change in plans and he stated that he would head straight there and secure our seats, and insisted I finish my drink, lest it go to waste. I thanked him and hung up, motioned to the bartender for the check and looked down at my three-quarter full glass, then back to my phone laughing to myself that he didn't want me to waste my drink. I took up the glass to his absence, laughed to myself again, and downed it in one shot as I signed the check and left.

When I arrived to check in with the hostess to point me in the right direction, he had overheard as he was seated at the corner of the bar in the two best seats, smiling ear to ear. He stood up to give me a hug. As we sat and settled, I looked down to see his nearly-empty Negroni.

"I thought you would be on martinis?" I asked.

"It's going to be a long night, I figured I would start slow," he replied, smiling with the glint in his eye; one he reserved for his friends in these types of situations.

As the bartender made his way over, Scott introduced us, having already made friends with the stranger.

"I'll take what he's having."

"And I'll take another," he added.

The bartender left and went about his business as we spoke, catching up about his wife, children, family, and Los Angeles (where he had moved back to after thirteen years in NY, post-pandemic).

Upon delivery of the drinks, we said cheers, and set about ordering the bottle of wine that would pair best with the gluttonous amount of food we were about to indulge in. As we waited for the sommelier to deliver the wine, we enjoyed another round of Negronis, and laughed about life and all its musings.

When the wine was presented and poured, he ordered the food. The business of dining complete, we tossed back our cocktails and set to the wine. We raised our glasses to one another, his new role at work and the future he envisioned from it, as well as to this book, my first opportunity to do what I loved and worked so hard for after a very long twenty plus-year journey, one in which he had been my biggest supporter throughout most of.

After dinner, we indulged in more cocktails and laughter, then moved on to continue in the vein, moving from spot to spot in the West Village. We planned our next golf outing and mused about making New Year's Eve in some exotic locales together a tradition, when I could afford it.

Around twelve thirty I was toast and about to call it when he insisted I come with him to Brooklyn to see his dearest friend Max. He bribed me with round-trip Ubers on him, knowing how much

I hate leaving Manhattan, especially for the hipster enclave of Brooklyn.

Of course, I acquiesced and found myself in the back of the car, quickly nodding off. As we hit a light not far from the bridge, I came to my senses and told him I had to call it. He said it was fine and laughed as he kicked me out of the car on Bowery and Prince. I left chuckling, telling him to send my best to Max and that I would see him the next morning for brunch.

When I awoke, Scott was not answering his phone. I was concerned as he doesn't usually sleep late, even after a night. I called a few times and texted and before I got to the point of going to his hotel to check on him, he called. He told me of his "second night" with Max, playing pool, drinking beers, and smoking cigarettes until four in the morning.

We decided to meet for brunch at Cookshop where I enjoyed a Bloody Mary and ironically, he had nothing but coffee and lots of food. We laughed about the night and then planned the following day to watch the NFL playoffs with a group of his friends. During the meal his son and wife FaceTimed him. We all exchanged hellos and joked that he was already out with "Uncle Nick."

We parted ways soon after and set about our days until we met the next morning for brunch and football. The day was long, filled with laughter, conversation, and some great football. We shared a cab back to Manhattan after the final whistle and as it pulled over to let me out on the side of 6th Avenue, we said our standard goodbye: a man hug and an "I love you buddy," with an added "See you in LA for some golf in April," as we had planned.

A few weeks later, on a cloudy Monday morning at eight thirteen, I got the call. He had died suddenly of a heart attack playing the sport he loved more than even golf, volleyball. I crashed to my floor like I had been hit in the gut. Heaving and crying, unable to contain myself as Max, the bearer of this awful news, sat patiently waiting for me to go through the beginning of the rest of our lives without him.

Having had the gift of seeing him so soon before was the only thankful element of this catastrophe. He was thirty-nine years old. He left behind his wife, Lauren, and his two little kids, Tyler and Crosby. As well as his sister, mother, father, his entire family of in-laws, his friends, coworkers, and associates. Every single person whose life he touched lost something that day.

I flew to LA a few days later, a puddle, for his celebration of life. There had been torrential rain in LA since the day after he passed. He was so loved, in the midst of a huge storm, many of the people whose lives he had touched so deeply came to celebrate him. So many, in fact, that it caused a traffic jam on the Pacific Coast Highway. That image made me laugh: him looking down and seeing all this love and support for his family at this time of sadness and confusion; all of us asking God, "why?" and "how could you?" seeing no silver lining for the passing of someone so much in his prime, full of energy and love and kindness.

I wanted to write this for him, his family, his friends and coworkers, and anyone who was touched by his life as a way for him to live on in print. For his memory, for that of his family, to know that he affected my life in a way so few people ever have and that with each passing day, although it gets easier, it will be with me forever; as it will with them and his children who were not old enough to have had fully experienced the wonderful father he was to them.

Scott, may you rest in peace and may your memory live on this earth for many years after we are all gone. My thoughts and prayers are each day with Lauren, Tyler, and Crosby as well as his parents Keith and Anita, and sister Ashley. And not to leave out his large extended family of Epsteins and all of his friends who were his family.

As you always said to me, I say it right back with tears running down my cheeks as I write it: "Miss you doggie!"